DEFEND I.T.

DEFEND I.T.

SECURITY BY EXAMPLE

AJAY GUPTA
SCOTT LALIBERTE

✦✦Addison-Wesley

Boston • San Francisco • New York • Toronto • Montreal
London • Munich • Paris • Madrid
Capetown • Sydney • Tokyo • Singapore • Mexico City

The publisher offers discounts on this book when ordered in quantity for bulk purchases and special sales. For more information, please contact:

U.S. Corporate and Government Sales
(800) 382-3419
corpsales@pearsontechgroup.com

For sales outside of the U.S., please contact:

International Sales
(317) 581-3793
international@pearsontechgroup.com

Visit Addison-Wesley on the Web: www.awprofessional.com

Library of Congress Cataloging-in-Publication Data

Gupta, Ajay.
    Defend I.T. : security by example / Ajay Gupta, Scott Laliberte.
        p. cm.
    Includes bibliographical references and index.
    ISBN 0-321-19767-4 (pbk. : alk. paper)
    1. Computer networks—Security measures. 2. Computer security. I.
Laliberte, Scott. II. Title.
    TK5105.59.G86 2004
    005.8—dc22

                                            2004004424

ISBN 0-321-19767-4
Text printed on recycled paper
1 2 3 4 5 6 7 8 9 10—PH—0807060504
First printing, May 2004

To my son, Rohan.
To my daughter, Ema.

Our pride and joy

Contents

PREFACE

What does a cyber security professional do? This is a question often posed by individuals who have heard a lot about security—especially the need to secure their electronic assets—but who are not entirely clear on what is involved. Cyber security involves a variety of things. Although we, the cyber security professionals, understand the various aspects of our jobs, it is often difficult to explain to people outside the profession (even our spouses) what exactly we do, and what exactly needs to be done to secure electronic assets.

The details of many professions are difficult to describe, so examples often offer the best means of explanation. Security is no different. In this book we hope to provide some insight into cyber security by using case studies to describe what a cyber security professional does.

We hope that this collection of case studies will serve as a tour of many of the issues that cyber security professionals face, not only in their careers but in their day-to-day lives.

One of the goals of this book, then, is to explain what we do; but there are other, more critical goals as well. Our primary aim is to provide practical examples of the types of issues that security professionals must be prepared to face in the execution of their duties.

How the Book Is Structured

The case studies are presented in five categories:

Part I: Basic Hacking

Part II: Current Methods

Part III: Additional Items on the Plate

Part IV: Old School

Part V: Computer Forensics

These categories certainly overlap to some degree.

Part I, Basic Hacking, covers some of the basic things that hackers do when attacking networks, often starting with mapping the network, which is also called *footprinting* (described in Chapter 1, Getting to Know the Enemy: Nmap the Target Network). Following from the discussion of mapping, Chapter 2, Home Architecture, presents a case study about a system compromised because of an architectural issue. Often during the mapping stage, a vulnerability becomes apparent and hackers use it to compromise the network. When no vulnerability becomes apparent, hackers have many options, one of which is to flood the network with traffic and make it unusable for legitimate users. This approach to compromising a system is typically referred to as a denial-of-service (DoS) attack (discussed in Chapter 3, No Service for You!).

Part II, Current Methods, covers methods that have received a great deal of attention lately, starting with a discussion of the security of a wireless network (Chapter 4, Look Ma, No Wires!) and continuing to a discussion of viruses (Chapters 5, Virus Outbreak I, and 6, Virus Outbreak II: The Worm). The subject of protecting systems against viruses is so important that it was deemed worthy of two chapters: Chapter 5 discusses how architectural choices led to the virus infection, and Chapter 6 discusses the case of a large-scale worm infection of a distributed network. Part II concludes with a case study presenting a Web server compromise (Chapter 7, Changing Face). This incident also pinpoints some of the "business" issues involved in performing security consulting.

Part III, Additional Items on the Plate, covers topics that one might not initially think fall under the purview of a security professional, but we are sometimes called upon to perform these services. This part starts by describing product selection for an intrusion detection system (Chapter 8, Protecting Borders: Perimeter Defense with an IDS) and includes cases that describe disaster recovery (Chapter 9, Disaster All Around), writing a formal security policy (Chapter 10, Security Is the Best Policy), and details of a security engagement performed in support of the HIPAA regulation (Chapter 11, HIPAA: Security by Regulation).

Part IV, Old School, discusses some of the older—but classic and still all too prevalent—means of compromising a network: namely, war dialing (Chapter 12, A War-Dialing Attack) and social engineering (Chapter 13, A Low-Tech Path into the High-Tech World).

Part V, Computer Forensics, presents three separate applications of computer forensics. Although it is not a new field, computer forensics has only recently entered the mainstream, and it is quickly gaining in popularity and importance. Topics covered in this part are industrial espionage (Chapter 14, Industrial Espionage), investigating financial fraud (Chapter 15, Executive Fraud), and investigating a network intrusion (Chapter 16, Cyber Extortion).

The book ends with a Conclusion that briefly touches on a few topics not discussed elsewhere in the book. Our hope is that the feedback we receive on topics included in this book and in the Conclusion will guide us in selecting case studies for a second edition—if we are so lucky as to be asked to write one.

FORMAT OF THE CASE STUDIES

The format will vary from case study to case study, but in general, here's what we'll cover.

- **Case background and description**. We will describe both the general environment and the specific security incident. The description generally will cover the people involved, time frames, issues encountered, and any political dynamics that may have existed.

- **The response**. We will discuss how the compromise was detected and what actions, if any, were taken to solve the problem. The discussion may cover any of the following topics: disconnecting the target machines, reloading the OS, performing computer forensics to ascertain the level of compromise, identifying root kits, and, possibly, prosecuting the attacker. Some chapters do not recount actual incidents, but simply describe the approach taken to resolve a specific type of issue or attack a specific type of problem.

- **Lessons learned**. We will highlight the lessons learned from each case study and identify what was done right, what was done wrong, and how to use this information to defend ourselves better in the future. We will determine what could have been done differently to avoid the losses incurred—whether such measures involve a different process for incident response or having better security countermeasures in place to begin with.

Along the way, supporting information such as network diagrams, tool screen shots, and other illustrations will be presented. As appropriate, the cases will discuss the tools used, as well as some of the sources available for researching current vulnerabilities and exploits. Technology in general, and security specifically, is a dynamic industry. What is true today may not be true tomorrow. And unfortunately, a "safe" or "secure" system today may be neither safe nor secure tomorrow. Constant research is crucial to keeping up with the latest technical advances and remaining current with the newest issues. At one time, all you needed to do to be safe from viruses spread through e-mail was to avoid clicking on and executing an e-mail attachment from an unknown party. That certainly is not the case now. With HTML-embedded e-mails, you may not have to download an attachment; the virus might be right in the HTML, and when an HTML-enabled e-mail application displays the message, the virus can launch automatically. This is just one example of how security threats evolve.

AUDIENCE

We hope that anyone within the information technology field who has an interest in cyber security or is entering a related profession will enjoy this book. One of the benefits of a case study format is that it can make the security issues discussed *real* and help security administrators and other security professionals relate the events to their own experiences. Through generalized case studies, people can share their own experiences and lessons learned that they might otherwise be reluctant to share, for fear of disclosing a weakness about their organization.

Current and aspiring IT security consultants can certainly get the flavor of a security consulting engagement from the case study descriptions. In addition, information technology auditors can learn about security issues that they will encounter during security audits. A better understanding of these issues will enable the IT auditor to audit more effectively.

This book addresses technical and management-level concerns and therefore can also be a valuable resource for security officers, CIOs, and other technology managers in the technical discussions they will have with their IT staff. Finally, we believe that this book is readable and understandable far and wide. Anyone who is curious about the security profession should be able to read this book and get a flavor of what we do.

ACKNOWLEDGMENTS

Many people made this book happen. We would like to acknowledge the efforts of the whole team at Addison-Wesley, especially our editor, Jessica Goldstein, who brought this project back from beyond the abyss; and our superb copy editor, Stephanie Hiebert, about whom enough can't be said. Certainly there would be many fewer complete sentences without her. An IT book is only as good as its technical reviewers, and we sincerely believe that the reader will find this a fine book. We would like to thank Roy Fernandes for putting together the book's Web site, www.gsecurity.com/DefendIT/, which we hope readers find useful. We would also like to thank our families for their support and encouragement—and for keeping dinner warm as we typed deep into the night on chapter after chapter. Finally, we would like to thank the following people for their technical contributions and assistance: Charles Barley, Jr., Howard Charnock, Ken Day, Fyodor, Jessica Goldstein, Kevin Greene, Sudeepa Gupta, T. J. Klevinski, Amy Korman, Beth Laliberte, Dhavan Mehta, Randolph Musgrove, and Ken Williams.

About the Authors

Adding more minds to efforts toward solving a problem leads to one of two things: either too many cooks in the kitchen or actually a better solution. We tested this premise in writing by reaching out to other professionals as contributing authors, and we sincerely believe that we have come up with the latter. Each contributing author added a unique skill or experience that helped round out the book. The book has therefore become a collection of knowledge of several experienced security professionals.

Primary Authors

Lead Author: Ajay Gupta, CISSP

Ajay Gupta is one of the coauthors of *Hack I.T.* and has more than ten years of experience in the security industry, focusing on cyber security, secure network architecture, computer forensics, and information privacy. He is a Certified Information Systems Security Professional (CISSP) and an expert in intrusion detection systems and penetration testing.

Ajay has held research positions focusing on developing new mechanisms for conducting intrusion detection and secure electronic commerce. In addition, he has held client service and project management roles in the Big 4, serving the banking, financial services, pharmaceuticals, energy, insurance, health care, education, and consumer media industries, as well as the government sector. In the Big 4, Ajay has managed a wide array of information and cyber security engagements, including penetration testing, intrusion detection system deployment, and performing security audits.

He currently runs Gsecurity, Inc., which provides cyber security and data privacy consulting services to federal, state, and local governments, as well as to commercial clients in the educational, financial, and health care sectors.

Ajay also serves as the Director for IT Security at Prince George's Community College and is on the faculty at Prince George's Community College and Golden Gate University. He has been an invited lecturer for organizations and universities around the globe and has published numerous articles on topics in cyber security, disaster recovery, and security awareness. He holds M.S. and B.S. degrees in electrical engineering from the University of Maryland, College Park, and expects to receive his M.B.A. from Georgetown University in April 2005.

SCOTT LALIBERTE, CISSP, CISM

Scott Laliberte, one of the coauthors of *Hack I.T.*, is now one of the leaders of Protiviti's Global Information Security Practice. He has extensive experience in the areas of information system security, network operations, incident response, and e-commerce. Scott has served clients in many industries, including health care, life sciences, financial services, manufacturing, and other industries.

Scott has managed many security engagements, including attack and penetration studies, Web application security reviews, systems vulnerability assessments, wireless security reviews, and security system implementations. Scott has also managed numerous incident response projects, helping organizations identify, stop, and recover from security incidents and attacks. Scott has implemented a variety of firewall, VPN, intrusion detection, and other security products. In addition, he served as an instructor for a five-day course on penetration testing techniques and methodologies. He has spoken on information security topics for a variety of audiences and industries, including the Information Systems Security Association (ISSA), the National Association of Foreign Student Advisers (NAFSA), the Information Systems Audit and Control Association (ISACA), the

Institute of Internal Auditors (IIA), and the Health Care Compliance Association (HCCA). He has been quoted as a security expert in the *Financial Times*, *Securities Industry News*, and other publications.

CONTRIBUTING AUTHORS

LANCE HAWK

Lance Hawk has more than 25 years of computer security experience. He conducts computer-related crime investigations and related computer forensic analysis at a Fortune 500 company. He is responsible for computer evidence handling and response, intrusion detection and response, computer emergency response, penetration testing, vulnerability assessments, security policies and procedures, and security consulting and review. He also handles disaster recovery and business continuity planning. Lance serves as a consultant and trainer to government and industry. He has been recognized by the Philadelphia FBI and FBI Director Robert Mueller for "exceptional service in the public interest."

Lance serves as a current board member and speaker for the Philadelphia chapter of InfraGard, which is a partnership between the federal government/FBI and industry. InfraGard's primary mission is to protect the nation's critical infrastructures. Lance is an active member/speaker for the High Technology Crime Investigation Association (HTCIA), the Information Systems Audit and Control Association (IIA, three-time president), the Institute of Internal Auditors (IIA), and the Association of Certified Fraud Examiners (ACFE).

Lance has investigated numerous cases of "black hat" computer hacking attacks and other advanced technology crimes, including computer viruses/worms, cyber extortion, cyber stalking, denial-of-service attacks, Internet tracking and tracing, Web defacements and threats, and competitive intelligence disclosures.

RODRIGO BRANCO

Rodrigo Rubira Branco is a Unix lover and chief security officer of Firewalls Security Corporation, located in Brazil (http://www.firewalls.com.br). He has contributed to many open-source projects—for example, Nmap, Snort, TCP-dump—and has experience in performing complete vulnerability scans, firewall evaluations, and other cyber security tasks. Rodrigo is certified in all Cyclades products and in network, security, and cryptography applications of the ISPA/Cyclades company.

DAVID TAYLOR, CISSP

David Taylor is the national leader of Protiviti's Incident Response and Computer Forensics team. He has more than 11 years of experience in information security and computer forensics. He is a former federal agent and computer crime investigator (CCI) for NASA's inspector general and for the U.S. Air Force Office of Special Investigations (AFOSI). As a CCI, David investigated computer intrusions and other violations of the law relating to computer and communications systems.

At Protiviti, David directs computer network security services and leads a national team of technology risk and incident response professionals. David has designed and assessed security programs and responded to security incidents at companies throughout the United States, including several financial institutions, technology manufacturers, and organizations in the hospitality industry, among others. He has spoken on information security topics for a variety of audiences and organizations, including the Information Systems Audit and Control Association (ISACA), the LegalTech trade show, the Florida Institute of Certified Public Accountants, the Institute of Management Accountants (IMA), and InfraGard, among others.

NELSON NEVES

Nelson Neves assisted with the case studies covering Web server compromise (Chapter 7) and war dialing (Chapter 12).

ERIC HODGE

Eric Hodge is currently managing security and infrastructure consulting engagements for Jefferson Wells in New York City. He has also been a consultant for Protiviti, where he delivered the engagement that is described in the wireless case study in Chapter 4. Eric spent seven years in the U.S. Air Force as a communications systems officer, gaining an intimate knowledge of encryption, information security, long-haul communications, and authentication methods.

Eric has managed and performed consulting engagements for five years, including work in vulnerability assessment, penetration tests, local and wide area network implementation, security infrastructure implementation, security due diligence, and application vulnerability assessment. He has performed much of his work with health care organizations and financial institutions. He has presented wireless security information to ISACA and for executive roundtables in Houston and Dallas.

CHRISTOPHER BROWN

Christopher Brown is an expert on denial of service and was the inspiration behind the distributed denial-of-service case study (Chapter 3).

Almost from the time he could crawl, Chris could be called a computer nerd. As a toddler he drew pictures on a Xerox Star, a Lisa, and various Apple Macintoshes. A great artist? Maybe not, but he did end up with a lifelong love of computing. Because all things electronic, especially computers and computing, were topics of discussion everywhere when he was growing up, Chris learned to do just about everything at a very early age so "he could talk at the big table," as he puts it.

An understanding and love of UNIX began in preschool, and the Internet was simply an extension of his computing domain. (Chris has never known a world that was not interconnected.) As the worldwide Web became a reality and TCP/IP exploits became more prevalent, he created a Web site defining the types of attacks lurking in early Net life. He researched much of his information in the test lab that he still maintains.

Eventually Chris began focusing on security, and major defense agencies and fortune 1000 companies visited his Web site. He identified vulnerabilities in the TCP/IP implementation of several operating systems that vendors subsequently fixed.

Chris still toys with his lab, but he now works as a network architect in the advertising industry and continues to focus on security as part of the team behind the Computer Security Now Web site.

KUMAR UPADHYAY

Kumar Upadhyay is currently Vice President of IT Operations for iSTRAT, an information technology and research consulting company. He has successfully handled several disaster recovery and risk management projects and is an adjunct faculty member with Golden Gate University, teaching disaster recovery and business continuity planning. Prior to joining iSTRAT, he spent several years working in the corporate sector in the areas of design, architecture, and implementation of IT networks and systems infrastructure to include configuring firewalls, routers, switches, and intrusion detection systems.

INTRODUCTION

The number of computer crimes and information security incidents continues to grow by leaps and bounds. Reports from the CERT Coordination Center (CERT/CC) at Carnegie Mellon University show this figure more than doubling each year, and projections for future years are only rising. Viruses and worms continue to take down organizations for days at a time. Approaches to securing systems and networks vary widely from industry to industry and organization to organization.

Security professionals continue to battle against external attackers, cyber terrorists, disgruntled employees, automated worms and viruses, and unfortunately, unknowing employees who mistakenly grant access to an attacker by falling prey to a social engineering attack. Amid this battle, the security professional must conduct another fight—a fight with management for the support and resources required to protect the company's information assets.

As if this were not enough, various regulatory bodies constantly mandate new requirements and regulations that the security professional not only must implement but also must monitor for compliance. Although the new regulations can sometimes be used to gain support for necessary security functions, often they add overhead and complexity to the security professional's world. The security professional must strike a balance between paranoia and vigilance, as well as between extreme measures to protect information assets and the need to do business and manage the cost benefit of security.

We see this fight each day and try to help security professionals and organizations manage this constantly evolving beast. In our first book, *Hack I.T.*, we shared the thoughts and techniques that our clients have found helpful.[1] Although the first book was well received, we heard a single common stream of feedback: "We loved your book, especially the case studies. Next time you should try to incorporate more." We accepted this feedback and saw the readers' point. We also reflected on the fact that when we give presentations on information security, our case studies are often the best-received portion of the talk. Then the idea came to us: Why not write a book consisting completely of case studies? That's when we decided to write *Defend I.T.*

We are both fortunate and unfortunate that the security field is still an emerging area. There is no Generally Accepted Accounting Principles (GAAP) for security. Efforts by the International Information Security Foundation (I^2SF) to create Generally Accepted System Security Principles (GASSP) are under way, but these efforts are still fairly young and have quite a way to go before they are as widely accepted as GAAP. No single guidebook has all the answers. We, the security professionals, must gather as much information and assistance as we can from books, publications, organizations, and colleagues. But in the face of adversity comes opportunity. In the fairly uncharted waters of information security, there is room for professionals to develop new ideas and blaze new trails in helping to defend information security.

There is not just one way to attack security. Numerous methods and approaches can all yield successful results. Usually by reaching out for ideas and lessons learned from our colleagues, however, we can see what worked, what did not, and what will probably work for us. By presenting case studies, we can share some of the approaches we have used and discuss what has worked and what

---

1. The primary authors of this book previously collaborated on *Hack I.T.—Security Through Penetration Testing* (Addison-Wesley, 2002).

hasn't. We hope you will benefit from this insight and learn valuable information that you can apply to your environment.

Each case study in this book focuses on a different issue in information security. Of course this book is not all-encompassing, but we have sought to develop a well-rounded mix of case studies that can build from the content of *Hack I.T.*, as well as cover new topics. In the case studies we try to highlight the technical issues, as well as the softer issues. Often the politics, policies, and personnel interactions are as crucial to an organization's security posture as are the technical issues. We have tried to provide some insight into how we as security professionals deal with these issues.

DISCLAIMERS

Because we are relating instances of real life, it is prudent to make several disclaimers. So here they are.

The events related in this book are based on actual events; however, every effort has been taken to hide the identity of the individuals, organizations, and institutions involved. As the saying goes—but for our own, "the names have been changed to protect the innocent." In each case study, dates, places, and some other information (not affecting the case) have been changed to protect all parties concerned. Some case studies may be compilations of multiple events or cases.

Any similarity to existing names (other than those of the authors), organizations, institutions, places, times, or procedures is purely coincidental.

In changing the names and selecting new names, we have attempted to be creative. For example, Chapter 2 deals with an application service provider (ASP) that we have called Aspen, Inc., because one of us has always wanted to go skiing in Aspen. In other cases, we have used the names of musicians of bands that inspire us, such as the Beatles, U2, and others. We do this for two reasons: First, it keeps things lively while driving home the point that the names are changed. Second, it doesn't seem very likely that anyone would believe the great Sir Paul McCartney to be a hacker.

Left unchanged are the titles of the individuals involved (for example, CISO, CFO) so that the reader can infer the type of work or responsibility that a particular position entails. This can be helpful in the course of fieldwork and in comparing the responses and actions of the organizations discussed in the book with those of your own organization.

Further, we have stayed honest in our description of the cases presented. Details may well have been omitted, again to protect identities, but we have attempted to provide sufficient details to give a clear picture of the security incidents—the losses incurred and the countermeasures that were or could have been implemented in defense. In all cases, the distinction between what was done and what could have been done is clearly made.

We trust that the descriptions, even under these conditions, will be helpful in educating the reader about the activities of a security professional and about the tasks involved in such a career.

Before we leave you to the body of the text, we wish you happy reading and hope this book will be as beneficial for you to read as it has been challenging for us to write.

PART I
BASIC
HACKING

Getting to Know the Enemy

Nmap the Target Network

Before actually breaking into a network, hackers—at least the good ones—spend a bit of time (and sometimes more than just a bit) getting to know the target network, mapping it out. The more information they can gather about the network, the better they will know how to break into it—and whether or not they really want to try.

This first chapter discusses such activity. There is no actual break-in in this case study; instead it looks at the preliminary activities that a hacker engages in before staging a break-in. After evaluating a network, sometimes a hacker decides that breaking in will require too much time and effort, and therefore simply moves on to another target. That's the desired result (from the network administrator's perspective). In other cases, mapping the target network clearly identifies a path onto the network.

1.1 Network Architecture

Throughout this book we will introduce diverse tools and techniques used by hackers and crackers to gain information on target networks that can be helpful in understanding how best to compromise and gain access to those target networks.

In this first case study we will introduce one of the most widely used tools available: Nmap (www.insecure.org/nmap). Nmap is one of the premier tools used for ping sweeps and port scans, as well as for operating system identification. We will see how these capabilities (among numerous others) are used by potential intruders to gather information about, or **fingerprint**, their targets in advance of a cyber attack. In addition, we will see how and where complementary tools are used to gain the maximum possible amount of information from the network.

The material in this case study depicts the actions that a potential hacker took in evaluating the network for attack. The process highlights many of the tools, capabilities, and general process of fingerprinting a network. As mentioned in the Introduction, all names have been changed to protect the innocent. In this and other case studies in this book, any similarities to real situations are strictly coincidental.

Let's start with a description of the target environment. Keep in mind that, when beginning to investigate a network, an intruder probably will not know this information; identifying this information is the goal. The network under examination in this case belongs to a medium-sized corporation and follows a typical network design supporting a 10/100 MB Ethernet network. There is an Internet router, providing connectivity to the Internet, followed by a firewall. A demilitarized zone (DMZ) lies behind the firewall, along with the firm's backbone switch. The corporate local area network (LAN) connects to this backbone switch, as illustrated in Figure 1.1.

Network fingerprinting attempts to capitalize on the information leakage from the network to draw a network topology map similar to or even more detailed than the one shown in Figure 1.1. Intruders often elect to begin their information gathering by examining the DMZ, as was the case here, because the DMZ generally hosts the public-facing Web server, and therefore it is the first place to connect to or interact with the target's network. The DMZ can often provide many bits of useful information relevant to the overall network. First of all, it is sure to have Internet-accessible hosts with open ports—that is, hosts that can be reached across the firewall from the Internet.

In addition to Web servers, DMZs often include domain name servers (DNSs) and mail servers. The DNS is needed to facilitate Internet routing to and from the Web server. Placing a mail server in the DMZ can allow for direct mail

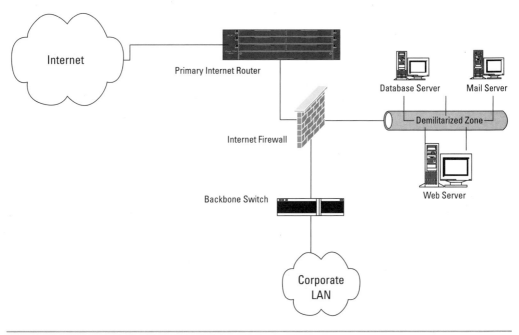

Figure 1.1 Typical Network Architecture

responses to queries on the company's Web site. It also potentially allows employees to access company e-mail over the Web. Because they expect so much anonymous Internet traffic, DMZs are usually not monitored by intrusion detection systems (IDSs) or other network-monitoring tools. This situation is changing, however. As IDS traffic-processing capabilities improve, more and more companies are starting to monitor the DMZ as well.

An unlucky few DMZ systems are misconfigured and provide a logical connection with the back-end network, increasing the attractiveness of these systems to hackers. Such a logical connection is shown in Figure 1.2.

The purpose of such connections is generally to allow Web developers to upload newly developed Web content from their development PCs to the production Web server. When such connections exist, they are effectively back doors that allow hackers to access network resources almost entirely undetected—undetected to the extent that they are not using the established route through the router

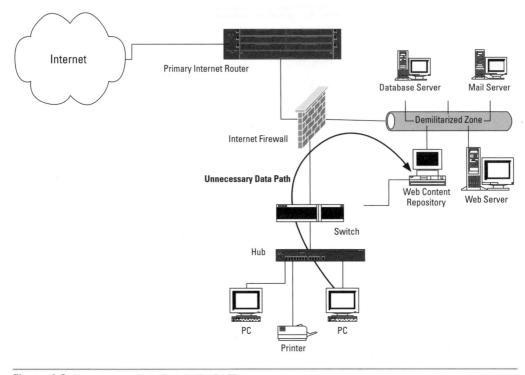

Figure 1.2 Unnecessary Data Path to the DMZ

and across the firewall. These connections can be discovered by examination of the routing tables on the hosts within the DMZ. In addition, when these connections are left in place for long periods of time or permanently, they can be identified through ping sweeps and traceroutes of the DMZ or by examination of the ARP (Address Resolution Protocol) table.

The firm in this particular case had a relatively simple and straightforward DMZ because there was no large-scale Web infrastructure. The more complicated the Web infrastructure becomes—consisting of, for example, numerous Web servers hosting a large collection of Web-based applications, each communicating with multiple databases—the greater will be the likelihood of identifying useful information on the target network or of finding a direct vulnerability.

Therefore, because intruders often spend time casing out the DMZ before launching attacks against other network resources, it is essential that security administrators follow a similar process to evaluate the installation of the company's DMZ in order to ascertain its security posture.

1.2 PORT SCANS

The intruder in this case study began the reconnaissance with a simple scan. The first scan is always simple, to avoid creating too much of a racket (noise), which could trigger network monitoring and intrusion detection tools. And in any case, the first step is to find out what hosts are listening and can be attacked at all, using the following Nmap command:

```
#nmap -p80 www.targetcompany.com/24
```

If the command executes successfully, the IP address of the company's Web server(s) will be returned. Here's the result of the command:

```
Starting nmap V. 2.54BETA7 ( http://www.insecure.org/nmap )
Interesting ports on target_machine_name(X.X.X.03):
Port     State   Service
80/tcp   open    http

Nmap run completed - 1 IP address (1 host up) scanned in 1 second
```

Old Is Gold

Astute readers may have recognized that the version of Nmap used here is more than 50 releases out-of-date. In fact, as of this writing, Nmap 3.49 was the latest stable version available, and even this version may be out-of-date by the time the book is printed. Between the time these events took place and the writing, many changes and enhancements have been made to Nmap that offer greater functionality and would likely make network footprinting, if not easier, at least more convenient.

For example, the initial port scan can include an -sV flag to perform version detection on the Web server. Nmap can identify the versions of numerous servers and daemons—including Web servers, FTP, Telnet, DNS, numerous UNIX daemons, and RPC programs—with the following command:

```
#nmap -p80 -sV www.targetcompany.com/24
```

Sample output generated by such a scan on a single host (felix, 127.0.0.1) looks like this:[1]

```
Starting nmap 3.40PVT16 ( http://www.insecure.org/nmap/ ) at 2003-09-07 02:56 PDT
Interesting ports on felix (127.0.0.1):

(The 1640 ports scanned but not shown below are in state: closed)
PORT       STATE SERVICE     VERSION
21/tcp     open  ftp         WU-FTPD wu-2.6.1-20
22/tcp     open  ssh         OpenSSH 3.1p1 (protocol 1.99)
53/tcp     open  domain      ISC Bind 9.2.1
79/tcp     open  finger      Linux fingerd
111/tcp    open  rpcbind     2 (rpc #100000)
443/tcp    open  ssl/http    Apache httpd 2.0.39 ((Unix) mod_perl/1.99 04-dev [cut])
515/tcp    open  printer
631/tcp    open  ipp         CUPS 1.1
953/tcp    open  rndc?
5000/tcp open  ssl/ftp     WU-FTPD wu-2.6.1-20
5001/tcp open  ssl/ssh     OpenSSH 3.1p1 (protocol 1.99)
5002/tcp open  ssl/domain ISC Bind 9.2.1
5003/tcp open  ssl/finger Linux fingerd
6000/tcp open  X11         (access denied)
8000/tcp open  http-proxy Junkbuster webproxy
8080/tcp open  http        Apache httpd 2.0.39 ((Unix) mod_perl/1.99_04-dev [cut])
8081/tcp open  http        Apache httpd 2.0.39 ((Unix) mod_perl/1.99_04-dev [cut])
Device type: general purpose
Running: Linux 2.4.X|2.5.X
OS details: Linux Kernel 2.4.0 - 2.5.20
Uptime 8.653 days (since Fri Aug 29 11:16:40 2003)

Nmap run completed -- 1 IP address (1 host up) scanned in 42.494 seconds
```

Right away the hacker can know what software the networks' Web servers are running. This information can then be used to discover known or potential exploits that may provide access to the network.

Scanning for port 80, while not necessarily a guarantee, does help to find all the hosts on the target network that are running Web servers. In addition to the public Web server, there may be staging, development, backup, or internal Web servers that are insecure or offer private information. In addition, port 80 is likely to be open on the firewall because Web traffic generally passes over this

---

1. This sample output was generously contributed by Fyodor and is available online at http://www.insecure.org/nmap/versionscan.html.

port. Nmap returns the IP address (X.X.X.03) of the target, potentially allowing the hacker to scan the related class C address space (X.X.X.x). But first the hacker must verify the class associated with the IP address. A popular method for doing this is to consult the whois service for the domain:

#whois *targetcompany.com*

Whois is available as a command-line tool on most UNIX flavors, as well as over numerous Web sites, such as arin.net (American Registry for Internet Numbers) and networksolutions.com, and sometimes whois is all that's necessary. The following information was returned on whois queries against the author's firm:

```
Registrant:
ANG Computer Technologies, Inc. (GSECURITY2-DOM)
   7215-C Hanover Parkway
   Greenbelt, MD 20770
   US

   Domain Name: GSECURITY.COM

   Administrative Contact:
      ANG Computer Technologies, Inc.  (025138-OR)    no.valid.email@worldnic.com
      ANG Computer Technologies, Inc.
      7215-C Hanover Parkway
      Greenbelt, MD 20770
      US
      301-345-7595
   Technical Contact:
      VeriSign, Inc.  (HOST-ORG)           namehost@WORLDNIC.NET
      VeriSign, Inc.
      21355 Ridgetop Circle
      Dulles, VA 20166
      US
      1-888-642-9675

   Record expires on 01-Aug-2005.
   Record created on 01-Aug-2001.
   Database last updated on 18-Mar-2003 20:37:00 EST.

   Domain servers in listed order:
```

```
NS.CIHOST.COM               216.221.162.81
NS2.CIHOST.COM              216.221.162.111
```

If the hacker is unable to identify the class of the network (as was the case here), the entire class C will have to be scanned, as follows:

```
#nmap -v -p 80 X.X.X.1-254
#nmap -v -p 53 -sU  X.X.X.1-254
#nmap -v -p 53 -sT X.X.X.1-254
#nmap -v -p 25   X.X.X.1-254
#nmap -v -p 110  X.X.X.1-254
#nmap -v -p 143  X.X.X.1-254
#nmap -v -p 139  X.X.X.1-254
#nmap -v -p 445  X.X.X.1-254
#nmap -v -p 6000  X.X.X.1-254
```

As we can see, the intruder uses numerous scans rather than one, larger scan in order to keep his activities quiet, beneath the radar of an IDS and watchful security administrators.

The intruder did not specify the protocol in the scan against port 80 (the Hyper-Text Transfer Protocol, or HTTP), because Nmap will default to TCP (Transmission Control Protocol), and there is little reason to scan for UDP (User Datagram Protocol) over this port. In successive scans against port 53 (the DNS port), the protocols UDP and TCP were specified. Over these ports, zone information is exchanged; in other words, the host name–to–IP address mappings for that zone are exchanged between DNS servers and routers. Although the DNS has primarily UDP traffic, it does switch to TCP if the traffic is larger than 512 bytes.

> **ASIDE:** A host that responds as "up" but with port 80 "closed" may be a DNS. Try a UDP scan (-sU) against port 53.

If DNS traffic is allowed through the firewall, a zone transfer might be possible. A **zone transfer** is a querying of the full DNS record, or potentially the entire host name–to–IP address mapping of the zone. We say "potentially" because an individual DNS may not contain information for all the hosts in the zone. Some zones can be split among multiple DNSs, and other hosts may have Dynamic

Host Configuration Protocol (DHCP), which allocates IP addresses from a previously specified range on demand—usually when the machine connects to the network. Still, capturing this information (a zone transfer) is one potential way to identify the data path to the corporate network. A zone transfer will be possible if the DNS allows transfers to unauthorized zones; however, many DNSs now block zone transfers except to specifically authorized IP addresses.

The intruder also checks ports 25 (SMTP), 110 (POP3), and 143 (IMAP). An open port 25 may indicate an e-mail server, especially in conjunction with ports 110 and 143 because these are interfaces at which the e-mail servers aim to allow users to download their e-mails to their machines.

Checks for ports 139, 445, and 6000 are an effort to identify the operating system of the target. Ports 139 and 445 are typical Windows ports (for NT and 2000/XP, respectively), and port 6000 is a typical UNIX port (the X11 service). Identifying the target's operating system is a large step in the direction of compromising the target because potential avenues of attack and known vulnerabilities can be explored. For instance, there are numerous, well-documented holes for Windows operating systems. Although Nmap has a specific option (-O) for determining the operating system of a target host, this "poor man's version identification" can be helpful early because the scans take less time than an OS identification scan takes. The savings in time is important because at this point the hacker is casting a wide net, and every effort needs to be made to keep the scans quiet. The -O scan is generally done against specific hosts, as we will discuss in Section 1.3.

In this manner, the intruder can perform numerous scans to find open ports on the firewall and identify hosts and running applications behind the firewall. Because the scans are kept small—only one port scanned at a time—this approach helps minimize the chances of triggering an IDS alert. Spacing the scans apart in time can further keep things quiet. Although there is no rule of thumb for how slow one should go, we have seen network mapping performed at a rate of just one scan per day over several months.

Identifying the applications not only helps to identify the vulnerabilities that they may bring to the network, but also indicates how to connect to the target. Once we know an application—for example, Telnet—running on a target

As Sly as a Fox

When stealth is not required, a more intrusive but informative scan of the whole class C network can be performed with the following command:

```
#nmap -A -T4 X.X.X.1-254
```

Going a step further, the option −p1−65535 could also be specified to scan all 65,535 TCP ports on each machine rather than just the default 1600+. The −P0 flag can be specified to do the full scan on each IP address even if the host doesn't respond to ping requests. Both of these options substantially increases the amount of time the scan takes to complete.

These scans are helpful for performing internal reviews or security assessments. They are a good way to obtain a sense of the services that are running on your machines and network.

network, we can research that application to identify its known holes and attempt to exploit those against the target. Sometimes during our research, we will also find exploit code for those vulnerabilities. Keep in mind that we must also identify the specific version and sometimes the maker of the application to research it thoroughly. Simultaneously, once we know that Telnet is running, we know that Telnet connections may be a way to access the network.

For example, once the attacker in this case had identified port 25 (SMTP) as being open, he attempted to identify the version of the application by making a Telnet connection to the port:

```
# telnet target_IP_address 25
```

The banner presented during the connection process will generally reveal all the information necessary. There are many applications for capturing application banners, including the freeware tools What's Running, netcat, and Grabbb. These tools are available at www.woodstone.nu/whats, packetstormsecurity.org, and ftp.firewalls.com.br/grabbb.tar.gz.

One way to use the Grabbb tool is to create a file with all the IP addresses to be scanned. For example, the following echo command can be used to create a file with the target IP address, in this case (for illustration) the address for the author's machine:

```
#echo " X.X.X.03" > example.txt
```

And now we run Grabbb, pointing to the example.txt file (through the –i flag):

```
#grabbb -i example.txt 22:25:80
```

The output generated by this command is as follows:

```
X.X.X.03:22: SSH-2.0-OpenSSH_3.5p1
X.X.X.03:25: 220 Welcome to Mail Server
X.X.X.03:80: Apache
```

We can see now the banners returned by applications running over ports 22, 25, and 80.

1.3 OS Identification

After identifying the availability of the popular ports, the intruder turns his attention to discovering the type of operating system (OS), and architecture hopefully, he is dealing with. The open ports give some idea of what the OS might be, as discussed already, but the following Nmap command string is used to reach a more reliable conclusion:

```
#nmap -O -sS -g 53 -v -F -oN filename --data_length 20 -n  -M 20
--max_parallelism 20 -randomize_hosts -iL targetIP_list -P0
```

The OS is identified with the -O command. The process of identification is to examine the target host's responses to the port scan SYN packets that it receives. RFCs (Requests for Comments) determine how such packets should be handled, but implementation details are left up to individual vendors. The differences in implementation details can allow a distinction between operating systems to be made.

In the preceding command, the intruder uses the -g flag to set port 53 (DNS) as the source port. This is an effort both to deceive the firewall and to convince the

DNS server that the request is a legitimate name resolution query. If the firewall is a proxy firewall, it is easier to deceive because it looks primarily at the source IP address and port to determine whether a connection should be allowed.

The -randomize_hosts flag, as its name suggests, randomly selects target IP addresses from those specified. The -v flag puts Nmap in the verbose mode, thereby increasing the tool's output (the -vv flag increases output even more). Inclusion of the -oN flag and a file name allows the output to be written to a log file so that the results can be referred to later.

Writing the output to a log file is highly recommended, especially if your efforts are part of a consulting engagement at a client site. By the same token, the –iL command tells Nmap to take the target IP addresses from the specified file (here, targetIP_list). This is a good way to record which IP addresses are being scanned. The -F flag scans for all ports in the Nmap_services file, which is a well-known list of ports that ships with Nmap. The -P0 flag tells Nmap not to ping the hosts, and just to proceed with the scan. This flag is important for scanning any hosts that do not respond to pings.

The other options used are not strictly necessary, but they do serve a purpose. We will describe them briefly; additional description is available on the Nmap man page (http://www.insecure.org/nmap/data/nmap_manpage.html). The --data_length option tells Nmap to pad packets with a specified number (here 20) of zero-filled bytes. Packets are padded to slow the scan down and reduce suspicion. The -n flag tells Nmap not to do a DNS resolution on the target.

The -M option sets the maximum number (here 20) of sockets to use simultaneously, thereby reducing the chance of placing too much of a burden on the target. Setting the maximum number of sockets is more critical for TCP full scans (-sT), which require more resources than half scans (-sS) do.

The --max_parallelism option tells Nmap the maximum number (here 20) of ping or port scans that Nmap can do simultaneously. Again, specifying this maximum can slow down the scan and help hide what's going on. In this case, it may be a bit of overkill to try to keep the scan quiet, but one can never be too safe—especially when breaking the law.

This scan can be run against only those hosts that have been identified as "up" by the previous scans. Therefore, scans are not performed on all 254 potential hosts within the class C address space.

1.3.1 ADDITIONAL OS IDENTIFICATION TOOLS

Other tools can be used to identify the OS as well, such as the freeware tools xprobe (available from numerous sources, including ftp://ftp.firewalls.com.br/xprobe.tgz and sourceforge.net) and Camal (ftp://ftp.firewalls.com.br/camal.tgz).

Xprobe is a simple UDP-based OS identification scanner and is launched with the following command:

```
#xprobe X.X.X.02
```

The result of the tool is as follows:

```
Xprobe ver. 0.0.2
------------------
Interface: eth0/<host>

LOG: Target: <host>
LOG: Netmask: 255.255.255.0
LOG: probing: <host>
LOG: [send]-> UDP to <host>
LOG: [98 bytes] sent, waiting for response.
FINAL:[3Com SuperStack II Switch SWNBBSI-CF,11.1.0.00S38
Nokia IPSO 3.2-2.3.1 releng 783-849
Ricoh Aficio AP4500 Network Laster Printer
Linux 2.0.x/2.2.x/2.4.x
Shiva AccessPort Bridge/Router Software V.2.1.0 ]
```

Another tool for identifying the OS is Camal, which uses ICMP (Internet Control Message Protocol) techniques to discover the OS of the target machine. Camal essentially runs a port scan of ports 1 through 1024, the ports assigned to well-known services. The tool is launched as follows:

```
#camal -S -O X.X.X.04
Enter the START PORT of the port range: 1
Enter the STOP PORT of the port range: 1024
```

The output of the tool looks like this:

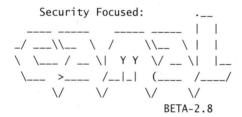

```
Address: A.B.C.02/ 1 to 1
PID: 2092
DNS Info: Working (good!)
OPENED PORTS:
```

ftp	21/tcp	# file transfer [control], file transfer protocol
ssh	22/tcp	# secure shell login
smtp	25/tcp mail	# simple mail transfer
domain	53/tcp nameserver	# domain name server, name-domain server
http	80/tcp http	# worldwideweb http, world wide web
httppop3	110/tcp pop3 pop-3	# pop version 3, postoffice v.3
sunrpc	111/tcp portmap	# portmapper, rpcbind, remote procedure call
netbios-ssn	139/tcp	# netbios session service
https	443/tcp	# secure http (ssl), http protocol over tls/ssl
pop3s	995/tcp	# pop3 protocol over tls/ssl
vsinet	996/tcp xtreelic	# vsinet, xtree license server

```
There are no filtered ports.

OS GUESS RESULTS:

Hex stack: 0xd016
Stack TCP/IP: Linux 2.4.2 - 2.4.9


Scan of X.X.X.04 completed.
1023 ports scanned, 11 ports open, 0 filtered ports.
```

1.4 PARTIAL PICTURE

At this point the intruder has identified critical ports open on target hosts and can make an educated guess as to their application (or function) and as to the host operating system. With this information, along with a traceroute to the target Web server, the intruder can draw a view of the target network. VisualRoute is a commercial GUI (graphical user interface) application that performs a traceroute, and can identify the data path between a source and its destination. A demo version of VisualRoute is available from the company's Web site, http://www.visualroute.com, along with an online demo. Traceroute is also a native tool on both Windows (`tracert`) and UNIX (`traceroute`). Analysis of the resultant data path, shown in Figure 1.3, can help identify Internet routers and firewalls.

The intruder must still trace a better profile of the firewall in question and chooses to use the Xmas scan:

```
# nmap -sX -P0 targetIP
```

An Xmas scan (performed with flag `-sX`) is a scan with all flags set, including the FIN, URG, and PUSH flags.

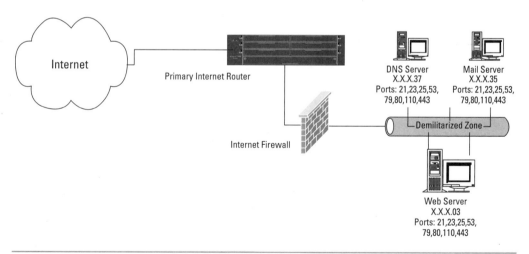

Figure 1.3 Partial View of the Target Network

Hide in Plain Sight

Keep in mind that many firewalls use an interesting option to hide from VisualRoute and other route-tracing tools. These tools send packets with a Time to Live (TTL) value of 1 when first tracing the route to the target. Because the TTL measures individual hops (moving from one router to the next) along the path, when the first router in the path sees the packet, it decrements the TTL and returns an ICMP-time-exceeded message. The route-tracing tools then send out a packet with a TTL value of 2 and receive an ICMP-time-exceeded message from the second router on the path. In this process, the tool is able to determine each step in the path between the source and the destination.

Firewalls, however, can increment by 1 the value in the TTL field so that the ICMP-time-exceeded message is sent back from the next upstream hop and not the firewall. To the route-tracing tool, it will look as if the firewall doesn't exist, helping to make the hacker's attempts more difficult.

If an Xmas packet passes through the firewall, it is an indication that the firewall does not analyze the TCP flags that are set in incoming packets. If a FIN scan can also pass, the implication is that the firewall is not tracking the connections (i.e., it is not a stateful inspection firewall) and thus is most likely a proxy firewall:

```
#nmap -sF -P0 targetIP
```

Having confirmed the type of the firewall, the intruder has another bit of information to add to his diagram, as shown in Figure 1.4.

Seeing Is Believing

The interested reader can confirm that the Xmas scan is a scan with all the flags set by monitoring the packet with tcpdump. When using the Nmap Xmas scan (try it against your own machine), monitor traffic with the following tcpdump command:

```
#tcpdump -I lo -w outputfilename.log
```

Tcpdump is a very useful network-sniffing utility and is widely used to view raw network traffic. The Nmap -packet_trace option, available in the current version of Nmap, allows the user to see the packets that Nmap sends and receives. This option can be used in place of analyzing tcpdump output.

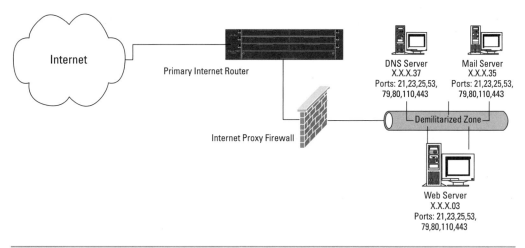

Figure 1.4 Proxy Firewall

To gain additional information about the firewall, we can scan the machine with invalid TCP flags (SYN/FIN), as follows:

```
#rsc -p tcp --saddr <your host> --daddr <targetIP> --sport 1025 --dport 23
--syn --fin
Raw Socket Constructor :
  src  ip : <your host>
  dest ip : <targetIP>
  src  port : 1025
  dest port : 23
  protocol : tcp
```

Multiple uses of the `rsc` command with different source and destination port pairs allow the user to test the firewall's filtering capabilities or configuration. For example, they can be set to reserved ports (<1024) to test if the firewall prevents connections between the known ports. The destination port (`--dport`) will have to be set to an open port on the firewall.

1.5 HIDING

The hacker in this case went to some lengths to keep his activities unknown to the target. Some additional options help Nmap to go unnoticed: the decoy scan

(-D) and the timing option (-T). As you might imagine, the decoy scan attempts to fool the target as to the source of the Nmap scan. Shown in the following command, the –D option allows the hacker to provide fake source IP addresses.

```
#nmap -O -sS -g 53 -vv -p 21,23,25,79,80,110,143,443 -oN filename –D
A.B.C.4-9 -T 2 -randomize_hosts -iL targetIP_list -P0
```

Nmap randomly selects from among the actual and the supplied decoy addresses when supplying the source address to the target. The -D option does not replace the true source address; however, it can increase the field of space that the target must investigate. It may also slow correlation of the scan to a particular entity.

In addition, the –T option sets the time between successive packets sent out by Nmap. Six canned timing policies are available: Paranoid (0, the slowest), Sneaky (1), Polite (2), Normal (3, the default), Aggressive (4), and Insane (5, the fastest).

Values of 0, 1, and 2 serialize Nmap and separate successive packets by 5 minutes, 15 seconds, and 0.4 seconds, respectively. Be careful with any of these options; they can make scans take an incredibly long time (scans running for days and weeks are not unheard of). Increasing the time between packets will certainly help avoid detection, but it requires a great deal of patience.

Conversely, if you are interested in speeding things up, the Aggressive and Insane options are available. These options add a timeout for each host (5 minutes and 15 seconds, respectively) so that the program does not wait very long for a response. This approach may well speed up scans, but it may cause you to miss some information. Alternative timeouts can be set for individual hosts with the –host_timeout command (note that this command takes a value in milliseconds).

In an even more advanced method of keeping scans hidden from observers, the attacker uses the –sI option to launch an idlescan. An **idlescan** is a "blind scan" of the network that intruders perform by launching a side-channel attack from a zombie host. Such a scan, as shown here, attempts to use predictable IP fragmentation ID sequence generation on the zombie host to gather information about any open ports on the ultimate target:

```
#nmap -P0 -sI <zombie_host> <targetIP>

Starting nmap V. 3.10ALPHA9 ( www.insecure.org/nmap/ )
Idlescan zombie <zombie_host> (<targetIP>) port 80 cannot be used because
IPID sequencability class is: All zeros.  Try another proxy.
QUITTING!
```

For the scan to work, the zombie host must, therefore, have the IPID sequence bug. As in the example shown, the zombie host did not have this bug, unfortunately for the hacker.

1.6 LESSONS LEARNED

As we have seen, a hacker can gain a great deal of information on the target network by simply using freeware tools over the Internet and gathering information that the network will voluntarily provide. It is also safe to assume that similar activities are under way, or have been performed, on most networks in operation today. There are two primary countermeasures to these preliminary activities.

The first is to have a finely tuned intrusion detection system (IDS) that can recognize such reconnaissance activity. Setting up such an IDS means fine-tuning thresholds for network-scanning activity. Granted, the more subtle the hacker's activities, the more finely tuned the thresholds will have to be. However, careful examination of logs at the firewall and router, in conjunction with careful analysis of (network and/or host) IDS alerts can warn system administrators of potential cyber attacks.

Second, system administrators should attempt to restrict, to the full extent possible, all information leakage. Measures taken should include strictly limiting DNS zone transfers to authorized hosts, as well as removing all identifying information from banners. (However, it is important to verify that removing or changing banners does not void any software warranty or support contracts.)

For example, as we saw in our discussion of the Grabbb tool (Section 1.2), in this case study complete information on the applications running over TCP ports 25 (mail) and 80 (Web) was not made available, whereas a great deal of information regarding TCP port 22 (SSH, Secure Shell) was available. The information is repeated here.

```
#grabbb -i example.txt 22:25:80
```

Here's the output generated by this command:

```
192.168.0.1:22: SSH-2.0-OpenSSH_3.5p1
192.168.0.1:25: 220 Welcome to Mail Server
192.168.0.1:80: Apache
```

To ensure the security of your server or workstation, it is important to restrict the information that the system volunteers. This example uses SSH protocol 2.0 and OpenSSH 3.5p1. Information volunteered by the system is not needed by anyone who should not have access. In fact, many authorized users also don't need to know this information or have it presented to them when they attempt to use the application. The Web server does not identify its version, but it does still announce itself as an Apache Web server. The mail server is another step ahead, offering even less information.

Restricting information volunteered by the system is sometimes derided as mere security by obscurity, but it can at least help reduce the network's information leakage and slow down a hacker's ability to gain information.

HOME ARCHITECTURE

In our society, having a second home is a mark of wealth. We often work hard and save money so that someday we can afford a second home in the mountains, or on a beach, or possibly in a resort city, or best of all, in Las Vegas.

In IT, there is the concept of a **dual-homed** host, in which a single host machine has two network addresses—placing it simultaneously on two different networks. Yes, this does somewhat describe a router. A router, however, is not a host, and a router has software specifically designed to allow it to serve as a checkpoint to control the flow of traffic among multiple networks.

A host (normal desktop PC) does not generally run such software and may not (likely does not) have the ability to control traffic flow between networks. Anyone with access to the host on one network probably has access to the other network as well. This dual access can cause problems, as we shall see.

In truth, a second network address is not so much like a second home as it is like a second driveway. Still, the term *dual home* is what has stuck.

2.1 INTRODUCTION

This case study dates to the early days of the application service provider (ASP) business model, when porting business applications and processes onto the

Internet to achieve great efficiency and cost reduction was just becoming a possibility. I mention this because this is another case, like so many, in which the jump into IT preceded accommodations for security.

2.2 BACKGROUND

The ASP, Aspen, Inc., was providing numerous commercial and custom applications to its customers, including enterprise resource planning and customer relationship management applications, as well as Web-hosting services. These applications were residing on the appropriately named Applications Network, or AppsNet for short.

Clients accessed the AppsNet through a VPN (virtual private network) link, as shown in Figure 2.1. Any client personnel who required access to the AppsNet

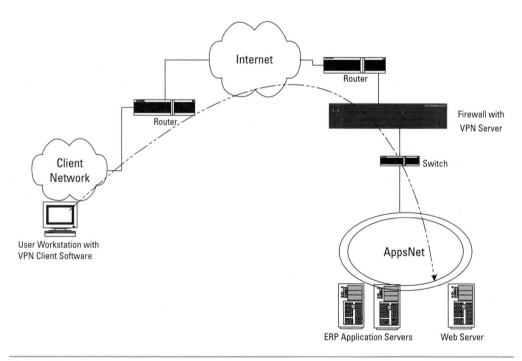

Figure 2.1 Aspen's Application Network

had VPN client software, with the required user name and password pair precon-figured, installed on their PCs. Unless a client specifically requested it, individual users were not tracked and everyone had the same user name and password. (There was one user name and password for each such client.)

The overall network topology, shown in Figure 2.2, included a DMZ hosting the corporate Web site, as well as the AppsNet, a development network (DevNet), and a corporate network. The corporate network for the ASP was essentially flat. Although the developers spent some time and energy in optimally designing the AppsNet, they spent very little in designing their own network or the DevNet. There's a finite collection of resources, after all, and the Aspen developers chose to put their money into the AppsNet, from which they make their money, and just get by with their own network.

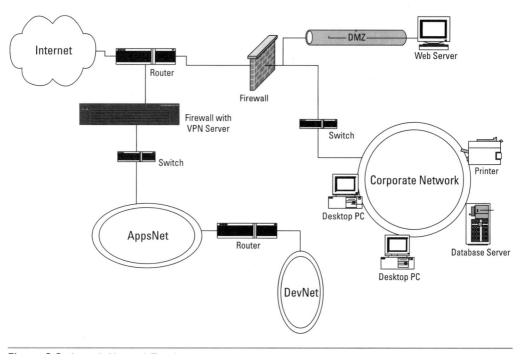

Figure 2.2 Aspen's Network Topology

2.3 THE INCIDENT

This incident was not discovered by flashing lights and alerts set off by an intrusion detection system (IDS) or through a noticeable decline in network speeds (see Chapter 6, Virus Outbreak II: The Worm). In fact, there was no early indication of a network compromise. There were hints, however—the kind that often require the benefit of hindsight to recognize.

2.3.1 THE MONTHLY BILL

One day, Aspen's billing department requested the network usage (access) report for REM & Associates (a client). This report documented the number of times that a connection from REM was made to the AppsNet over the VPN and the duration of each connection. Because a component of Aspen's bill to REM was dependent on the amount of time spent using the software, this report was requested monthly and was used to determine the final billing amount.

Aspen's account representative for REM compiled the system usage report from the access logs. The review of the access logs indicated that although most of the connections were made during normal working hours, there was activity in the middle of the night, especially between 11:00 PM and 4:00 AM. Even though this was a break from the pattern established during the previous year, the account representative and others at Aspen thought nothing of it, since clients do sometimes alter their usage patterns and long days are common whenever a firm is up against a deadline, such as an end-of-year or end-of-quarter deadline. So the account representative bundled off the report to the billing department and kept a copy in her file. The billing department processed the report and calculated the total bill, which was a bit higher than in previous months, and sent it off to the client.

REM received the bill and noticed that it was higher than usual. The difference was attributable mostly to the increased system usage reflected in the nocturnal connections. Perhaps the increase wasn't substantial enough to warrant further attention, though, for REM paid the bill and filed the invoice. This pattern repeated itself the following month, but the fee was even higher, due again in large part to the nocturnal connections.

This time, REM launched an internal investigation to find out who was pulling the all-nighters. Since Aspen was not tracking individual usage, REM management asked all of its employees with access to the AppsNet if they had been working longer shifts. All users confirmed that they were using the system strictly during working hours. Management then checked the staff time sheets, and sure enough, everyone with the VPN client software had stamped out between 5:00 PM and 6:00 PM on days when activity deep into the night was reported on Aspen's bill.

REM did not know what to make of the usage report or the high bills. They brought the situation up with Aspen, who said that the logs clearly showed connections coming in from REM to Aspen. Aspen offered REM a more detailed log report, as well as the opportunity to inspect the logs if they wished. REM did request the access log to be shared on a weekly rather than monthly basis so that they could track the usage more closely.

> **ASIDE:** REM management had considered asking Aspen to cut off access after hours, but doing so would have hampered REM's own productivity on nights when they really did need to access applications on the AppsNet. Further, REM felt the evidence suggested that an outside individual was accessing their network—something they needed either to verify or to disprove.

It quickly became clear that someone from REM was in fact accessing Aspen's application network, but who?

2.3.2 THE E-MAIL

At about the same time, Aspen had started to receive e-mails, from a source address on Aspen's e-mail server, requesting politely (read: demanding) certain sums of money and various online benefits (e.g., free e-mail address for life, free online storage space). Naturally, the sender was interested in receiving these things as a part of an equal exchange and not just for free. The sender was prepared to abstain from releasing Aspen's customers' names and financial information, which the sender had obtained from Aspen's databases, to the highest bidder.

The e-mails were written in a jovial, comical tone, but the reader was left no doubt of their seriousness. These e-mails contained a partial collection of sensitive customer information, as well as the name, IP address, and MAC (media access control) address of the server from which the information originated. This situation called for an immediate investigation.

2.3.3 THE INVESTIGATION

A computer forensics and cyber crime team was brought in immediately. The team reviewed everything related to the case up to that point and suspected the e-mail sender to be the hacker involved. This could not be assumed, however; it had to be explicitly proven (presumed innocent until proven guilty). The cyber crime team was successful in baiting the sender into talking through e-mails and sharing how he was able to access the information.

ASIDE: We are all thankful for loquacious crime culprits.

The crime team learned that access to the back-end server was obtained originally through the AppsNet, which was accessed from one of Aspen's clients. The sender also claimed now to have access to all of Aspen's clients' data and accounts on the AppsNet.

2.3.4 THE DISCLOSURE

The statements made in the sender's e-mails were deemed reliable enough for Aspen to issue a disclosure to all of its clients on the AppsNet. Aspen account representatives had to contact all of its clients, including REM, to inform them of the potential compromise at Aspen, and to report that although there was no specific evidence of data tampering, Aspen was not able to ensure the integrity of its clients' data.

When Aspen mentioned this to REM, REM management put two and two together and began to fear that they were also compromised, and that this was somehow responsible for the nocturnal connections shown on the recent monthly bills.

2.3.5 THE INVESTIGATION AT REM

With this new information, REM had more faith in the usage reports they were shown and now believed that this unknown hacker was the one creating the connections after hours.

The first thing they did, with the assistance of the cyber crime team, was to check the machines on which the VPN client software was running. They were looking for anything suggesting that an outsider had access to the machine, such as Trojan horse files, hidden files, root kits, or unknown users with remote access or administrator access.

The fact that REM did not have a standard image complicated this search. However, no unknown users, hidden files, or Trojan horses were found. A check of the scheduler also revealed that nothing unexpected was preconfigured to run automatically. REM did not keep audit logs on its network or at its firewall, and it did not have an IDS, so there was little way of learning whether anyone from the outside may have gained access to its network.

2.4 INCIDENT RECONSTRUCTION

As mentioned already, a cyber crime team was brought in to track, capture, and potentially prosecute the hacker. Since other cases (see Chapters 14, 15, and 16) deal with forensics efforts, we will skip some of the technical details and present the results of the effort here. The cyber crime team conferred with Aspen's IT staff and examined historic and ongoing logs (firewall, router, and other network logs) maintained by Aspen. The team also spoke with the IT personnel at REM and reviewed any information that they could provide. The team determined the following as the most likely means by which the hacker had compromised the network:

1. Having gained access to the REM network, the hacker discovered the existence of VPN client software on a group of computers and an outgoing VPN link. This discovery attracted his attention, and the hacker set off to find out who was on the other side. Accessing those machines, the hacker then noticed that the user name and password were preconfigured, offering a secure avenue onto another network.

2. Once the hacker reached the other side of the VPN link, a little snooping around turned up some ERP applications, suggesting that this network was an ASP to whom companies could outsource components of their IT and business application needs. The hacker was able to find the ASP's name and look up some information on the company over the Internet and other public sources.

3. On the Apps network, the hacker discovered that a routine window from 2:00 AM to 4:00 AM existed for all system and server maintenance, as shown in Table 2.1. During this time, the path between the AppsNet and a second network was open. In other words, the internal router connecting these networks appeared to block all traffic at all times, except during this maintenance window. So during that time, the hacker sent a root kit from the AppsNet to stake his flag on the second network. However, he wasn't able to compromise the router and was restricted to activity between 2:00 AM and 4:00 AM.

4. After a bit of snooping, the hacker learned that this network performed operations such as running system backups and installing patches. (This is the network that Aspen called the Developer Network, or DevNet.) There were only a few machines on this network, so it did not take long to look through all of the hosts to discover the one that would allow the network intrusion to proceed further.

5. On the DevNet, the hacker stumbled onto a dual-homed host, as shown in Figure 2.3. One of the machines was dual-homed between the DevNet and Aspen's corporate network. One of Aspen's developers had purposely added a second NIC (network interface card) to a development machine and plugged it into the corporate network so that he could share files between the development box and his desktop PC. He had planned to disconnect the machine from the corporate desktop, but he went back and forth between the two so much that he just left it dual-homed.

Table 2.1 Filtering Rules for the Router Connecting AppsNet and DevNet

To	From	Protocol	Ports	Time	Rule
Any	Any	Any	Any	Any	Deny
Any	Any	Any	Any	200–400	Allow

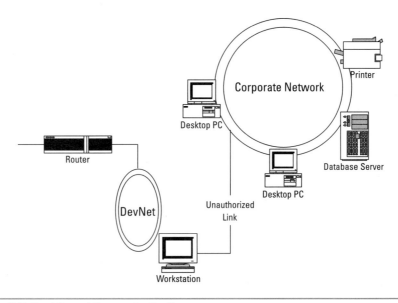

Figure 2.3 Dual-Homed Host on the DevNet

6. The dual-homed host was the connection the hacker needed. This machine
   allowed the hacker access to Aspen's flat corporate network. At this point the
   hacker was able to find and access the corporate databases and capture critical
   client information.

In summary, from the REM network the hacker had accessed Aspen's AppsNet
through the existing VPN link. During a normal maintenance window, he
reached the DevNet and, through a dual-homed host, made his way onto the
corporate network, where he was able to access all the information needed to try
to blackmail Aspen's management.

The cyber crime team wrote up a report highlighting this information and presented it to Aspen. Copies were also made available to REM, as well as to the
appropriate authorities. The report did not proclaim the hacker's guilt—that
would be for a court to decide—but merely presented the facts of the case.

With this report and all the gathered evidence (and a properly maintained chain
of custody), Aspen would have the option to seek criminal or civil action.

2.5 REPERCUSSIONS

In this case, the repercussions of the compromise, although felt most strongly by Aspen, were shared among many parties—all of the clients on Aspen's application network.

All of Aspen's clients had to check the integrity of their data, which in some cases meant restoring their systems to the last known good backups and reprocessing all of the data from that date forward. As you might imagine, this was an expense that the clients were very interested in sharing with Aspen.

Further, some of the clients wanted simply to drop their contract with Aspen and find another ASP to provide the desired services. The loss of several clients' monthly payments, as well as the demands of other clients for restitution related to the data-reprocessing expenses, placed a severe strain on Aspen's cash flow. The news of the network compromise also led to a drop in Aspen's stock price. Aspen was severely limited in its options for raising additional capital either through the equity markets or by assuming additional debt.

2.5.1 THE HACKER

Through continued e-mail communication, the hacker was tracked and captured. Logging mechanisms were initiated at REM, which was confirmed to be the origination point for the unauthorized access to Aspen's back-end database servers, to assist in the tracking process.

> **ASIDE:** All information gathered as a result of this logging effort was not admissible in a court of law. For reasons why, see Chapters 14 and 16.

With the aforementioned report in hand, Aspen had to decide whether or not to pursue criminal or civil action against the hacker. Two points led Aspen to pursue neither option. First, it was determined that the hacker might not have the resources whereby a favorable civil judgment could actually help Aspen in its current financial situation. Second, Aspen's true interest was to have the matter over and done with as soon as possible. They certainly didn't want the kind of publicity that might surround a trial. A full confession, along with a promise never to do it again, was sufficient for Aspen, Inc.

2.6 Aspen's Response

Naturally, Aspen did take some steps to put out the fires. A new public relations campaign aimed at customer retention efforts rather than new customer recruitment was planned. However, the campaign had to wait until the negative press could be suppressed and countered, or simply forgotten. Remember, this was early in the Internet days, and security still wasn't on a lot of people's minds.

One of the items that Aspen chose to advertise was the new focus on network security that it had undertaken. A new network security officer was brought in and charged with redesigning the network to avoid such situations in the future. Needless to say, but unfortunately, one move that management thought would help dam the exodus of clients was to fire the developer whose action had led to the existence of a dual-homed host.

2.7 Lessons Learned

Numerous lessons can be learned from this case—from the lack of access logs to help verify and track the potential hacker's actions and whereabouts, to the fact that a dual-homed host provided the final link to the bridge that the hacker used to threaten Aspen.

2.7.1 Access Logs

It is a good idea to keep access logs that are as detailed as possible—at least with respect to inbound and outbound connections to and from your network, and with respect to access to critical data repositories, such as databases of client information. Though you may not use these logs on a regular basis, for those instances when you need them, especially including investigations of network compromise, they are invaluable. And nothing else can be used to get the kind of information available in the logs.

Not only do you have to record and keep logs, but you have to take actions to ensure that they are secure and accurate, even when the overall network is compromised. We will talk about this more in later chapters.

2.7.2 RESPONDING TO CHANGING USAGE PATTERNS

Aspen should have discussed the change in usage patterns with REM when it was first observed. Changes in technology and network usage patterns can certainly be due to changes in business practices or even corporate culture. However, they may also be due to an unknown and unauthorized intruder, as in the case here.

Anomaly-based intrusion detection systems are developed under the philosophy that changes in usage patterns suggest potentially suspicious activity. A simple discussion between Aspen's account representative for REM and REM's point of contact might have identified the nocturnal connections as suspicious. In addition, such a discussion might have allowed all parties to respond to the intrusions a month earlier, before the threatening e-mails started arriving.

Often service providers are afraid to bring up such topics with clients, for fear of being wrong and having their technical knowledge come into question. However, we believe that in such cases it is best to err on the side of caution. Aspen doesn't have to come out and say that REM is being hacked, but simply ask whether REM is aware that its usage patterns have changed and suggest an investigation if they are not aware of this fact.

2.7.3 USER NAMES AND PASSWORDS

It may not be wise to have the user names and passwords preconfigured into client software. Certainly it is more convenient, but asking employees to enter passwords (even if they are common passwords) adds one extra level, albeit minor, of security. If we could get all clients to the level of individual user accounts (user names and passwords for each person), that would be a plus.

2.7.4 ARCHITECTURE

If companies believe that their employees will be tempted to dual-home hosts, it may be wise to design the physical workspace to discourage this possibility. For example, the physical space used for one purpose (e.g., the development lab) need not have wall jacks that are connected to routers on separate networks (e.g., the corporate network). This logical separation will have to run throughout the infrastructure in order to be effective, but efforts toward this end can help remind all employees that they should not change the network topology. (Naturally, this approach relies on having a well-thought-out network topology in the first place.)

2.7.4.1 Network Segmentation

Aspen used a flat network architecture for its corporate network. Although such a structure might have served their needs, there is some wisdom in placing database servers that store critical corporate information on a separate subnet, to allow for some traffic filtering and security between these servers and the general corporate network.

2.7.4.2 Maintenance Windows

Rather than creating a maintenance window during which all traffic is allowed to pass, you may want to restrict as much as possible specifically which traffic will be allowed to pass. For example, traffic can be restricted to only those hosts that will be involved in the maintenance. If any ports and communications protocols can be identified, they should be incorporated into the filtering rules. If the maintenance will include installing patches or making backups, such tasks may well be undertaken over predefined ports and protocols. It may also be possible to restrict such traffic to one direction (DevNet to AppsNet), especially if maintenance will involve only a push, rather than a pull. Again, the filters should be as detailed and granular as possible. Although these measures may not block all access attempts, they can certainly erect another hurdle to be crossed.

2.7.4.3 Dual-Homed Hosts

One of the main lessons to learn from this case study is to avoid, at all costs, the dual-homed host. The problem with such hosts is that they create connections within the network that were not anticipated by the network designers and most likely haven't been addressed in terms of security measures. Even well-segmented networks have been known to be compromised by a machine that someone unwittingly connected to two places at the same time, allowing unscrupulous individuals into areas where they aren't otherwise allowed.

Although the most common instance of the dual-homed host is of a desktop user, with a LAN connection to the corporate network, who is dialed out to the Internet through his own modem and ISP (such as AOL). Just as in the case discussed here, an insecure path is created that the company did not know about—and can lead to terrible consequences, like the loss of a job or the demise of a company.

No Service for You!

Denial of service is a concept that pre-dates information technology. In the past, for example, people used to cut the rope attached to the bucket or cut holes in the bucket so that other people could not get water from the well. It's quite likely that these activities continue today in areas served by well water.

The case study that follows discusses a situation in which a company found itself the target of an electronic denial-of-service (DoS) attack from unknown sources and describes the steps involved in resolving the situation. Measures that can potentially help networks be less susceptible to such attacks are also discussed. (For the type of attack described in the previous paragraph, one suggestion is to carry your own bucket and not leave it in the well.)

3.1 The Discovery

The day began as any other at our victim company, when suddenly the help desk began getting a flood of calls from people reporting not being able to surf, e-mails not reaching clients, and other Internet-based traffic problems. After confirming that Web surfing was indeed a problem and that they could not send test e-mails from an external mail source (e.g., yahoo.com), the help desk staff escalated the situation to the network team.

In investigations of this and any other congestion issues, the mail server was the network team's first place to investigate because e-mail is an essential network service. Any interruption in communications is of critical importance.

Was mail indeed queuing or was it getting through? When had the last inbound mail message been received? And what about outbound mail? Mail throughput would give the team an approximate timeline if they needed to call their Internet service provider (ISP). Generally, a "usual" or "normal" service interruption was short-lived and was corrected in a timely manner, even without a call to the ISP.

Review of the mail log files showed that mail hadn't been going in or out for about an hour. This was out of the norm and suggested a need for further action.

The next stop was the firewall. The system was up and running, and everything seemed normal except for unusually high traffic on one interface. The fact that only one interface was experiencing high traffic certainly gave cause for suspicion. So, next, the "network detectives" examined the Internet switch and router and noticed high utilization on both. What was happening?

This was the call to action. A member of the network team connected a laptop to the Internet switch. Fortunately, all the tools necessary for diagnosing network issues were already on this machine, for being unable to surf or FTP, let alone download software, the firm would have been at a loss to acquire any new tools it might immediately need.

Even though Windows was the victim's predominant operating system for both desktops and servers, the network team chose Linux as the operating system for the diagnostic laptop. Although there was a learning curve for using an operating system foreign to the environment, the strength of the TCP/IP (Transmission Control Protocol/Internet Protocol) implementation in Linux and the availability of free or moderately priced networking and diagnostic tools made the choice easy. (We'll see these tools in a bit.)

The laptop had multiple Ethernet interfaces; a large, fast disk; and plenty of RAM, allowing for maximum flexibility. A few of the free diagnostic tools installed were tcpdump, Snort, Ethereal, and IPTraf, as well as those available as part of the operating system installation, such as RFmon and ping.

Tcpdump and Ethereal are freeware network-sniffing utilities that are quite adept and can be configured to identify the network traffic of specific interest. Snort is a freeware intrusion detection system (IDS) that is very fast and can handle a great deal of traffic. IPTraf is an IP-based LAN monitor that generates and records statistics including TCP and UDP counts, ICMP and OSPF (Open Shortest Path First) information, Ethernet load information, IP checksum errors, and others. RFmon is a monitoring tool for communication over radio frequency networks, and ping is a network-tracing utility that, to be fair, is a part of all operating systems.

The laptop was connected to the Internet switch directly off of the network's primary (backbone) Internet router, as shown in Figure 3.1. Using the OS's standard

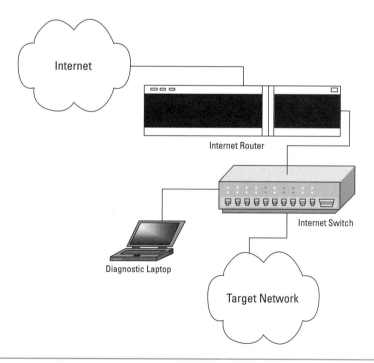

Figure 3.1 Location of the Diagnostic Laptop

ping utility, the network team could reach the Internet router, but with unexpectedly long ping times to a device on the same switch. Could anything beyond the router be reached? Yes, pings of devices beyond the router returned with even longer extended ping times, but they were successful. However, packets were being lost traveling to just the first hop into the wide world of the Internet. Again came the question, What was happening?

Although some people might have called the ISP at this point and passed the buck by suggesting that the ISP's router was having a problem, the network team decided that they really needed to know exactly what type of traffic was reaching their primary router. The more information they knew about the situation, the better they would be able to respond to it.

In order to see the traffic running on their network, the team set the switch port to which the diagnostic laptop was connected to promiscuous mode and enabled tcpdump. After watching a bit of the traffic (a dump log is shown in Listing 3.1), they noticed that the feed was certainly being hit by a huge amount of traffic—specifically, TCP SYN packets. Could this be a large denial-of-service (DoS) attack, or perhaps a distributed denial-of-service (DDoS) attack, they wondered?

Listing 3.1 First Dump Log of Network Traffic

```
09:34:07.319386 attackers.38871 > victim.490: udp 1024
09:34:07.319389 attackers.1893 > victim.68: P ack 1 win 65535
09:34:07.320346 attackers > victim: icmp: echo request
09:34:07.320349 attackers > victim:  ip-proto-0 0 [tos 0x7,CE]
09:34:07.320399 attackers.29579 > victim.68: . win 16384 [tos 0x8]
09:34:07.321353 attackers.38871 > victim.491: udp 1024
09:34:07.321356 attackers.1893 > victim.69: P ack 1 win 65535
09:34:07.322319 attackers > victim: icmp: echo request
09:34:07.322325 attackers > victim:  ip-proto-0 0 [tos 0x7,CE]
09:34:07.322368 attackers.29579 > victim.69: . win 16384 [tos 0x8]
09:34:07.323324 attackers.38871 > victim.492: udp 1024
09:34:07.323329 attackers.1893 > victim.70: P ack 1 win 65535
09:34:07.324285 attackers > victim: icmp: echo request
09:34:07.324289 attackers > victim:  ip-proto-0 0 [tos 0x7,CE]
09:34:07.324336 attackers.29579 > victim.70: . win 16384 [tos 0x8]
09:34:07.325293 attackers.38871 > victim.493: udp 1024
09:34:07.325296 attackers.1893 > victim.71: P ack 1 win 65535
09:34:07.326254 attackers > victim: icmp: echo request
```

```
09:34:07.326257 attackers > victim:  ip-proto-0 0 [tos 0x7,CE]
09:34:07.326306 attackers.29579 > victim.71: . win 16384 [tos 0x8]
09:34:07.327261 attackers.38871 > victim.494: udp 1024
09:34:07.327264 attackers.1893 > victim.72: P ack 1 win 65535
09:34:07.328223 attackers > victim: icmp: echo request
09:34:07.328226 attackers > victim:  ip-proto-0 0 [tos 0x7,CE]
09:34:07.328274 attackers.29579 > victim.72: . win 16384 [tos 0x8]
09:34:07.329232 attackers.38871 > victim.495: udp 1024
09:34:07.329235 attackers.1893 > victim.73: P ack 1 win 65535
09:34:07.330192 attackers > victim: icmp: echo request
09:34:07.330196 attackers > victim:  ip-proto-0 0 [tos 0x7,CE]
09:34:07.330246 attackers.29579 > victim.73: . win 16384 [tos 0x8]
09:34:07.331199 attackers.38871 > victim.496:  auto-rp type-0x29 Hold
1h26m24s
09:34:07.331202 attackers.1893 > victim.74: P ack 1 win 65535
09:34:07.332165 attackers > victim: icmp: echo request
09:34:07.332170 attackers > victim:  ip-proto-0 0 [tos 0x7,CE]
09:34:07.332214 attackers.29579 > victim.74: . win 16384 [tos 0x8]
09:34:07.333171 attackers.38871 > victim.497: udp 1024
09:34:07.333175 attackers.1893 > victim.75: P ack 1 win 65535
09:34:07.334133 attackers > victim: icmp: echo request
09:34:07.334140 attackers > victim:  ip-proto-0 0 [tos 0x7,CE]
09:34:07.334182 attackers.29579 > victim.75: . win 16384 [tos 0x8]
09:34:07.335141 attackers.38871 > victim.498: udp 1024
09:34:07.335147 attackers.1893 > victim.76: P ack 1 win 65535
09:34:07.336388 attackers > victim: icmp: echo request
09:34:07.336390 attackers > victim:  ip-proto-0 0 [tos 0x7,CE]
09:34:07.336402 attackers.29579 > victim.76: . win 16384 [tos 0x8]
09:34:07.337106 attackers.38871 > victim.499: udp 1024
09:34:07.337109 attackers.1893 > victim.77: P ack 1 win 65535
09:34:07.338068 attackers > victim: icmp: echo request
09:34:07.338188 attackers > victim:  ip-proto-0 0 [tos 0x7,CE]
09:34:07.338255 attackers.29579 > victim.77: . win 16384 [tos 0x8]
```

A DoS attack against a victim is essentially an attempt to flood a target—in this case the victim's router, switch, and network—with so much extraneous traffic that it can't handle, or route, the actual legitimate traffic. In DDoS attacks, more than one system is used to launch the attack, thereby improving the chance of success. These types of attacks are very hard to defend against because of the potentially large number of compromised systems (called *zombies*) on the Internet that are used to conduct the attacks. These attacks are aimed at a network's bandwidth. If someone has more bandwidth than the target (the network being attacked), the target's resources can be brought to a standstill, and its ability to access the Internet can be cut off for the duration of the attack. You can fend off some of the attack, but in the end the larger connection generally wins.

Concerned about the excess traffic, the network team started dropping some of the attacker's traffic, but there was still a performance hit on the network because these extraneous packets had to be inspected. Even though the network team had denied or dropped attack packets at the firewall, the bandwidth was still being tied up with those attacks (the very inspection process leading to being denied or dropped uses bandwidth, system processing capabilities, and time). Remember that these attacks usually come from spoofed IP addresses that are randomly generated, so there are many IP addresses that must be set to DENIED or DROPPED.

At this point it's obvious that the inbound attack packets were not the only problem. A TCP SYN message is the first part of the TCP three-way handshake (Figure 3.2).

The TCP SYN message tells the recipient (the destination host) that the source host wants to open a channel and the destination host responds with a TCP SYN/ACK message (*ACK* stands for *acknowledgment*) saying, I'm willing to talk to you. In accordance with this setup, the victim's network was replying to some of the spoofed hosts with SYN/ACK messages and in the process using up even more of its own bandwidth. The same pattern was seen in the traffic logs, as Listing 3.2 illustrates.

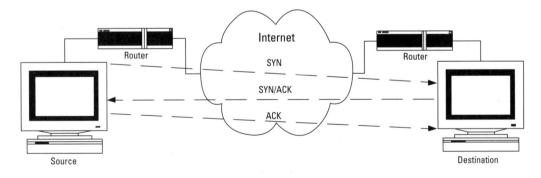

Figure 3.2 TCP Three-Way Handshake

Listing 3.2 Second Dump Log of Network Traffic

```
09:41:45.303931 attackers.933 > victim.36962: . win 16384 [tos 0x8]
09:41:45.303985 victim.36962 > 193.128.201.59.933: R 0:0(0) ack 16391776
win 0 (DF) [tos 0x8]
09:41:45.304131 attackers.1701 > victim.42075: . win 16384 [tos 0x8]
09:41:45.304265 attackers.2213 > victim.26790: . win 16384 [tos 0x8]
09:41:45.304310 victim.26790 > attackers.2213: R 0:0(0) ack 100277856 win
0 (DF) [tos 0x8]
09:41:45.304333 attackers.2469 > victim.60396: . win 16384 [tos 0x8]
09:41:45.304604 attackers.3493 > victim.55419: . win 16384 [tos 0x8]
09:41:45.304650 victim.55419 > attackers.3493: R 0:0(0) ack 184163936 win
0 (DF) [tos 0x8]
09:41:45.304671 attackers.3749 > victim.46968: . win 16384 [tos 0x8]
09:41:45.305011 attackers.5029 > victim.17411: . win 16384 [tos 0x8]
09:41:45.305057 victim.17411 > attackers.5029: R 0:0(0) ack 284827232 win
0 (DF) [tos 0x8]
09:41:45.305347 attackers.6309 > victim.949: . win 16384 [tos 0x8]
09:41:45.305391 victim.949 > attackers.6309: R 0:0(0) ack 368713312 win 0
(DF) [tos 0x8]
09:41:45.305619 attackers.7333 > victim.14146: . win 16384 [tos 0x8]
09:41:45.305668 victim.14146 > attackers.7333: R 0:0(0) ack 435822176 win
0 (DF) [tos 0x8]
09:41:45.305687 attackers.7589 > victim.60734: . win 16384 [tos 0x8]
09:41:45.305821 attackers.8101 > victim.7172: . win 16384 [tos 0x8]
09:41:45.306094 attackers.9125 > victim.52889: . win 16384 [tos 0x8]
09:41:45.306429 attackers.10405 > victim.15441: . win 16384 [tos 0x8]
09:41:45.306630 attackers.11173 > victim.53830: . win 16384 [tos 0x8]
09:41:45.306677 victim.53830 > attackers.11173: R 0:0(0) ack 687480416 win
0 (DF) [tos 0x8]
09:41:45.306698 attackers.11429 > victim.26333: . win 16384 [tos 0x8]
09:41:45.310788 attackers.106.11685 > victim.25312: . win 16384 [tos 0x8]
09:41:45.310972 victim.25312 > attackers.11685: R 0:0(0) ack 721034848 win
0 (DF) [tos 0x8]
```

3.2 THE RESPONSE

As mentioned already, the network team had begun to drop as much of the harmful traffic as possible. In addition, the team contacted the firm's ISP and had some of the attack blocked at the router in front of them, as well as some temporary data rate limits imposed. Implementing data rate limits on a temporary basis removes the burden of having to remember to call the ISP back and restore the default rate.

After a while the attacks ended. Mail flowed freely, tide on the Internet was high, and the entire IT department heaved a collective sigh of relief. That was not the end of the day for the network team, however. Why had the firm been attacked? What could they do to stop such an attack or limit its effects if it happened again?

The reason that attacks like this are of such concern is that they represent a potentially high cost in terms of lost business and professional reputation as a result of being out of business for even a short period of time—especially if the cause is a cyber attack. Because of this threat, management, always interested in limiting the firm's exposure to and liability for these attacks, wanted plans to be developed ensuring that such an attack would not happen again.

We will come back to possible prevention methods later. First let's take a look at another side of this story: the attacking system. How does the attacker play into all this?

3.3 The Process

Depending on the attack method used to compromise these systems, several things could have happened to turn the attacking hosts into "zombies." The term **zombie** in this lexicon refers to an Internet-connected host that has been compromised by a hacker and is then used to launch DoS attacks. Although the system may simply *belong* to a hacker, we generally think of a zombie as being a machine that is unwittingly (to its owner) used as part of a DoS attack.

3.3.1 DoS Root Kit

One highly popular method of mounting a DoS attack is to gain either authorized or unauthorized access to a system, and install what is known as a **root kit**, including a set of DDoS tools. Several packaged root kits available on the Web are specific for use on certain operating systems.

Following a basic client/server setup, the hacker sits on a *client* machine and dispatches commands (identity of target, type of traffic to use, and so on) to *handlers*, also known as *master servers*, who communicate the attack information from the client to the actual attacking host, called the *agents*, or *zombies*, which do the attacking two degrees of separation away from the perpetrator.

Different DDoS attacks may use different methodologies. However, Figure 3.3 illustrates the general topology of a DDoS network used in the attacks. The attacker or attackers can control one or more master servers, each having a list of agents.

Note that the attacker does not necessarily need to have root or administrative access on the zombie machines. All that is required is the presence of the DDoS software, which a hacker can load simply by getting the user of the machine to download and run an e-mail attachment, for example.

3.3.2 DDoS IRC Bots

IRC (Internet Relay Chat) programs called **dosbots** connect to IRC networks and sit in channels waiting for someone to give them the command to attack a host. This is a popular method of invading a system because of, naturally, its ease of use. Compromised Windows machines connected to IRC channels can be used to perform DDoS attacks against specified targets.

Perhaps as important as the ease of implementing this dosbot approach is the wide availability of exploitable Windows systems that can be compromised. And with more and more homes getting broadband access (Cable modem or always-on DSL) and the overwhelming preponderance of Windows, dosbots form a large DDoS network waiting to happen.

> **Aside:** DSL features fast download speeds, which is great for downloading movies and MP3 files, but slow upload speeds, which may make it seem unfit for a zombie. However, ADSL (often called business DSL but available in homes), features both fast upload and download speeds and makes an attractive network connection for a zombie machine.

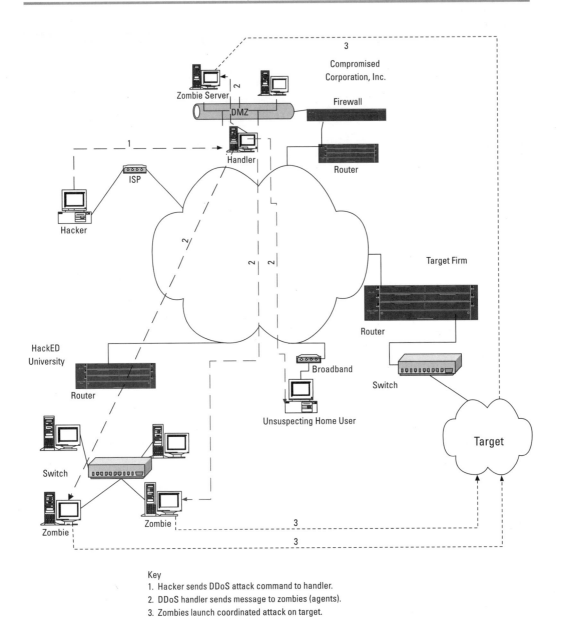

Key
1. Hacker sends DDoS attack command to handler.
2. DDoS handler sends message to zombies (agents).
3. Zombies launch coordinated attack on target.

Figure 3.3 Distributed Denial-of-Service Network

Defending against such actions are the vigilant IRC opers (operators) who K-line (i.e., use the KLINE command to ban) many of these types of bots. Anyone who finds your channel can use your "DDoS network." To counter this threat, many such dosbot networks require the use of passwords to communicate between components and have individual dosbots connect to different IRC channels in an attempt to remain hidden even if some are discovered.

> **ASIDE:** Windows 2000 and XP allow the source address to be spoofed at the raw socket level, making spoofed source addresses more convincing. (This is a change to the Windows OS; the 9x versions didn't allow this functionality.)

3.4 LESSONS LEARNED

To protect your network from being used as a DDoS zombie, secure your systems by keeping current with all patches and hot fixes. (Yes, you've heard this a thousand times, and yes, it is important. Patches are often driven by the discovery of vulnerabilities in existing code.) Change default configurations on operating systems and applications to include only needed and used services. Taking the cautionary measures a step further by denying services not needed at the firewall or router level is always a good thing.

Ingress traffic filtering, recommended by RFC 2267 (http://rfc-2267.rfc-index.com/rfc-2267-8.htm) and RFC 2827 (http://www.ietf.org/rfc/rfc2827.txt), is another good way to help defend specifically against the threat of your machines being used as zombies in a DDoS attack. If someone does break into your network to use your machines as DDoS handlers or agents, packets originating from inside the network but with IP addresses that don't correspond to your IP block will be dropped at the router.

Similarly, **egress traffic filtering** (dropping packets coming in from the outside with an internal source address), although it may not directly affect the success of any DDoS attack, can certainly help. These mechanisms cannot stop DDoS, since there really isn't a way to stop it, but they make tracing the source a lot easier. Figure 3.4 illustrates ingress and egress filtering.

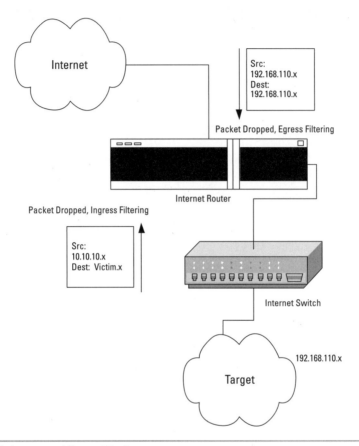

Figure 3.4 Ingress and Egress Filtering

An intrusion detection system can help track and alert administrators of an attack in progress. Here is an alert from the Snort IDS that identifies traffic that potentially corresponds to a DDoS attack in progress:

```
Date 10:02:16 laptop snort: [1:249:1] DDOS mstream client to handler
[Classification: Attempted Denial of Service] [Priority: 2]: {TCP}
attackers:18589 -> victim:15104
```

As with many things, early detection is the key to preventing an attack. If you have identified an attack in progress, the data rate of the network can be limited. Taking this measure should cut the rate of incoming traffic (TCP SYN messages) from the attacker and thereby at least slow down the attack. DoS attacks last for a finite period of time. Their intent is to knock down your ability to conduct business *now*, not necessarily forever. Eventually the attacker will call off the dogs, stopping his/her legions of handlers and zombies from sending extraneous traffic to your site, and eventually the large queues that have built up in your routers and Web servers will empty out (or you'll just kill the machine and reboot). Then you will be back up and running. So if you can just weather the storm, you'll be OK. Naturally, you will still have to identify and clean out any zombies to try to stop the hacker from repeating the attack.

In this light, increasing your processing capacity will help. For example, for a Web infrastructure, the key may be to augment your bank of Web servers and place them behind load balancers, such as in Figure 3.5.

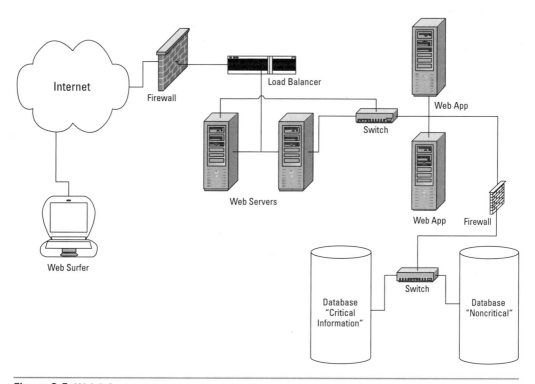

Figure 3.5 Web Infrastructure

3.5 REFERENCES

The following links provide additional information on topics discussed in this case study:

- **DoS attacks:** http://packetstormsecurity.nl/distributed
- **DDoS attacks:** http://staff.washington.edu/dittrich/misc/ddos
- **Intrusion detection system:** Snort: http://www.snort.org
- **Network-sniffing utilities:**
  - Ethereal: http://www.ethereal.com
  - Tcpdump: http://www.tcpdump.org
- **Ingress and egress filtering:**
  - http://rfc-2267.rfc-index.com/rfc-2267-8.htm
  - http://www.ietf.org/rfc/rfc2827.txt

PART II
CURRENT METHODS

Look, Ma, No Wires!

Not all security engagements are a response to hacks. Sometimes we're called in during the initial stages of a project. This case study discusses such a situation. A bank was interested in implementing a wireless network, but because of concerns about the lack of security associated with wireless networks, it requested an initial design and implementation review and evaluation of the proposed wireless network.

We were asked to evaluate the existing implementation and recommend measures to improve security that could be taken *prior* to the launch of the network. This is a good situation, and we are always happy to take part in this early stage (the earlier the better). Often, only so much security can be retrofitted into an existing system. The stumbling blocks to retrofitting are not only technical, but financial and political as well.

For example, deploying encryption into a running network involves updating the router configurations and may require the installation of all new routers to ensure that they can properly decode and route encrypted traffic. In addition, end devices, such as e-mail servers and potentially numerous clients on user desktops, have to be changed (updated) to perform encryption and decryption. Similarly, installing an access control server (ACS) as a central repository for verifying user names and passwords may mean that all applications must be configured to interface with the ACS at every log-in attempt. Setting all this up is a monumental task.[1]

Making such changes to a network can involve the purchase of new software and/ or hardware, and it will involve manpower—potentially a significant monetary expense, especially because firms rarely budget for such retrofitting. The ROI (return on investment) calculations are not always attractive. Further, a certain amount of political muscle is needed to push changes through.[2] Changes to a working system make people very uneasy, especially the people whose livelihood is tied to those machines. The potentially poor ROI, the internal hesitation, and the technical challenges have often led to potential countermeasures being pulled off the table.

Implementing countermeasures during the initial installation does cost something, but rather than being reactive and patching holes as they come up, it's far better to be proactive and design the network from the beginning to have the desired level of security. Clearly, this approach may increase the initial costs in terms of time and money, but these costs should be more manageable than the costs that would be incurred if the security measures were implemented after the system was launched. Getting security in place before the system is launched also does not necessarily mean that it will take longer to launch the system. In the case that we will describe here, for example, the security review was performed outside of regular work hours and prior to the scheduled launch date, so it did not delay the overall project. And a system that experiences fewer (no?) security compromises should have a better ROI picture as well.

4.1 INTRODUCTION

Much has been made of the inherent insecurity of wireless networking systems. One can find hundreds of articles outlining the relative ease with which a few

---

1. The costs and technical challenges of configuring diverse applications to communicate with a central access control server become an issue with the deployment of a single sign-on environment.

2. It is often said that to overcome the resistance to change, a security compromise is necessary. Only after things go bad and the network is shown to be broken will the security team have the ammunition it needs to force the necessary changes—and even then it is a challenge.

academic groups managed to defeat the "flawed" wireless encryption standard (Wired Equivalent Privacy, also known as WEP). We have all heard presentations by experts claiming that there is no way to secure a wireless network to a satisfactory level—at least not without their help. In addition, any company that has a mailing address has likely been bombarded with sales literature describing how vulnerable its wireless network is liable to be—that attacking a wireless network can be as easy as pulling up in the parking lot with a wireless card and a laptop and simply connecting to the network. However, although it is true that the simplest network attacks are often via wireless connections, it is not true that a wireless implementation is, by its very nature, insecure.

As security professionals, when we talk about network security with a new client, we try to find out just how secure they need their information to be. Inevitably, this is what we hear: "We need to protect our data from hackers, but it's not like we're the Department of Defense or a bank or something." Well, the National Security Agency (NSA) and the Department of Defense have recently finalized a set of recommendations[3] that will allow the military to send top secret information over wireless data channels, including 802.11 devices and RIM (Research In Motion) BlackBerry devices, and several banks (as well as coffee shops and fast-food restaurants) around the country are rolling out wireless architectures in their branches.

The subject of the following case study is a bank that has implemented a wireless network at one of its branches.

4.2 BACKGROUND

General Savings & Loan (not a real name) is a regional financial institution with assets in the tens of billions of dollars. Its area of operation covers four states, and it has over 200 branches. General has traditionally been an early adopter of new technology, from online banking to innovative extranet solutions, and it is now

---

3. These recommendations were published online at http://www.fcw.com/fcw/articles/2002/1115/web-wire-11-20-02.asp.

in the early stages of rolling out another cutting-edge technology: wireless local area networking.

General would like to create an environment in which its tellers, loan managers, and customer service representatives are not tied to a certain desk in the branch. Instead, the bank would like to enable its employees to move around the building without having to reconnect to the network. Such a setup would allow representatives to sit down with customers in a private room and then meet with the loan officer in another part of the building without having to log on and off the wired network at each location. Site managers would also be able to move around the bank without losing a connection, and General would not need to install additional cabling when it grew or changed its capabilities.

When they decided to go forward with a wireless network, General's senior executives deemed it necessary to develop a design first (with a particular branch in mind) and test the design in a laboratory environment. This testing satisfactorily proved the concept to the executives, and a prototype implementation at the test branch was ordered.

There Are Always More Tests to Take

The testing of a new technology in a laboratory environment is an important step to help ensure that the technology will work and the imagined capabilities can be realized. We do not discuss this process in greater detail here because our focus is the security assessment of the wireless network. Note, however, that such testing should be performed before real-world implementation.

The branch that General chose as the site of the prototype wireless network is located in a busy suburb, and it presented numerous challenges to securing a wireless environment. General felt that successful implementation of the concept at this branch would provide the necessary assurance for implementing a similar design at an initial set of 30 bank branches. The new branch was being built in the ground floor of an existing building, and the grand opening of the branch was set for a Thursday.

4.3 THE PROJECT

General needed an objective party to check the design and implementation that the bank had put in place, so it hired an outside IT security firm (us) to assess the vulnerability of the wireless network, highlighting all exposures. Testing began on the Sunday evening prior to the planned opening, the results of which would determine whether the branch would open as scheduled. All that we were told was that one or more wireless access point(s) was located within this particular branch facility.

The tools involved in the testing included two laptops: one running Linux, and one running Windows 2000. The Linux laptop was loaded with tools to detect vulnerabilities: Kismet, the best wireless security scanner we knew of at the time of the assessment (and this writing); AirSnort, a freeware application that cracks wireless encryption; and Ethereal, our preferred network sniffer. The Windows laptop was intended for exploiting any identified vulnerabilities, including cracking network passwords with L0phtCrack and a handful of snooping tools. Other hardware included several wireless cards with Hermes chipsets, a GPS (Global Positioning System) receiver, and two wireless antennas: One was a 5-dBi omni-directional antenna; the other, an 11-dBi directional antenna (shown in Figure 4.1).

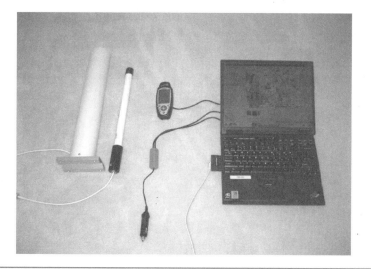

Figure 4.1 Wireless Vulnerability Assessment Toolkit

The security firm's wireless white-hat team chose to spend the first day and night probing the network the way a sophisticated hacker might. They parked outside the site under cover of darkness and configured the Linux laptop to detect components of the wireless infrastructure within. We connected a Zcomax wireless card to the 5-dBi antenna, and then, using Kismet, we were able to detect a good signal from each of the two access points within the bank. Through Kismet we noted that the access point service set identifiers (SSIDs) both had long names with numbers in them, and that it would be difficult to identify those points as belonging to General Savings & Loan on the basis of the SSID. We also noted that both access points were using encryption.

Kismet, the GUI interface shown in Figure 4.2,[4] is a passive detection tool, unlike the more commonly used Windows-based NetStumbler. Whereas NetStumbler

Figure 4.2 Kismet Output with Sensitive Information Obscured

---

4. Figures 4.2, 4.3, and 4.4 have been blurred to help proect the identities of those involved, but they do convey the types of information these tools provide.

emits a signal to query the access point forits SSID, Kismet listens to the emissions of the access point and other devices that are connecting to the access point and is therefore able to sniff the SSID of the access point from these packets without announcing its presence. An access point can emit a beacon signal that advertises its presence in response to a query, if desired. This is often referred to as *broadcasting* its SSID.

Access points are often set not to broadcast the SSID, which makes it harder to detect them. NetStumbler learns the SSID from the beacon, so if the beacon is not present, NetStumbler does not detect the access point. Kismet reads the SSID from normal wireless packets as they travel from wireless device to access point. The SSID (and other parts of the packet header) are not normally encrypted, even though the payload portion of the packet may be encrypted. The output from Kismet and NetStumbler, combined with GPS and overlays, can be used to create maps that show access point locations, as Figure 4.3 shows.

Figure 4.3 Map Created from Kismet and NetStumbler Output, Showing Access Point Locations

We configured the Windows laptop to connect using the SSID names that we had learned. However, we were unable to guess or crack the password required either to configure the access point or to make the initial connection to the network.

We then set up the Ethereal sniffer (see Figure 4.4) and AirSnort to capture packets for a period of four hours. AirSnort is a freeware tool that uses the flaws in the WEP encryption algorithm to attempt to derive the encryption key. The weakness in WEP stems from the first portion (24 bits) of an encrypted wireless packet, which makes up the initialization vector. Initialization vectors are sequenced in a predictable way, and they repeat over a period of time. Once AirSnort has identified a few packets with the same initialization vector, it can conduct a statistical attack against the encrypted portion of the packet, which can result in derivation of the key. This technique was first performed successfully at the University of California, Berkeley, in 2001; and shortly thereafter, AirSnort, a Linux-based WEP-cracking tool, became available.

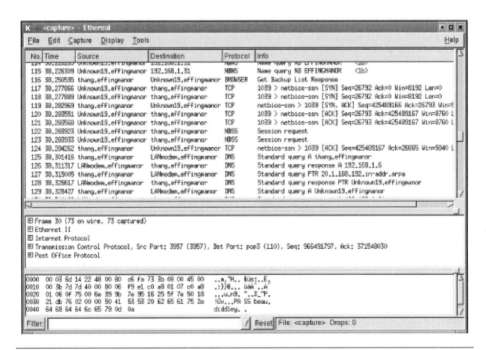

Figure 4.4 Example of Ethereal Sniffer Output

After four hours, AirSnort had not captured enough packets to be able to identify two that had the same initialization vector. We hadn't expected to capture very many packets at 10:00 PM outside of a network that was not in use. However, using Ethereal to review the packets that we did capture indicated that the encryption key was changing every 20 minutes or so, probably automatically, since no one was at the bank at the time.

After analyzing the types of packets we had captured, we concluded that the system was using a Cisco authentication protocol called LEAP. This fact was evident from the EAP (Extensible Authentication Protocol) authentication markers on the packets when we examined them. There also appeared to be an access control server that required authentication.

We switched over to the Windows laptop to try to gain access to network services. On the assumption that the internal bank clients would be using nonroutable IP addresses (192.168.x.x, 172.16.x.x, or 10.x.x.x), we tried setting our client with these different IP address ranges. We used the SSID that we had sniffed, but we were challenged for a password by the ACS on the network. We spent some time guessing at the password—favorites like local sports teams, misspellings of the name of the location, and important dates. We even scripted a procedure to try a list of about 15,000 passwords in a cracking dictionary, but we were unable to get beyond the ACS. (There are so many such password-cracking tools available that we don't include our script here.)

The next morning (Monday) we set up some equipment in rented space across the street from the branch location and began capturing packets again. We met with our point of contact at General, and we worked with General's personnel to generate simulated traffic on the network, hoping to gain more information than we had the previous night. We found a spot from which hackers would be able to operate without being observed, and we left our laptops there over lunch to sniff what they could.

While the laptops were gathering packets, we performed a site survey by walking around the area using a laptop with Kismet and the directional antenna that we had brought. We found that, with this equipment, we were able to gain a strong enough signal to connect to the access point from more than a block away to the

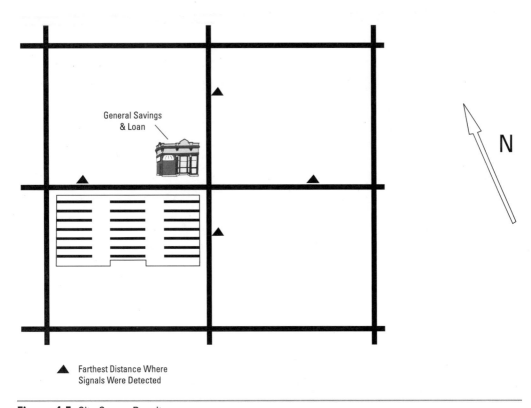

General Savings
& Loan

N

▲ Farthest Distance Where
Signals Were Detected

Figure 4.5 Site Survey Results

north, east, and south, as shown in Figure 4.5. Due west was effectively screened by the building across the street from the bank, but we were able to gain a good signal from inside that building. We also got a very good signal from the second and third floors of the building in which the bank was located. We reconnoitered at the site, looking for particular security problems with the physical layout.

After lunch we recovered our laptops and took a look at the packets and overall traffic that we had been able to capture. From Ethereal, we could tell that authentication was occurring between several clients and the ACS. However, these packets looked similar enough to make us think that all clients authenticating to the ACS were using the same account. Other than this information, the methods employed in the LAN were well concealed, and AirSnort was not able to make any progress toward deriving the WEP key. It had captured surprisingly few "interesting packets." (AirSnort considers packets whose sequence it understands to be interesting.) It has to capture about 6GB of interesting traffic before it can effectively conduct its statistical attack algorithm. The shortage of interesting packets was probably due to the fact that the initialization vectors were being obscured by LEAP.

On Tuesday we met with our General point of contact again and explained what we had found. We explained that we could gain a good wireless signal from up to a block away and from the rented space across the street. We talked about the ACS and reported that it seemed to be sharing one account for everyone, but that we were not able to gather enough packets to crack the encryption, nor were we able to defeat the ACS authentication. Then, with our attack and penetration fieldwork finished, we sat down to review the internal network architecture.

4.4 EXISTING SECURITY

General Savings & Loan had implemented a multifaceted wireless network defense:

- Wireless laptops were to be configured and distributed on the premises, and they were not to leave the confines of the bank.
- These laptops were configured to use WEP encryption when connecting to the access points.
- Once connected, users were directed to a Cisco ACS running EAP, which required them to enter a difficult-to-guess user name and password. However, the user name and password were the same for all users.
- Cisco's LEAP was employed to change the WEP key dynamically every 20 minutes. This feature also obscured the initialization vectors to help defeat attempts to derive the WEP keys.

These measures had been effective in denying us network access over the course of a day and a half. But General, as a financial institution, needed to be concerned about more concerted attacks. Further, the fact that our attempts to guess the password were not detected showed that General's monitoring systems were not as effective as they should have been. Could they stand up to a team of motivated hackers who might set up in the same quarters that we had been using, but for a longer period of time? One thing hackers are often known for is their patience. Were General's defenses adequate to protect against malevolent current and former employees who might have information about the workings of the network? Perhaps they were, but we were able to make suggestions that would help the folks at General sleep easier at night.

In addition, although current defenses were effective against current threats, methods of attack evolve. An attack for LEAP could be developed and widely disseminated next week; or ACS could prove to have a previously unknown vulnerability. We needed to make sure that General's defenses were optimized to reduce future risks.

4.5 RECOMMENDATIONS

The first thing we recommended was that General slightly lower its emitted power settings to continue to permit connections from everywhere inside the branch but not from so far away. We spent several hours testing different power settings, both inside the bank using their wireless cards, and outside the bank with our attack and penetration tools. We eventually arrived at settings that would permit employees to connect, but would not allow hackers to detect the network from more than half a block away. We were able to detect the network from only a small corner of the building from which we had based our attack, and we were still able to connect from the second floor of the building in which the branch was located. General decided that this was an acceptable risk. Some amount of leakage was, of course, inevitable.

An alternative to turning down the emitted power settings would have been to obtain directional antennas for the access points, which could then be focused toward the center of the branch and away from the street or the upper floors. In addition, the facility could be shielded. Although 802.11 signals can propagate through concrete and drywall, a metal screen (like chicken wire) can contain virtually all emissions. In this case the chicken wire solution would have been prohibitively expensive because it would have required complicated remodeling of an existing facility, but it might be practical when a facility is being built from the ground up.

Next we recommended adding another layer of authentication. General's solution of an ACS with a difficult password and WEP keys seemed at first glance to meet the standard for "strong authentication." Strong authentication is usually defined as *something you have*, like a token or a key that is already loaded on your laptop, combined with *something you know*, like a user name and password. The idea of having strong authentication is not only to make it more difficult for an external hacker to break in, but also to diminish the ability of an insider to hack the system. Internal security is especially important in a bank, where employees could be tempted to use inside knowledge to steal money or work with someone on the outside to perpetrate a crime.

The ACS user name and password pair that General had in place *is* something that a user would have to know, but it is not information unique to that user. The "something you know" should ideally be something that *only* the individual user knows. When a user name known only to a specific user is used, it is possible to determine exactly who accessed the system (nonrepudiation), and it is less likely that the unique password will be compromised. In a bank, nonrepudiation is more important than in other industries, so the method used by General was not a good solution.

We recommended simply adding domain authentication (user name and password) to the authentication process and continuing to make sure that personnel were using secure user name and password combinations. This change prohibits any access beyond the ACS until the user has supplied something that he, and only he, knows. General Savings & Loan implemented this recommendation right away, and we sniffed packets within the network to verify that the authentication was working properly. We were able to see authentication packets being exchanged between the domain and the ACS. We noted that it would be important for General to develop a strong password policy, and to develop controls that would help them make sure that employees were using complex passwords, were changing them regularly, and were not divulging them.

In addition, it made sense to configure the wireless access points to include media access control (MAC) filters that permitted only a specific set of laptops, identified by MAC address, to connect to the access point. Doing this helps reduce the likelihood that a hacker will drive up to the network and connect to the access point with his own laptop and wireless NIC. The hacker may be able to sniff the traffic and determine what MAC addresses are permitted and use one of them when they disconnect; however, using the MAC address to authenticate wireless access points does add at least one additional layer of security.

Our final major recommendation was to develop controls to keep the laptops within the confines of the bank branch. We provided several options for laptop tracking systems and theft deterrence systems. General had recognized the importance of keeping a laptop with an encryption key already loaded on it from leaving its control, because once a branch laptop left the building, a user would need to know only the log-in information in order to access the LAN. Thus, again the bank would be made vulnerable to attacks with insider complicity. The simplest solution was a proximity alarm that detects a small device attached to a laptop when it passes through the doors, much like anti-shoplifting devices in department stores.

Along with these recommendations, we left General with a suggestion that they regularly perform wireless scans and monitor activity on the network. We suggested conducting the scans at least quarterly, and monitoring the network for intrusions each day, using standard intrusion detection methods. These final recommendations were intended to address the fact that no countermeasures to brute-force password guessing were yet in place.

4.6 THE END STATE

The final solution, combining our recommendations with the wireless architecture that General and its consultants had developed, included the following elements:

- A system of physical controls to make sure that laptops containing wireless keys would never leave the premises.
- WEP encryption combined with LEAP's dynamic rekeying of the WEP key every 20 minutes. (Plans were in process to upgrade to WEP+ as it became available.)

- LEAP architecture to obscure the initialization vectors and to enforce the dynamic rekeying.
- ACS authentication using a complex user name and password.
- Domain authentication to require that each individual user supply a user name and password pair that only he knows.
- Power settings to reduce the leakage of wireless emissions to a small area immediately outside the bank branch.
- Authentication of wireless access points on the basis of MAC addresses.

To return to the original issue, can an organization that needs the highest level of security safely implement a wireless architecture within its LAN? Let's look at what would be required to compromise such a system from the outside.

First, we demonstrated how to detect the access points and the important settings on those access points. That step is not too difficult. A hacker could park outside late at night as we did, and the only people who might notice would be local law enforcement—unless the company implemented 24/7 video camera monitoring of all its facilities.

Once the hacker knew the SSIDs, he would need to crack WEP. In order to crack WEP (using known methods, such as the statistical attack against the initialization vectors), he would need to capture about 6GB of traffic. We don't foresee General ever transmitting as much as 6GB of traffic over the wireless link in the period of time between successive dynamic rekeyings. The hacker would need to gather and analyze that much traffic and derive the key in one 20-minute period—no small feat.

Added to this, the LEAP method obscures the initialization vector before it can even be analyzed in the first place. A handful of people might be able to decrypt the LEAP hash, and a handful of people might be able to crack WEP without a prohibitively large volume of traffic, but finding the two skills in one team parked outside a bank branch is extremely unlikely as of today. However, new hacking tools and new attacks are always being developed. After the release of WEP, it took less than a year for AirSnort, with its WEP-cracking capabilities, to be freely distributed.

Naturally, an upgrade to WEP+, when available, will offer increased protection for General Savings & Loan's data.

The internal attack is more of a threat. A knowledgeable internal user could open a laptop and remove the proximity alarm device. He could use his own password to connect from outside the building and pilfer information or perhaps funds. However, it would be easy to identify the perpetrator. He might be better off just robbing the bank himself; that is, he might be more likely to get away with it.

There are other recommendations that would make this network even safer, but we thought they would be overkill. For example, the access points could have been sequestered in a demilitarized zone (DMZ) or on a virtual local area network (VLAN), and the traffic from the access points could have been filtered to allow only a very narrow range of traffic to resources within the bank.

The information that we provided convinced General Savings & Loan that its wireless architecture was secure enough to open for business on Thursday. General eventually decided to go ahead with the broader rollout at its remaining branches.

With the right tools and know-how, and a periodic review of the state of the wireless network, wireless networks can be secure, even when a high level of security is a primary concern for operations.

Virus Outbreak I

This chapter details the case of a virus attack, highlighting the potential harm that viruses can cause. It shows that virus investigations involve not only identifying the source of the infection but also determining the depth of infection.

It is widely believed that protecting e-mail, the most common way for viruses to propagate, should be enough to mitigate the risk of being hit with a virus. However, this case shows that poor firewall configuration, combined with a lack of patch management, can also leave a network open to a virus infection.

5.1 Introduction

Some time ago we received a call from a biomedical research firm for which we had previously installed several UNIX systems. The firm was having trouble with its systems and asked us to come in to troubleshoot—and hopefully fix—the problem.

Upon arriving, we found that the company's Sun servers had run out of disk space and the CPU utilization was at almost 100 percent. We began to research the problem. We asked how long this had been going on and were told it had been like this for three days. They kept assuming that the machines were hung on a process and rebooting them, but the machines would shortly return to full utilization, slow down, and sometimes freeze up.

The 100 percent CPU utilization suggested a possible denial-of-service (DoS) attack or a runaway process. But rebooting can help with both of those. So we needed to look at the process list to see if anything jumped out right away as a potential problem. We did this by issuing the following command:

```
# ps -ef
```

A few processes commanded a closer review:

- `/bin/sleep 300`
- `/bin/sh/dev/cuc/sadmin.sh`
- `/bin/sh /dev/cuc/uniattack.sh`
- `/bin/sh /dev/cuc/time.sh`
- `/usr/sbin/inetd -s /tmp/.f`

We looked up the sadmin daemon on the cert.org[1] Web site, which led us to Advisory CA 2001-11 (http://www.cert.org/advisories/CA-2001-11.html) discussing the sadmind/IIS worm, which compromised, appropriately, the sadmind process on vulnerable Sun boxes.

Before concluding that this worm was the cause of the client's problem, we needed to verify as many of the details as possible, in addition to the positive match for the entries on the process list. The advisory suggested that the worm opens a root shell listening on TCP port 6000 and included a list of potential syslog entries. We wanted to check the client's logs to see if any entries matched those included in the advisory.

Generally, when systems are compromised, the logs can no longer be trusted because they may very well have been altered by the hacker, along with any evidence of such tampering. We do still review the logs, however, in the hopes that they will offer an insight into what took place—and the hacker may not have

---

1. This is the Web site for the CERT Coordination Center of the Software Engineering Institute at Carnegie Mellon University.

bothered to alter the logs. This client was exporting the syslogs onto another machine, and we were able to take a look at entries from around the time the systems became unusable. Several entries were found to match those in the advisory:[2]

- `Apr 9 09:10:05` *sun.biorsrch.com* `inetd[139]: /usr/sbin/sadmind: Bus Error - core dumped`
- `Apr 9 09:10:00` *sun.biorsrch.com* `inetd[139]: /usr/sbin/sadmind: Segmentation Fault - core dumped`
- `Apr 9 09:10:09` *sun.biorsrch.com* `inetd[139]: /usr/sbin/sadmind: Segmentation Fault - core dumped`
- `Apr 9 09:16:20` *sun.biorsrch.com* `inetd[139]: /usr/sbin/sadmind: Killed`

Further, the advisory included evidence that the `/dev/cub` directory is used to store a log of compromised machines and the `/dev/cuc` directory contains tools used by the worm. Both of these directories were indeed included on the compromised UNIX hosts.

This research made it clear that the client had fallen victim to the sadmind/IIS worm (also known as the China worm because it is believed to have originated in that country[3]), which exploited a known vulnerability in the sadmind processes of unpatched Solaris 2.6 systems, among others. (The "IIS" in the name indicates that it also compromises Microsoft IIS Web servers.) The machines had been totally "owned," but it did not appear to the client that any data files had been destroyed. (This status was determined by a comparison of the data files to the backups that had been made the night before.) By "owned," we mean that it was clear that the hacker not only had access to the machine, but had root privileges and was potentially in position to extend his reach deeper into the company. We were able to discover a few text documents written by the hackers boasting about how clever they were and how stupid the system administrators were (the latter apparently because the system was running at a fairly old patch level).

---

2. The host name here (sun.biorsrch.com) is in italics in these entries as a placeholder; biorsrch.com is not the URL of the client company. Any firm owning and operating the URL biorsrch.com bears no resemblance to the company discussed here.

3. According to an article published online at http://www.das.utah.gov/cc/may2001/techcorner.html, the launch of the China worm is believed to have been part of an effort aimed at cyber retaliation "for the accidental U.S. bombing of the Chinese embassy in Belgrade, Yugoslavia, on May 7, 1999."

5.2 HOW DID YOU GET IN?

We started doing a bit of detective work to discover two things: (1) how the worm found the Sun boxes in the first place and (2) the extent of the compromise. When we originally worked on the configuration of these UNIX systems, as shown in Figure 5.1, the network was essentially a stand-alone network supporting a single research-related application. This setup was similar in nature to a demilitarized zone (DMZ) in that it was located behind a firewall with a default Deny All rule for inbound traffic and was monitored with a network-based intrusion detection system (NIDS). Other security safeguards were in place as well. So even with the old patch level, we were interested to know how the virus had made its way in.

We examined the firewall rule set and found that it had been changed, and the Deny All rule itself had been dropped. Was this the work of the hacker? We

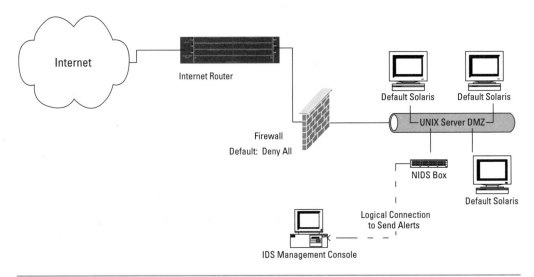

Figure 5.1 Original Connectivity to the UNIX Server DMZ

brought this to the attention of the client and soon learned that this certainly was not the work of the hacker. The client informed us that two changes had taken place since we had last been with them.

First, the firm had recently joined forces with a university lab and had needed to grant access to researchers at the lab so that they could conduct the necessary research. The university lab did not have access to the client's corporate network, but it did have basic Internet access through a local Internet service provider (ISP). Naturally, the lab was originally unable to see our client's Sun boxes because of the firewall rules.

Second, the firm had gone through some restructuring and had added some additional staff to this project internally. To facilitate a greater number of people working on the project, two things had been done: First, the university lab's research network had been connected to the firm's corporate network, as we'll see shortly; and second, the firewall rules again had been modified.

Table 5.1 shows the original firewall rules that denied access to both of the new groups.

The UNIX servers were grouped into a list and collectively called UNIX_DMZ. Apparently, traffic out to the Internet was allowed, possibly to allow research (e.g., Web queries and queries against various databases) and to post research results to industry consortiums. The short-term solution to the problem of the firewall rules was simply to drop all the rules and restrictions for connectivity to

Table 5.1 Original Firewall Rules

Action[a]	Source Host/ Network	Destination Host/Network	Interface	Service	Description
X	Any	UNIX_DMZ	Outside (inbound)	Any	Deny all access
✓	UNIX_DMZ	Any	Inside (outbound)	Any	Allow traffic out to the Internet

a. X = deny traffic corresponding to the rule; ✓ = allow traffic.

Table 5.2 Modified Firewall Rules

Action[a]	Source Host/ Network	Destination Host/Network	Interface	Service	Description
✓	RSRCH_Group	UNIX_DMZ	Outside (inbound)	Any	Allow inbound traffic from corporate network
✓	Any	UNIX_DMZ	Outside (inbound)	Any	Allow all access
✓	UNIX_DMZ	Any	Inside (outbound)	Any	Allow traffic out to the Internet

a. ✓ = allow traffic.

the Sun servers! The firm literally went from a `Deny All` setup to an `Allow All` setup, as shown in Table 5.2.

The group `RSRCH_Group` was a listing of the hosts belonging to project members who accessed the system from within the corporate network. So now, users in the university lab could see the servers, applications, and data. And consequently, the boxes were exposed to anyone with Internet access, as shown in Figure 5.2.

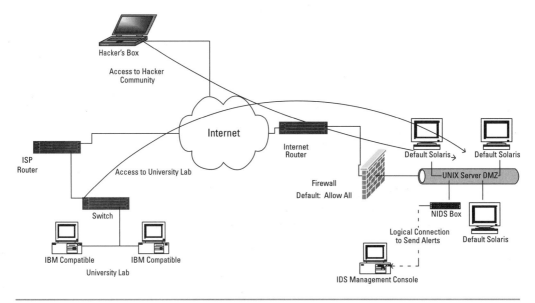

Figure 5.2 Modified Connectivity to the UNIX Server DMZ

The definitions of the rules in Table 5.2 suggest that the rule to allow access to RSRCH_Group was added first, and the more comprehensive Allow Any rule was added afterward to accommodate the university lab. The organization's long-term plan was to implement a VPN at the university location, create a VPN user group (similar to RSRCH_Group), and allow inbound access to that group while restricting all other inbound access. However, this change did not take place—at least not in time to prevent the virus attack.

So now we see how the worm got in. However, how the worm was able to inflict its damage without being identified by antivirus software or the intrusion detection system was left to be determined. Half of the problem was easily identified: The client was not running antivirus software on these machines. Because these were not user machines and were not expected to experience heavy user or Internet traffic, the client did not believe that installing antivirus software was necessary.

This situation was further exacerbated by the fact that the Sun Solaris operating system was a completely unpatched, default installation. Numerous patches had been released since the machine had been installed. As we will see, the sadmind/IIS worm that attacked and compromised the machines exploited a vulnerability that had been fixed by one of these uninstalled patches.

As for the IDS, the client was running a network-based intrusion detection system within the UNIX server DMZ to identify signatures of potential hacking or cyber attack activity.

By checking the IDS logs as well as the system logs, we hoped to discover how the worm had reached the systems. Again, even though the logs may have been compromised, we can turn to them for clues in situations such as this. The logs in this case indicated that an Anonymous FTP session between an unknown host and one of the servers in the DMZ had been created just a few hours before the problem started. Here are the log entries:

```
09:41:45.305687 attackers.7589 > victim.21:     ftp  send file
09:41:45.305821 attackers.8101 > victim.55434: ftp  send file
```

This FTP session led to a file being uploaded onto the server. We presumed that this file was the sadmind/IIS worm, and that presumption was verified by later examination of the file. Once the file was loaded, all the hacker needed was to have it executed. To do this, the hacker saved the file with the file name `netcsape.exe` and placed it in the same directory as the actual Netscape Web browser executable. (Because this was a default installation, the attacker was able to guess the path to the appropriate directory.) The attacker was hoping that a user would mistype "netscape" when attempting to launch a Web browser, entering "netcsape" by mistake. This error would then launch the worm, and it would do the rest. It would continue to spawn instances of the vulnerable process until stopped, or until the machine crashed. In addition, the sadmind/IIS worm is self-propagating, meaning that it automatically sends itself to other vulnerable Solaris hosts.

FTP sessions and instances of the running sadmin daemon, however, would not set off the IDS, because these are not contained in the signature database as evidence of potential hacker activity. FTP sessions and instances of a normal system daemon were simply not defined as unusual traffic. Once one machine was compromised, they could all fall in turn, courtesy of this worm.

The worm appeared to have just spawned a large number of the sadmin daemon processes to effectively overload the box and render it essentially unusable. In addition, the worm added the line + + to the `.rhosts` file in the root user's directory, thereby allowing any user from any host to access the server. This modification is what allowed the hacker to access the machine, write taunting files, and potentially steal the client's research data.

As a short-term remedy for the high CPU utilization, one could consider simply cycling the box—that is, rebooting (turning the machine off and back on). It sounds reasonably simple. However, doing this would not address the problem of the worm itself. There is no reason to believe that the worm wouldn't just start up again. There would have to be a way to scrub the machines of the sadmind/IIS worm.

The company also did not have a standard baseline for these UNIX servers identifying their proper configuration—the proper applications and files existing on the systems. Therefore, when the machine came back up after a reboot, there would be no way of knowing if there were any other problems, such as a root kit installation or a back door planted for the hacker's convenience, allowing him access to the machine. As far as we could tell, however, the backup files were untouched. System backups were being performed nightly, written to tape, and saved to a separate system.

The infected servers had to be rebuilt completely, starting with the operating system—this time with all relevant patches in place. To complete this process, the applications running on the servers needed to be tested on the new base operating system.

The fact that patches can potentially affect the applications running on a machine often makes system administrators hesitant to install the patches. Not all applications will be compatible with *new* patches. And some patches may not be backward-compatible; that is, they may not support all previously running applications. Finally, the patches themselves may have untold vulnerabilities. However, given that the vulnerability experienced in this case was directly treated by the existing vendor patches, the client was committed to their immediate installation.

After the OS was reloaded, the applications were tested and reloaded, and the data had to be reloaded as well. Luckily, the client had been backing up the data nightly, thereby significantly limiting any potential loss of data processing or research findings.

5.3 HOW MUCH HAVE WE LOST?

As for the second piece of detective work—that is, determining how far into the company the compromise extended—the listing of compromised hosts within the /dev/cub directory offered a starting place. We couldn't consider this a complete listing, because once the hacker had access, he may have been able to compromise additional hosts separate from the use of the worm and without recording the conquest.

The lack of a baseline again complicated the review of additional hosts, especially outside of the DMZ. We returned to the logs to review entries from within the DMZ, its firewall, the Internet router, and the corporate firewall (as shown in

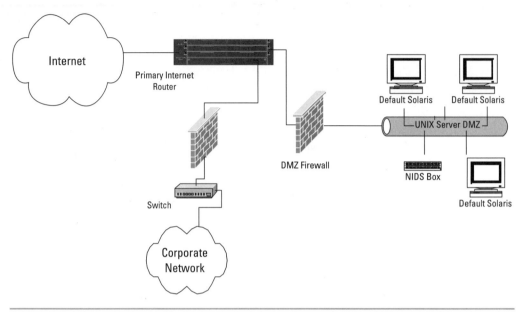

Figure 5.3 Overall Network Architecture

Figure 5.3). Our goal was to see if connections had been made between the DMZ hosts and machines on the corporate network that were not a part of normal business. Figure 5.3 also shows how the research network, the DMZ, was connected to the rest of the corporate network. The firewall was simply attached to the company's primary Internet router.

We were lucky in that the log entries matched up and indicated that connections had been made with a few hosts:

```
10:14  accept  FW_DMZ  inside  tcp  src_IP:4240  dest_IPa:23
10:16  accept  FW_DMZ  inside  tcp  src_IP:5329  dest_IPb:23

10:14  accept  FW_NET outside  tcp  src_IP:4240  dest_IPa:23
10:16  accept FW_NET  outside  tcp  src_IP:5329  dest_IPb:23
```

All of the hosts potentially touched by either the sadmind/IIS worm or the hacker were then subjected to a complete forensic review to identify a "fingerprint" of the hacker, which was then used to evaluate other machines and hosts for compromise. This is a rather involved process that will be discussed further in Chapters 14 through 16, but it revealed no large-scale compromise of the potentially affected computers.

However, the company did lose valuable research time. Throughout the period of the infection and while this investigation was being conducted, they were unable to access their data, run simulations, and conduct research. Once lost, this time could not be recouped.

5.4 LESSONS LEARNED

A general point here is that a compromise normally consists of more than one building block. Antivirus software should be installed on all machines regardless of their system load or Internet connection. The open connection to the Internet would have mattered less if the OS had been correctly patched. Sun Microsystems had released patches, well in advance of the virus infection in this case, that were specifically developed to fix the hole that this worm exploits.[4] However, it is always wise to adopt a layered defense strategy rather than to rely on strengthening just one aspect of a system.

The client should have developed a more secure architecture in the first place. It is not necessary to connect the servers directly to the Internet to allow access from a satellite office, and the company knew this. A short-term strategy had been implemented to get things up and running *today*, with the intention of fixing the process *tomorrow*. Such an approach may be acceptable and, let's face it, perhaps necessary to get the job done and stay ahead of competition, but it is imperative to make sure the procedures are fixed before a problem arises.

The planned VPN, along with a list specifying users to whom access across the VPN would be allowed, needed to be implemented. This setup could potentially have allowed the university researchers working from their location to access the systems without also granting that privilege to the general Internet community. Such a rule set is shown in Table 5.3.

---

4. Patch ID 108661-01 (http://sunsolve.sun.com/pub-cgi/findPatch.pl?patchId=108661&rev=01) was the specific patch called for in this environment.

Table 5.3 Suggested Firewall Rules

Action[a]	Source Host/ Network	Destination Host/Network	Interface	Service	Description
✓	Uni_Lab	UNIX_DMZ	Outside (inbound)	Any	Allow access to IP addresses in the university lab
✓	RSRCH_Group	UNIX_DMZ	Outside (inbound)	Any	Allow inbound traffic from the corporate network
X	Any	UNIX_DMZ	Outside (inbound)	Any	Deny all access
✓	UNIX_DMZ	Any	Inside (outbound)	Any	Allow traffic out to the Internet

a. X = deny traffic corresponding to the rule; ✓ = allow traffic.

Firewall rules are read in their order of appearance. Therefore, the Deny All rule in Table 5.3 effectively denies access to all but members of the Uni_Lab and RSRCH_Group networks. In addition, access does not have to be granted to "any" services, but can be further restricted to the specific services (ports) that the users of the applications will require to perform their duties. This will likely be a small subset of "any."

The operating systems, especially for any Internet-connected hosts, should be configured in accordance with a **minimum secure baseline** that includes all configuration settings, running applications, file structure, permissions, user account status, current patch level, and so on. In the event that a box has to be rebuilt, such a baseline gives clear guidance on how to rebuild that box. Once a machine has been set up in accordance with these configuration settings, the entire machine can be burned to a CD-ROM. This CD (sometimes called a *golden CD*) can then be used simply to load up new hosts.

A minimum secure baseline also provides a great deal of information about how the box will look. This information helps in searching the box to identify root kits, as well as changes in configuration settings, such as the creation of new accounts, added files, and Trojaned files. A minimum secure baseline should also identify any and all unnecessary applications (such as Anonymous FTP) that can be disabled, as well as the list of all executable files, such as `netscape.exe`. Therefore, along with host-based monitoring on the hosts, the organization can be alerted to the creation of extra world-writable and/or world-executable, such as the Trojaned worm, `netcsape.exe` in this case. This may be more of a response than is necessary, but tracking the usage of the system can do a lot to help secure the network.

VIRUS OUTBREAK II
THE WORM

In Chapter 5 we discussed the case of a virus and the potential harmful effects that a virus can have on the availability of IT resources and the overall productivity of a firm. Virus incidents can certainly be harmful events. Potentially even more deadly than a virus, however, is a worm, especially the polymorphic worm that we will discuss in this chapter.

Viruses and worms are often thought of as one and the same thing; they can certainly be considered to belong to the same family. In layman's terms, a worm is a virus on steroids. A **polymorphic worm** is one that can change itself after each infection so that its signature is slightly different on each infected host. This ability to change signature makes it more difficult to develop signatures that identify, quarantine, and delete the worm, and thus gives the worm more time in the wild to do its damage.

6.1 INTRODUCTION

Local governments often operate under the classic stovepipe syndrome. Although their systems may be linked to a common backbone for access to the Internet, or attach to the same Web infrastructure (e.g., http://www.city.gov, http://www.co.<county>.zz.us, or http://www.zz.us[1]), often each individual department has an independent IT infrastructure, complete with its own secondary Internet connection, software applications, security tools, and so on. It is also not unusual for agencies within a department to have their own, separate IT networks as well. Naturally, in such cases each domain (stovepipe) has its own IT management, including its own network security personnel.

Stovepipe setups like this do not seem to bother the progress of a worm. Worms seem to have little problem navigating the political landscapes and moving from department to department, crossing jurisdictional and political hurdles in a matter of moments. This case study involves just such an instance. A worm infiltrated a state government[2] at one location and quickly spread to many agencies throughout the government. Even operations offering necessary citizen services, such as the motor vehicle, police, and health departments, were not spared.

6.2 Background

Before we get into the details of the case, let's spend a minute looking at the victim's network, shown in Figures 6.1 and 6.2. The purpose of the network is to provide backbone communications and Internet access. Multiple data centers provide Web site hosting and numerous additional applications to the various agencies. From the backbone there is visibility into the agencies; however, the IT department that manages and operates the network pays little attention to what takes place on the other side of the agency routers. Nevertheless, it is known that the agency networks are predominantly Windows environments with numerous hosts running different versions of the Windows operating system.

---

1. Where *zz* is the two-letter abbreviation for the state.
2. To hide the identity of the government body in question and for clarity's sake, we will simply refer to it as a *state*, but we certainly make no claim that this case study reflects any incident that may or may not have occurred in any of our 50 states.

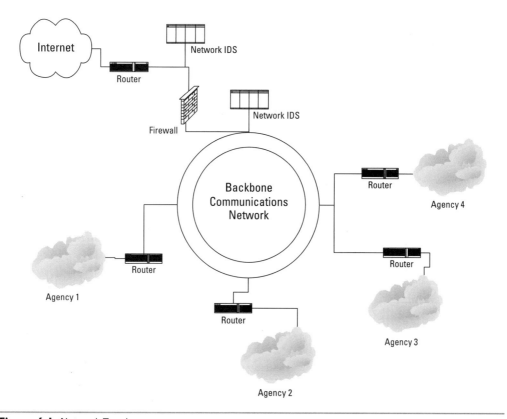

Figure 6.1 Network Topology

6.3 THE WORM INFECTION

In the early morning hours of August 12, 2003, a user in the state's Department on Aging was performing the common morning ritual of browsing through her e-mail using a Web-based e-mail client (similar to yahoo.com or the numerous other free e-mail providers). As this user scrolled through her e-mail, she came to one that looked especially appealing. She double-clicked on the e-mail and opened it to view the entire HTML-embedded e-mail message.

And it started.

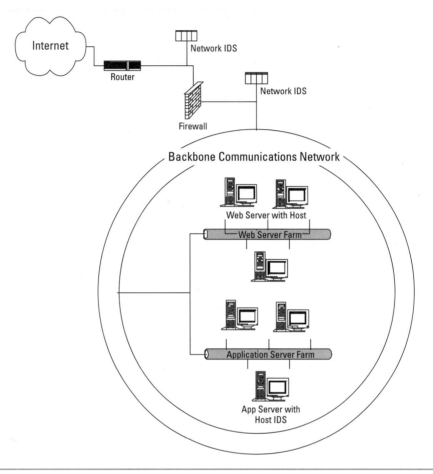

Figure 6.2 Backbone Network

Simultaneously, an employee across the state in the Department of Sanitation plugged his personal laptop into the network to download some music. The state may have had something to say about the downloading of music, but the employee was entirely permitted to connect his personal machine to the network. Using Kazaa, this user surfed the Internet for his favorite songs, leaving the default configuration options in place.

That was it. The worm was off to the races.

Soon after these events occurred on that morning, staff members in many offices throughout the state government began to notice that the Internet had become very slow. A similar observation was made in the security department (part of the state's cyber security department), which immediately began to look for potential reasons that CNN.com and MSNBC.com were both unavailable at the same time. The network help desk (also a part of the cyber security department) began fielding calls from curious—and sometimes irritated—end users asking why they couldn't browse the Web or download their e-mail.

To get to the bottom of the problem, the security staff turned to reports from their intrusion detection, firewall, and antivirus tools. The antivirus software had indeed detected the presence of a virus; the intrusion detection system had begun sending alerts. The security staff quickly gulped down their morning coffee and logged into their systems to see what was happening.

One especially judicious security staff member checked the firewall log and sent the following e-mail requesting an immediate review and some information from another IT professional within the state government.

```
From: G. Harrison (SecOps)
To: J. Lennon (Dept. Aging)
Cc: Information System Security Officers (ISSO)
Sent: Tuesday, August 12, 2003 4:04 PM

Subject: Virus Outbreak II: The Worm

Please look at the firewall log below for the source machine
10.x.x.3; it may be infected. This is the machine identified in
the first alert this morning. Can you determine what the user did
right before the infection started? The destination of the HTTP
activity, shaded in the log below, didn't resolve. If we know how
the outbreak got started, it'll help down the road if we need to
put up any blocks.

G.
Security Operations
```

Firewall Log on the Morning of the Worm Outbreak:

Time	Action	Service	Source	Destination[a]	Proto
09:13:47	accept		10.x.x.03	132.y.y.201	icmp
09:13:48	accept		10.x.x.03	132.y.y.210	icmp
09:13:49	accept		10.x.x.03	132.y.y.208	icmp
09:13:50	accept		10.x.x.03	132.y.y.206	icmp
09:14:48	accept	NCP	10.x.x .03	132.y.y.206	tcp
09:09:21	accept	http	10.x.x.03	64.z.z.36	tcp
09:09:22	accept	http	10.x.x.03	64.z.z.36	tcp
09:09:24	accept	http	10.x.x.03	64.z.z.36	tcp
09:09:25	accept	http	10.x.x.03	64.z.z.36	tcp
09:09:27	accept	http	10.x.x.03	64.z.z.36	tcp
09:09:28	accept	http	10.x.x.03	64.z.z.36	tcp
09:09:38	accept	http	10.x.x.03	165.z.z.103	tcp
09:16:14	accept		10.x.x.03	132.y.y.206	icmp
09:16:15	accept		10.x.x.03	132.y.y.208	icmp
09:16:16	accept		10.x.x.03	132.y.y.210	icmp
09:16:17	accept		10.x.x.03	132.y.y.201	icmp
09:17:16	drop	TCP-135	10.x.x.03	1.a.a.1	tcp
09:17:16	drop	TCP-135	10.x.x.03	1.a.a.2	tcp
09:17:16	drop	TCP-135	10.x.x.03	1.a.a.3	tcp
09:17:16	drop	TCP-135	10.x.x.03	1.a.a.4	tcp
09:17:16	drop	TCP-135	10.x.x.03	1.a.a.5	tcp
09:17:16	drop	TCP-135	10.x.x.03	1.a.a.6	tcp
09:17:16	drop	TCP-135	10.x.x.03	1.a.a.7	tcp
09:17:16	drop	TCP-135	10.x.x.03	1.a.a.8	tcp
09:17:16	drop	TCP-135	10.x.x.03	1.a.a.9	tcp

a. Not actual IP address

In short order, machines across the government were setting off alarm bells, similar to those already mentioned and all related to the virus. The state's computers were getting hit faster than the security operations (SecOps) group could send out e-mails to agency IT personnel (such as the preceding e-mail) requesting information.

As the virus spread, systems became unavailable and state personnel became unable to access information that they required to provide citizen services. For example, parole officers and social service case workers could not access their case records—all stored electronically—to contact and follow up with case subjects and parolees. Even with those they could call (because they had their numbers jotted down or still carried paper notes and files), they could not enter notes from the conversations into the official record online. In many of these cases, if there was no record confirming that contact was made (and all was well), the "status" of the individual in question changed in the computer records automatically, and for the worse. The state was left with two options: pursue everyone the system claimed to be in violation, or give everyone a waiver and attribute it to the system outage. In either case, this technical problem led to administrative and procedural problems in providing effective citizen services.

6.3.1 DIAGNOSIS

The problem that the state experienced was being attributed to a "virus" solely because of the alerts from the antivirus software. To deal with the problem effectively, however, it would be important to identify the cause of the problem more precisely.

If the problem was a virus, then which virus was it? What targets would be most susceptible? Was a patch available? Or was there a script to disinfect any infected hosts? The ultimate diagnosis was performed by comparison of what was being seen on the state's network with what were being reported as telltale signs of the viruses currently in the wild.[3]

On the basis of all the information available, it was determined that the state had been hit by the Lovsan worm, a variant of the MS Blaster worm. Of course, the diagnosis had to be reviewed whenever additional infected hosts exhibited unexpected behavior, because many worms were taking advantage of the MS RPC bug at the time, so even greater than the worry of misdiagnosis was the fear that multiple worms were running amok on the state's network.

6.3.2 PLAN OF ATTACK

What the state needed (and lacked) at this time was a clear plan for responding to this situation.

---

3. Some sources of industry information are included in the Recommended Reading section at the end of the book.

The security department immediately set up a task force consisting of members throughout the agency who were in any way responsible for responding to the virus incident. Included on this task force were representatives of the firewall operations group, IDS operations, the antivirus deployment group, e-mail, network operations, and agency management. Also included were representatives of the agency's public relations group because regular and periodic reports to the governor and the public would probably be required.

All security staff members of the IT Agency were added to the e-mail list to be kept abreast of the situation, not only for their edification, but also so that they could be ready for action if they were deployed somewhere to put out fires. In addition, members of the IT and/or security staff of all other individual agencies of the state were included on the task force e-mail communication list so that they could contribute to efforts to fight the worm and be kept apprised of progress made. Table 6.1 lists the members of this task force and their specific roles.

Table 6.1 Task Force Members

Member	Role
Cyber security department management	Coordinate all activities related to containing and eliminating the worm
Network operations	Monitor the network and identify potentially infected subnets and hosts
E-mail group	Ensure that virus scans were taking place on the e-mail servers
Antivirus deployment group	Update antivirus status on all hosts
Intrusion detection system group	Monitor the IDS to identify infected hosts and subnets
Firewall group	Monitor firewall and router logs to identify and block suspicious traffic and all traffic between suspected compromised hosts
Public relations	Properly communicate the status message to the governor and the media as necessary
CIO/CSO/director of victim agencies	Contribute whenever possible, and keep abreast of the current status of the antivirus efforts

The task force needed to be in constant communication, and no time could be wasted in reacting to the worm, so rather than having physical meetings (which involve arranging conference rooms, and having various parties travel from multiple locations to the specific conference room), all meetings were held via regularly scheduled teleconferences, allowing parties to dial in from any telephone (with the conference pass codes), and minute-by-minute status updates were communicated over the e-mail distribution list already described.

By the time the task force was in place, it was clear that they were dealing with one of the numerous worms developed to take advantage of a recently announced Microsoft vulnerability. The first thing that had to be done was to come to a consensus on exactly what was happening. Therefore, an immediate message had to be sent to all government personnel (IT staff and end users) to ensure that the antivirus software was updated to the latest virus definitions and engine versions on all of the state's computers. It was agreed that the chief security officer (CSO) would prepare a memo to this effect, and for greater impact, it would be cosigned by the governor himself. Here's what the CSO wrote:

FROM: P. McCartney, Chief Security Officer

TO: All State Employees
TO: All Antivirus Administrators
TO: All Cyber Security Personnel
TO: All Agency Chief Security Officers
TO: All Agency Chief Technology Officers
TO: All Agency Directors

DATE: Tuesday, August 12, 2003

RE: Emergency DAT 4.0.4284 for McAfee VirusScan released 08/12/03

This morning we are in the midst of an outbreak of what is believed to be a variant of the W32/LOVSAN.WORM exploiting the recently reported Microsoft Windows RPC DCOM flaw, and a close relative of the Blaster worm featured in the recent Department of Homeland Security/FedCIRC W32/Blaster Worm Advisory FA-2003-20 (attached) dated 08/11/03.

Our antivirus software vendor has provided an emergency release of DAT file ### to detect and identify this particularly harmful strain of the RPC DCOM exploit. It is imperative that you implement this emergency DAT file on all hosts immediately. The DAT file will be available today at the following locations:

<<URLs listed>>

Thank you,
P. McCartney
Chief Security Officer

It was hoped that updating the antivirus software on all the machines in the network would prevent any further infection and would help identify the subnets and hosts on the network that were infected. Once identified, infected subnets and hosts can be blocked from the network at the router level so that the infection (and the worm) can be isolated and the cleanup process can begin.

Another mechanism that can help identify infected machines is to create new signatures for the intrusion detection systems to identify the virus and send alerts about it. Such signatures are based on information obtained from industry reports, research into the worm, and activities being witnessed right on the affected network. The IDS vendors, also actively working on creating defensive signatures, were consulted in this endeavor.

The effort to identify infected hosts and subnets included careful examination of the firewall logs. During the review of the firewall logs, a great deal of *incoming* traffic on TCP port 135 was noticed. This activity suggested that there were infected subnets on the state government's side, as well as infected machines—or the attacker's machine—on the sending side. The router blocks to be installed would also block incoming traffic over this port to these subnets. Two members of the firewall operations group were assigned to review the firewall logs in greater detail to develop access control lists (ACLs) that would effectively block the unrecognized source addresses for the unusual inbound traffic. Outbound blocks were also put into effect for this port at both the routers and the firewall.

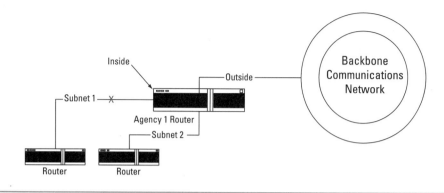

Figure 6.3 Subnet-Level Blocking

Once an outline of infected subnets and hosts—as comprehensive as we could make it—had been developed, the decision was made to put blocks at the routers. Such blocks start at the individual IP address level; however, if the number of infected hosts grows fast, as it does during an outbreak and certainly did in this case, blocking individual IP addresses is not feasible for very long. The blocks simply have to be placed on the entire subnet, as illustrated in Figure 6.3.

The access control lists that achieve the blocking described here are shown conceptually in Tables 6.2 and 6.3 for the inside and outside interfaces, respectively, of the router.

Table 6.2 Inside Interface

	Rule	**Protocol**	**Source**	**Destination**
Access list	Deny	Any	Any	Subnet 1

Table 6.3 Outside Interface

	Rule	**Protocol**	**Source**	**Destination**
Access list	Deny	Any	Subnet 1	Any

Because the infection was rather widespread, the blocks were placed through a wide cross section of the state's network in order to quarantine the infected subnets and protect the uninfected subnets. As you might imagine, when such blocks are implemented far and wide, many network services became unavailable—perhaps chief among these, electronic mail. Disconnecting people from e-mail capability resulted in some fallout, including the following, hand-delivered memo:

FROM: Y. Ono, Communications Director
TO: P. McCartney, Chief Security Officer
DATE: Tuesday, August 12, 2003

RE: Loss of E-mail Communications Services

I cannot believe that users were simply cut off from their e-mail. I do not understand how you can simply disconnect such a critical service. In the future, you must not take actions affecting e-mail services without discussing this with us.

What you have done is make it impossible for any user who is on Lotus Notes to access e-mail to send or receive messages. This is a major outage for all Exchange users. The help desk and e-mail operations are being flooded with phone calls from users who cannot access mail or cannot send or receive mail. Please resolve this problem and restore our connectivity immediately.

I thank you in advance for your immediate attention to this matter.

Y. Ono
State Communications Director

In response to this complaint, a list of the Lotus Notes e-mail servers to and from which communication should specifically be allowed was compiled. However, before altering the block to allow communication to the servers, security personnel had to be sure that none of the machines involved were infected. A plan to deal with the many infected hosts had to be developed anyway, so a plan was developed for restoring e-mail services. This plan had to ensure that all servers received the same treatment and that the machines were cleaned effectively.

In another conference call, the engineers hammered out the details of a plan to clean each infected machine, including the following measures:

- Disconnect the machine from the network
- Update the antivirus software
- Scan the machine
- Disinfect the machine
- Decide whether to reconnect or rebuild the machine

Naturally, any infected machine had to be immediately disconnected from the network. Its antivirus software had to be updated (and in all too many cases, loaded for the first time). Once disconnected, the new virus signature files could not be downloaded from the Web, so before the engineers could begin working on the machines, the necessary files (and software) had to be saved to a CD so that they could be loaded onto the machines manually.

Once the latest virus signatures had been loaded, the machine was thoroughly scanned for infection by the antivirus software. The machines were also scanned by commercial vulnerability scanning tools, such as Internet Security Systems' System Scanner (and Database Scanner where appropriate) and eEye Digital Security's Retina Network Security Scanner. Soon after Microsoft released the patch for the RPC DCOM flaw, numerous security vendors had released scanners to detect whether the patch was present and whether the machine was still vulnerable. Many of these scanners were offered as free downloads.

For each scan, the infected machine was placed onto a hub (that the security staff brought with them) that also had a laptop on which the scanning tool was loaded. This second scan was just to double-check the cleanliness of the host and to verify that the hole the worm had compromised was fixed.

Efforts were made to disinfect the machine. The antivirus software was able, in most cases, to quarantine and delete the worm. However, an additional script had to be run to clean out other changes (such as to the Windows Registry) that the worm had caused.

After these steps, the machine was rescanned to verify that it was truly clean. If so, it could be reconnected to the network. But if not, it had to be sent to be rebuilt. If there was any doubt, the machine simply had to be rebuilt. You can't play around with polymorphic worms.

On the basis of the success of the process to check the e-mail servers, more-formal emergency response teams were formed, assigned to specific lists of infected hosts and subnets, and charged with doing whatever was necessary to disinfect those machines.

Throughout the process, the governor required periodic but irregular updates. Naturally, whenever there was a change in the number of infected hosts, a report was to be made. And whenever the public inquiry in the governor's office was too great to quell, again a report needed to be made.

This process went on for many days. With a limited security staff, and a manual cleanup process that was combating a worm with a replication rate rivaling that of fruit flies, things were not back to normal just overnight, as you might well imagine.

6.3.3 Count Your Losses

Given the large-scale nature of this incident, everyone from the elected officials to agency directors and news reporters was demanding to know how much this worm outbreak was costing the state (and hence the taxpayers). The state had spent over two months fighting the worm. Although the worst of the problem was right at the beginning, when the worm first hit, there were flare-ups throughout the period in which machines that had not yet been patched and updated became infected and started filling the network bandwidth with communication over port 135.

To determine the total cost of the worm attack, two security staff members were coupled with accountants from the payroll office to ascertain the losses. It is very difficult to measure and quantify the loss caused by a virus, but the attempt had to be made—if only to build a case for preventive measures in the future. Therefore, the four-member team set about the task of identifying categories of loss and then figuring out ways to ascertain the level of loss in each category. The following categories were identified:

- Lost productivity
  - System and server downtime
  - Loss of access to information
- Time spent rebuilding machines
- Lost data
  - Time spent reentering lost data
  - Time spent reprocessing data
- Loss of machines
- Loss of software and software licenses
- Loss of image and public trust

6.3.3.1 Lost Productivity

Any downtime caused by the worm would result in lost productivity. Downtime came in the form of down network systems and servers, as well as periods when employees were unable to access information. Damages caused by lost productivity were measured at the same rate as is calculated for paid time off for government holidays or emergency snow days.

6.3.3.2 Time Spent Rebuilding Machines

In a sense, the time that security staff spent disinfecting machines and the time that agency IT staff spent rebuilding machines can be considered periods of lost productivity. Although such activity is certainly part of the job description, it is an emergency function that pushes day-to-day activities aside.

6.3.3.3 Lost Data

On several machines that were hit, data was wiped out as well and had to be restored. In some cases backup data was available; in others, data had to be reentered manually. In all cases, the data had to be reprocessed. Naturally, this data reprocessing put the affected agencies behind schedule and caused delays into the future.

6.3.3.4 Loss of Machines

It's not often that machines are lost because of worms or viruses. In this case, however, for some of the older machines (e.g., running Windows 95) that were completely corrupted, it made more sense simply to scrap the machine and replace it rather than attempting to reload the original operating system. These machines were valued at their replacement cost.

6.3.3.5 Loss of Software and Software Licenses

In just a few instances, the original media for software loaded on an unrecoverable machine was no longer available (it had been lost over time). In these cases the only choices available to the state were to go without the software or to buy it again. (Naturally, appeals to the vendor would be made for concessions, given the nature of the need and the potential for future sales.)

6.3.3.6 Loss of Image and Public Trust

The most difficult loss to measure was the loss or damage done to the public trust. However, some reflection of the public's dissatisfaction had to be included, if only to convey the message to the state and its personnel.

• • •

After the assessment was completed, it was determined that during the two months the state had spent actively fighting the worm outbreak, thousands of man-hours of productivity were lost, forcing numerous IT and other projects to be placed on hold and citizen services to suffer. Many machines had to be dumped (though, truth be told, they were so old that everyone was just looking for a reason to dump them), and several software packages had to be reinstalled, or worse, repurchased from the vendors. The lost data in more than a few cases meant that the progress that had been made in many projects, job tasks, and government initiatives throughout numerous state agencies would simply have to be redone. The dollar amount attached to the whole incident reached the middle eight figures.

6.4 LESSONS LEARNED

Viruses and worms are taken very seriously now, not only in the government but in commercial organizations as well. Given the media coverage they receive, people are getting the message that a virus can very seriously and adversely affect an organization—from causing the loss of data to forcing severe and prolonged network downtime. Therefore, at even the hint of a virus, the security staff have learned to mobilize quickly into "firefighting" units to seek out infected hosts and disinfect them—by any means necessary. Countermeasures certainly include disconnecting infected machines from the wire.

However, the ad hoc nature of the emergency response groups limits their reach because security staff don't necessarily know who they may be working with and must wait for assignments. It would be preferable, and likely take less time for deployment, if these teams existed on a permanent basis. Thus, numerous additional measures were identified to improve the state's overall security posture and defense posture against worms.

6.4.1 SYSTEM BACKUPS

Every time a machine was ordered rebuilt, the end user and agency IT staff learned another valuable lesson in the virtues of keeping system backups. Recent backups, while not a defense against system downtime, can protect system data so that not all of it is lost.

6.4.2 CONSTANT MONITORING

After this awakening to the potential dangers of viruses and worms, the state felt that it would be better to remain vigilant in monitoring its antivirus posture. Even after the worm was finally under control, the security operations group continued its sweep throughout the state's network to identify machines running outdated virus signature files. Those that were outdated were updated immediately.

Further, the firewall and IDS logs were modified to report on evidence of potential virus-related activity. Such reporting required constant monitoring of industry sites to incorporate into these reports the latest virus signatures (such as ports and protocols that infected hosts use to communicate).

6.4.3 CONTINGENCY PLANS

The government agency's lack of contingency plans (also called *continuity of operations plans*) was certainly exposed. Numerous agencies were unclear on how to revert to paper mechanisms when the IT mechanisms became unavailable. In some ways this lack of preparedness is not inconceivable. So much time and money is spent on making business processes electronic, for the anticipated efficiencies and time savings, that the need to allow the old paper-based processes to continue can easily be overlooked.

In addition, the IT department determined that a comprehensive strategy for responding to virus incidents was needed. Such a plan was developed, and a flowchart, shown in Figure 6.4, was created to communicate the plan to all necessary parties. Note that the process contains a feedback loop (in dashed lines) to ensure that the process will be reviewed and modified after each virus incident, in the hope that such review will improve the overall defense against viruses.

6.4.4 CORRECTIVE ACTIONS

All of the precautions that we have described already are certainly helpful in defending against viruses and worms. Under pressure to enact measures to avoid such losses in the future, however, the security operations group identified the measures necessary to prevent the actions that introduced the worm in the first place. Had these been in place earlier, the entire incident might have been avoided. Specifically, the following actions were identified as the original source of the infection:

- Allowing users to access Web-based e-mail
- Allowing people to plug any machine into the network and receive an IP address (through DHCP, Dynamic Host Configuration Protocol) to go out to the Internet and access network resources

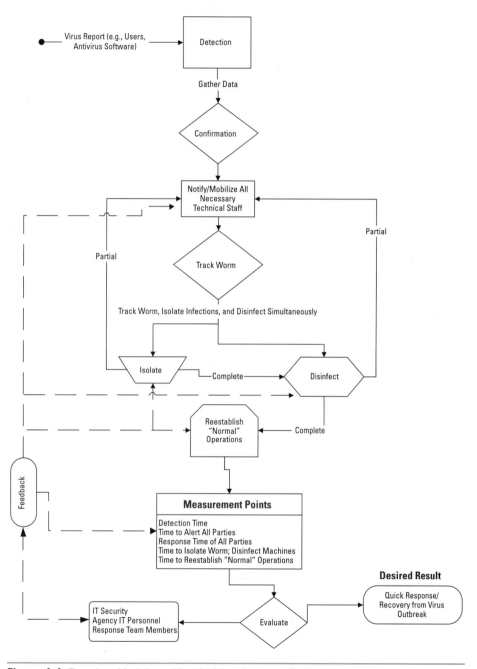

Figure 6.4 Flowchart Modeling a Virus Incident Response Strategy

6.4.4.1 Web-Based E-mail

Everyone loves to Yahoo! As responsible as anyone else for bringing e-mail to the masses, Yahoo! has been imitated by countless firms across the Internet. However, many of these Web-based e-mail services present two problems: (1) They support HTML-based e-mails, and (2) they don't all scan their e-mails for viruses. The latter problem is the one we're interested in here.

Not performing a virus scan on the e-mails means that users must rely solely on their desktop antivirus software to catch anything harmful in the e-mail. However, the "office" e-mail that goes through the state's e-mail servers can be scanned at the e-mail server prior to reaching the desktop, adding another layer of defense.

The other issue of allowing HTML-based e-mails is potentially more dangerous because encoding viruses directly into the HTML is becoming a popular means of spreading the virus. This means that users don't have to download and open attachments; they simply open the e-mail and the virus is started.

How can this be stopped? Because there is no way to get all Internet-based e-mail providers to scan all e-mail messages for viruses, it is easier just to block Web-based e-mail. The security operations staff in this case developed a list of Internet e-mail services and the associated IP addresses to block; a very partial listing is shown in Table 6.4. Actually putting such a block into effect certainly involves a great deal of political maneuvering; however, given the worm outbreak that had just occurred, the security operations group had all the ammunition it needed.

Table 6.4 Partial Listing of Internet E-mail Service Providers

Internet E-mail Provider URLs
http://email.excite.com
http://mail.hotmail.com
http://mail.yahoo.com

6.4.4.2 Hot Network Jacks

The issue of what to do about people plugging their own laptops into hot network jacks and connecting to the network is much more complex. On the surface, there seems to be little that can be done to avoid the problem. All unused network jacks could be made cold. Jacks could be locked to specific MAC addresses. However, how would you know which jacks were being used and which weren't? What would happen when a user who was connected to one jack was moved to another floor in the same building? With numerous government buildings, it is almost inconceivable that there would be an effective way to manage the status of all network jacks. And even if that were possible, managing the jacks would not fully address the issue, for someone could simply pull the network cable from a computer that was connected to the network or simply place a hub on any network jack that was hot.

A potential solution is to bar any outside laptop or desktop from being used on government facilities and to make sure that all government computers are running updated antivirus software. This is a policy-based solution. By itself, it doesn't prevent anyone from plugging a laptop into the network illegally and causing the same types of problems. However, when coupled with security education and training, as well as the threat of strict penalties, it can certainly have a positive effect.

Laptops and desktops, after all, are not items that are easily snuck into a building. Well-trained security personnel can be trained to spot them and ask the individuals carrying them for the proper authorization (for laptops that are issued by the government) or simply refuse to let them enter (should the laptop in question not belong to the government). As you might imagine, however, there would always be gaps in such coverage, and it would be hard for such a mechanism to entirely stop the use of personal digital assistants (PDAs) on the network.

7

CHANGING FACE

This chapter deals with a Web site defacement performed as part of a security assessment for a university client. The case description will not only cover the technical process, but will also address some of the things that can go wrong when the consultant/client relationship is not clearly defined.

7.1 INTRODUCTION

The security department of a local university issued a Request for Proposal (RFP) seeking a security assessment of one component of their Web infrastructure. Specifically, they were interested in reviewing the security posture of the machine hosting the HTML pages for their Web site. Because the task seemed fairly straightforward and the individual in charge of security of the Web site at the school was an old colleague, we submitted a proposal, hopeful of winning it. (Contacts really can come in handy.)

After reviewing our proposal, the old colleague called to give us the green light. During this call we discussed the specifics. He told us that we were to do what "any good hacker" would do to try to corrupt the Web site. We discussed the specifics of the Web site; the limitations on the assessment; the level of criticality of the site, its data, and the servers involved; and a host of other issues. We told him we would document all of these issues in a memo and fax it to him along with our standard contract, and once the memo had been signed by a designated signator of the school, we would begin. Our colleague agreed to this arrangement and said that he had the authority to sign the document on behalf of the school.

We told him that he should look over the memo and contract carefully and that, although we understood that there was some urgency in having the assessment performed, it was important to make sure we were all aware of exactly what the assessment would involve—what might and would happen, and what should not happen. He agreed, and in a couple of days, we received the return fax and were ready to start.

7.2 THE ASSESSMENT

Along with the signed contract, our colleague provided the client's IP address, and we were off. We started the engagement by spending some time quickly mapping out our activities. The first step was to ascertain what kind of computer and operating system we were dealing with.

That task was simple enough. We ran Nmap to unveil the mystery, using the following command:

```
bash# nmap -O <target_machine> -oN <filename>
```

The result told us that the machine was an `i386 Red Hat 7.0` operating system. The second step in this footprinting process was to identify the applications and services or daemons that were loaded and running on the Web server. Again we turned to Nmap:

```
bash# nmap -sS -F <target_machine> -oN <filename>
```

Just our luck, the server was running the httpd, sshd, and mysqld daemons. The httpd daemon was more than likely being used to support an HTTP server. The sshd daemon supports the Secure Shell (SSH) service, which is essentially just an encrypted version of the Telnet application. The mysqld daemon supports—as you may have guessed, given the obvious syntax formula—the Mysql service that allows database query language from remote clients to database servers.

Mysql is a popular open-source database. Given the knowledge that these three daemons were running, we attempted to capture their banners to identify the version and, we hoped, the patch level for each. This information would allow us to research the applications and find vulnerabilities and exploits (if any existed) that might allow remote access.

Because the SSH service is similar to Telnet, we attempted to identify the banner with the following command:

```
bash# telnet <target machine> 22
```

SSH runs over port 22; therefore, attempting a Telnet connection to port 22 might give the SSH version. We did in fact get the version, and we made note of it.

Identifying the version of the httpd daemon was even easier, because it could be done with a Web browser pointed to an invalid URL on the host server. We used the Links browser, like so:

```
bash# links http://<target_machine>/<some_invalid_URL.html>
```

which returned the HTTP 404 Not Found HTML error page (system administrators leave this as the default) and of course an <hr> tag and the apache daemon that was being used at the time.

This method of identifying the daemon being used works because system administrators often leave the default HTML error pages in place, and any request for an invalid URL generates the 404 Not Found HTML error page. In addition, on Apache Web servers, as well as others, the Web server version is returned. It is recommended that these default pages be customized by an organization so that they don't allow such information leakage. (Perhaps it is better to misinform.)

As for the third service, we decided to try connecting to the mysqld daemon, but our attempts were immediately cut off. We verified this a couple of times. Our guess was that mysqld did not allow remote connections—a check mark in the plus column for the client's security posture. We had to remember also to ask if the client was logging these connection attempts; that would be two check marks.

Nonetheless, we had two open doors: the httpd and the sshd services. One or both of these would have to be our way in. So we started some research to discover the security flaws of the particular versions of these services that were running. We checked out the usual sites: www.securityfocus.com, astalavista.box.sk, and packetstormsecurity.org, as well as redhat.com, since this was a Red Hat machine. We suggest you pick your own favorite vulnerability/exploit sites.

We found it interesting that a lot of denial-of-service (DoS) attacks were possible, and we were confident that these attacks could be used to bring the Web server down. However, we had to pay careful attention to the task we had been given: determining whether the server could be compromised by an intruder, not whether it could be affected by a DoS attack. So, although we did make a note of these potential attacks to bring to the client's attention, we continued with our research.

What looked interesting was a potential buffer overflow in the userhelper program (http://packetstormsecurity.nl/advisories/redhat/rhsa.2000-001-03.userhelper). Apparently a segmentation fault could be caused in the userhelper program to give local users root access. We were not entirely sure we would be able to use this, but we downloaded this tool and bookmarked the page just in case.

The versions of the daemons running on the server did not have a lot of holes that would allow remote access. However, we did find some that were quite interesting if we could manage to get a shell on the computer. So we started wondering if the Apache server itself was well configured, or if potentially it could give us a shell. We had already seen the default HTTP 404 Not Found HTML error page, so we tried making a connection with an SSH client to the the server. It was successful. We thought to ourselves, "Why didn't we just try this in the first place?"

If we had just been lazy, we might have saved the time spent researching. In the long run, however, research was certainly the right thing to do; at least we had identified potential DoS attacks to bring to the client's attention.

The only thing now was to discover a valid user to work with to gain a shell. We had some good ideas to try at this point. We knew a colleague's name (Rob Thomas) and had met with two other individuals at the university whose names we could try. We could try a lot of the common permutations of their names to see if we could get in (Table 7.1 shows several common permutations of the name Rob Thomas). We also knew Rob Thomas's e-mail address (rthomas@universityofhigherlearning.edu), which was a good guess for the account name.

In addition, we could try the httpd daemon user, Apache. These almost certainly weren't root permission users, but what the heck, all we wanted was shell access to perform some exploit magic, and this was as good a chance of getting access as any other, so we simply tried

```
bash# ssh <target machine>
login: apache
password: apache
```

and

```
bash# ssh <target machine>
login: user123
password: user123
```

And what did our eyes behold, but nothing—nothing except wrong passwords and wrong user names. Our old colleague must have known a bit of the game himself. We weren't worried, though; we just kept trying because we knew that this was the way to get access. If some of the more obvious or default user name/password pairs weren't working, we would simply have to find a better way than just educated guessing.

Table 7.1 Some Possible User Names for Rob Thomas

Name: Rob Thomas

rob.thomas

rthomas

robthomas

thomas_rob

thomasr

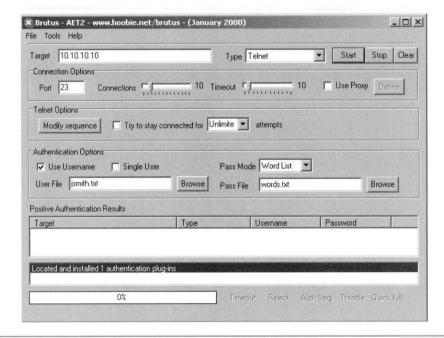

Figure 7.1 GUI for Brutus, the Brute-Force Connection Tool

After researching a bit more over the Internet, we came across just the tool that might do the trick: Brutus (shown in Figure 7.1). This tool makes connections over Telnet, FTP, and other connection-oriented applications; and then it can run through user name/password pairs. Essentially, it is a brute-force connection maker. We went back to trying to establish the connection using some information that we had already found. Essentially, what we were doing now was trying to make a connection by entering variations of the user name and by using brute force to concoct the password.

It took some time, but the effort paid off, and finally we got a user shell by entering the user name `rthomas$`, which we had been able to extract from our colleague's e-mail address:

`<target machine>/rthomas$`

We now had a shell on the target machine.

I then downloaded one of the exploits I had discovered doing research (we were glad that the research was coming to some good). After testing it out on our own machine until we were comfortable with it (a very critical step that deserves attention and should be highlighted strongly), we copied the exploit onto our new "host" machine—the client's machine on which we had just gained a shell. Now the idea was to escalate our privilege up to the root level. We had already walked half of this path. The exploit was the simple shell script that we had found earlier, `Userrooter`, which grabbed the signal sent to the userhelper application and just performed a simple buffer overflow on it, giving this result:

```
bash#
```

Root permissions—yes!!! We immediately sent an e-mail to our contact at the school. (This is what we had been instructed to do if we gained access at this time of night. If we had gained access during the day, we would have called the contact person, and if we didn't reach him, we would have left a voice mail for him, as well as a message with someone who could contact him.)

But now that the message had been sent, it was time to compromise the computer. We accessed the `/usr/local/apache/html/htdocs/` directory and renamed the `index.php` file `index_orig.php` and saved it in a new directory: `/usr/local/apache/html/orightdocs/`. We created our own splash page and placed that in the directory under the name `index.php`. This was the first page presented to Web visitors when they surfed to the Web site.

We wrote some warnings and completely reformatted the HTML and PHP code in the pages, and we created some interesting GIF and JPEG files to include in that code. Of course, all of the original Web code was saved into the `orightdocs/` directory.

After working on our HTML and PHP coding skills, we altered the permissions over the files contained in the `htdocs/` directory. The reason for changing these permissions is that hackers would be likely to take this step to make it more difficult (or at least add another step) for system administrators to reload the original, true Web page. We also created a back-door user for ourselves, by modifying the `/etc/passwd` file, altering the Apache user profile, giving our user a shell of its own to access, and of course, selecting a truly tough password (at least we thought it was tough).

Finally, we altered our colleague's password so that he couldn't access the network and we could. We did this to make it clear that he was not responsible for the Web defacement. After all, we didn't want to get the friend who had awarded us this engagement in trouble. The fact that an employee's remote access password was changed immediately following a Web defacement (or at the same time) would be something of an indication that a hacker had compromised that account in order to do the defacement and that it wasn't an action taken by that user. Certainly, an employee could deface the Web site and just change her own password, but often when an insider (a disgruntled employee, for example) hacks the system, she doesn't necessarily change her own user password.

The whole server was now fully compromised. We checked the time—5:00 AM— so we packed up our stuff, leaving the server as it was, hoping to show the client in the morning what we had done, how we had done it, and what needed to be done to prevent the situation from occurring during production.

The next morning, a couple of hours later, we went to the university early, and everyone looked at us and grinned. At first we didn't realize what was going on, but then it hit us: They had just seen the Web page. The senior officer at this site was the first person to speak to us. He came over and said, "Great job, but that guy [our colleague] is pissed off at you." That seemed odd. Why would our colleague be mad at us? He had asked us to hack the system, and we had done that. What was going on?

As it turned out, our colleague had forgotten to provide one critical piece of information. When we got to the meeting with the client at which we had been planning to report what we had done and how, as well as to give our recommendations for securing the site, we learned that missing bit of information.

The client had intended to bring the Web site online first thing that very morning. Immediately we understood the dilemma and all the looks we had received. That wasn't going to happen now! Our colleague was mad at us for modifying the Web pages, and because the files couldn't be accessed in the htdocs directory, the client thought that the original site content had been deleted. And, naturally, there was no backup.

However, the university's representatives started to calm down when we told them that the files were all there, that we had just changed the permissions and renamed the splash page. We also tried to explain that they really should have done the security review a bit (much) earlier in the process than the night before the whole site was supposed to go live. What if a hacker had done what we had done a month after they had been online? That would have made the situation they were now facing look like Utopia.

Still, the client was not easily appeased, and our old colleague and friend wanted to pin the mess on us. Looking at things from his perspective—encountering a delay on the very morning of the launch—we could understand his anger. However, we calmly pulled out the agreement memo and contract that he had signed, as well as the original RFP, and showed our colleague and the university's management that it contained no statement that the site was scheduled for launch on this morning. Nor were any of the actions that we had performed listed among the restrictions and limitations stated by the university and agreed to in the contract. We explained that we fully recognized and appreciated the current situation, but if we had known the site was going live that day, we would have conducted the review differently.

Ultimately, the delay was substantial. Management now wanted to do a full security evaluation and penetration test, get a full assessment of the security posture, and implement the necessary countermeasures to ensure that something like this would not happen again. And they wanted a full report detailing all of the steps that we had taken to deface the Web site. They also wanted to reevaluate the security risk they were willing to assume in their Web presence.

7.3 LESSONS LEARNED

It took over two months for the university to take its Web site online with all the recommendations we had made for changing the security posture in the server and Web environment. The process took that long because the operating system had to be updated, and all the daemons had to be secured and patched, including altering banners to reduce information leakage. For example, the Web server banner included with the default errors was changed, and, as shown in Figure 7.2, reference to Apache was removed. The page was made to mirror the typical error format received from a Microsoft IIS browser, including a link to Microsoft's site.

We removed all reference to the Apache daemon and said it was a 48K Spectrum computer. All the user rights and privileges were reduced to the minimum

Figure 7.2 Default 404 Error Page

privileges required with respect to job functions. Every service ran with the "nobody" user, which limited permissions and serves only as a bridge between the end user application and the signals sent to the processor on the host machine. Monitoring and updating of patch levels were added to the normal maintenance routine.

The changes made the server safer, but not totally intrusion-proof. So in order to be able to track intrusion attempts, we rigged the host with every syslog and application log service available, including the iptables daemon. Logs were sent to a log repository from which a log analysis tool would, well, analyze the logs for evidence of intrusion. We were impressed that the client had made a commitment to reading the logs to sense, visualize, and respond to potential intrusion attempts. The university was also in the process of setting up an incident response unit.

We made sure that all network communication files were correctly configured, including the /etc/hosts.allow and /etc/hosts.deny files. Fortunately, the situation is still under at least some level of control, at least in the sense that the client doesn't recall having been defaced again.

It is important that security reviews be done with enough time to (1) perform the analysis, (2) assess the results, and (3) enact the appropriate countermeasures *without* delaying production schedules. These requirements imply that security considerations are built into the overall project planning and life cycle. Performing a security review the night before a launch date runs the risk that the launch will be delayed (possibly significantly) if a serious security weakness is discovered, as was the case here.

7.3.1 AND WHAT DID THE CONSULTANT LEARN?

We did ask the client to read the agreement memo and contract before signing, but we should have made sure that our contact really understood what we were trying/planning to do. Though the client wanted to have the review done as soon as possible, we should have taken one additional step and asked about the state of the overall project. Doing either of these two things might have gotten the client to disclose that the scheduled launch date was in the very near future. With this information, we would certainly have proceeded differently.

In addition, we should have e-mailed our colleague a status report as soon as we gained access and when we moved the original content. Documenting this information in an e-mail would have minimized the anger we experienced when we arrived in the office the following day.

Nothing could have prevented the delay in launching the site, however. Whatever the consequences, bringing the security lapses to light was an absolute must.

This was an expensive lesson: To appease the client, we billed at only half our normal rate throughout the follow-on review. Though the "mistake" may very well have been on the client's end, the ultimate responsibility for maintaining a solid relationship remains with the consultant. In the long run, it seems to have worked out. Our old colleague has remained a friend to this day.

PART III

ADDITIONAL ITEMS ON THE PLATE

PROTECTING BORDERS
PERIMETER DEFENSE WITH AN IDS

This case study presents another instance in which the client was proactive about security and sought assistance with the selection, design, and implementation of an intrusion detection system (IDS). This forethought was due in part to this client's belief (and there were reasons) that it would increasingly be the target of cyber attacks.

Considering themselves a "likely" target, they specifically wanted to improve their ability to monitor their network. They were also interested in being able to capture network traffic and data and use that in future forensic investigations, should any be necessary.

8.1 BACKGROUND

Around the turn of the millennium, the U.S. government, through regulations,[1] strongly suggested that all government agencies deploy intrusion detection systems. Many government agencies are still working to comply with this regulation. The

---

1. The regulations were actually released earlier than the year 2000, but it was around this time that the government became more concerned with enforcing them.

regulations did not apply to private-sector organizations, but organizations that worked with the government, especially the Department of Defense, or whose networks touched government networks, were expected to meet certain security standards.

One specific firm, a New England company called OverSeas Financial Services (OverSFS), had developed a mechanism to allow U.S. expatriates to access financial information on U.S. and global markets and manage their financial assets, including trading securities online. Expatriates are mainly U.S. government employees and military personnel; therefore, the client felt it needed to pay extra attention to security. The company commissioned a security audit of its online infrastructure that revealed numerous shortcomings in its IT security posture, none drawing more attention than the lack of an IDS.

The auditor specifically gave the client a timeline—actually a deadline—by which it needed to have an IDS deployed, but no specific technical guidance was offered. Therefore, the client found itself with a requirement to have a fully deployed and functional IDS in a short turnaround time. However, OverSFS did not want to compromise on its standards and simply plug any IDS into its environment just to meet the auditor's requirement. Rather, OverSFS was determined to perform the appropriate testing and validation efforts to select a product solution to fit its needs.

We were called in to assist with this problem. Specifically, we were asked to

- Determine the requirements for an IDS solution
- Perform market research to identify potential IDS solutions (vendors and products) that met the requirements
- Pilot-test the top two potential solutions
- Implement the best solution
- Configure and train operators in the operation and maintenance of the IDS

In our initial meeting, representatives from OverSFS stressed the strict timeline and the fact that the company was not in a position to experience any delay or slippage. They explained that their auditor had established the deadline and that they were dedicated to full compliance.[2]

So we got right to work. The first thing we did was try to understand the environment so that we could help the client develop the criteria for an IDS solution.

8.2 THE COMPANY

OverSeas Financial Services (OverSFS) provided its members with the capability to check the status of their accounts online, much like online banking. The membership was initially restricted to members of the military, but in an effort to reduce costs through economy of scale and to compete with larger institutions, the company expanded its membership to include relatives of active-duty military personnel, then opened it up to all federal government employees, and finally to state and local government employees as well. Expanding to serve the general public was always a topic of discussion, but most members still were military and their relatives.

The heaviest days of traffic on the network were payday and the day after, when members logged in to check if their direct-deposit payments had come in. Paydays were the first and fifteenth of the month, or the next business day if these dates fell on a weekend or holiday. Other days were expected to be heavy as well, such as days following major events affecting financial markets (e.g., corporate bankruptcies, mergers, and acquisitions).

In terms of services, members could access international news feeds covering the financial markets, international events, politics, and general business issues. In addition, they could perform online banking if their banks, U.S. or foreign, offered online banking; and they could buy and sell stock on the U.S. stock exchanges. OverSFS was also seriously considering adding automated bill payment and credit card services.

---

2. The deadline corresponded with OverSFS's planned go-live date, implying that the auditors had suggested that the service not be launched before an IDS was added, offering some teeth to this recommendation.

There was some rationale behind the auditor's demand for the near-term deployment of an IDS. Financial assets were considered prime targets (for both cyber criminal and cyber terrorist attacks). The target would affect U.S. citizens overseas and potentially throughout the world, offering an additional psychological component. Therefore, OverSFS wanted to implement an IDS to improve its ability to monitor its network for potential intrusions.

On its internal LAN, OverSFS was a Windows NT/2000 shop with Dynamic Host Configuration Protocol (DHCP) addressing. The company was in the process of migrating to Windows 2000, and this process was occupying a good portion of the IT staff's time and attention. For security reasons, however, the network infrastructure related to its online banking application was entirely UNIX. In addition, no Internet-facing machine was allowed to run a Microsoft operating system. All hosts in the Web infrastructure had internal addressing, and Network Address Translation (NAT) was performed at the firewall to allow for external access to the Web servers. The company's high-level network topology is shown in Figure 8.1.

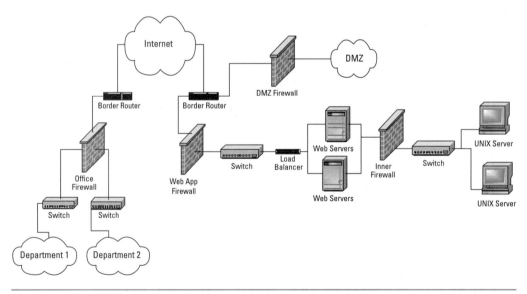

Figure 8.1 Overall Network Topology

What Figure 8.1 does not show is that the Web servers were load-balanced, and the application servers resided on the UNIX servers in a separate subnet.

8.3 DEVELOPING REQUIREMENTS

At a high level, the requirements were intended to ensure that the selected IDS solution met the goals specified in Section 2.2 of Special Publication 800-31 of the National Institute of Standards and Technology (NIST): "Intrusion Detection Systems" (available at http://csrc.nist.gov/publications/nistpubs/800-31/sp800-31.pdf). The main goals were stated in that document as follows:

1. "To prevent problem behaviors by increasing the perceived risk of discovery and punishment for those who would attack or otherwise abuse the system" (i.e., to add a visible deterrent to discourage attacks).

2. "To detect attacks and other security violations that are not prevented by other security measures."

3. "To detect and deal with the preambles to attacks (commonly experienced as network probes and other 'doorknob rattling' activities)." (OverSFS had experienced a sharp rise in such [preamble] activity recently and wanted a means of discouraging and thwarting the activity before it became full-blown cyber attacks.)

4. "To document the existing threat to an organization." (Learning the risk to the online application was a major concern for OverSFS.)

5. "To act as quality control for security design and administration, especially of large and complex enterprises."

6. "To provide useful information about intrusions that do take place, allowing improved diagnosis, recovery, and correction of causative factors."

These guidelines served as an excellent starting point for developing a set of requirements tailored to the client's specific needs. Therefore, we talked with members of the IT staff and those responsible for managing the online banking application to assess their true needs. We also made ourselves very familiar with the auditor's report to understand that point of view.

Although interviews can sometimes be quite tedious, a great deal can be learned from them, and this instance was no exception. While focused primarily on monitoring its Web infrastructure for external attacks, OverSFS was open to a solution that also offered, to the internal LAN, IDS protection against attacks from external sources and, to a lesser extent, from internal sources—as long as the additional criteria would not place too much load on either the current systems or the eventual IDS infrastructure. Further, it was clear that OverSFS wanted a solution representing "industry best practices," without necessarily knowing exactly what those were.

We wanted the IDS to feature customizable signatures (see criterion 2.02 in Table 8.1) and a flexible system for creating new signatures (criteria 2.03 and 2.04). For instance, we wanted the IDS to take into account the known network traffic characteristics. Because we knew that traffic hit a maximum on payday and the day after payday, we wanted to require the IDS to sound an alert when traffic hit or exceeded certain levels on other days. Detecting high levels of network traffic was also seen as a possible way to detect certain types of DoS attacks.

OverSFS was also interested in establishing a cyber forensic group within its security department to assist in analyzing cyber attacks and in identifying and prosecuting attackers. They hoped that the IDS would be a good lead-in to this long-term goal by providing another source of data that could be used in forensic analysis. To assist in forensic efforts, a reporting tool that would help clarify how often the network was being attacked would be a benefit (see criteria 3.16 and 3.17 in Table 8.1). The IDS needed to be able to generate reports in a format that could be read by the client (Crystal Reports and the Microsoft Office suite pretty much take care of this requirement) (criterion 3.15). More importantly, however, the IDS needed to be able to process data in the formats available (criterion 3.23), especially for the host-based components.

We were seeking an IDS with the ability to send alerts primarily to the IDS management console and pages to the network administrator (criterion 3.05), but if other options were available, they might very well be pressed into service.

OverSFS was intrigued by the ability to use the IDS in a preventive fashion. An IDS with the ability to block traffic from certain IP address spaces and/or ports (criterion 3.06), as well as to terminate connections by injecting TCP reset packets into suspicious connections (criterion 3.07) was sought.

Clearly, new vulnerabilities and attacks would always be possible, and any vendor would need to keep up by diligently and expeditiously releasing new signatures and sometimes new product releases. Therefore, the signature history over the period of one year was requested from the vendor (criterion 4.07), along with all product updates.

The IDS's compatibility with the existing IT infrastructure and ability to scale (grow) with the client's network was also evaluated (criteria 4.11 and 4.13).

On the basis of the organization's network and security needs, we determined that the optimum IDS would be a hybrid solution with both network-based and host-based components. We were interested in expanding the network-based component's ability to securely monitor a large infrastructure with a small number of sensors that were nearly invisible to attackers. In addition, we were interested in the host-based component's ability to monitor events local to the host, identify integrity breaches such as a Trojan horse, and read log files.

On the basis of our understanding of the client's needs, we developed criteria for the IDS, a partial listing of which appears in Table 8.1. The criteria were broken into four main categories: (1) performance, (2) detection, (3) analysis and reporting, and (4) integration and implementation.

Table 8.1 Partial Listing of IDS Requirements

Criteria		
1	**Performance**	
1.01	The IDS application should cause no network- or host-level performance degradation.	
1.02	The IDS must achieve the following success rates:	
	Load	**Success Rate[a]**
	Average	95%
	80% of peak	80%
	Peak	75%

a. *Success rate* here means the percentage of attacks that are correctly detected.

Table 8.1 *Continued*

Criteria

1.03	The IDS should meet the performance requirements with the rule set and signature database tailored for this environment.
1.04	An impact assessment (of both the network and the host) must be performed.
1.05	The IDS should be able to monitor network traffic on 10Base-T Ethernet networks.
1.06	The IDS should be able to monitor network traffic on 100Base-T Ethernet networks.
1.07	The IDS must provide network-monitoring capability on TCP/IP and UDP/IP networks.
1.09	The IDS must be able to capture and replay user-initiated TCP/IP sessions from authentication through termination.
1.15	The IDS should be fault-tolerant; that is, it should not lose stored information if the host system crashes.
2	**Detection**
2.01	The IDS must allow users to view its existing rule set and signature database.
2.02	The IDS must allow users to modify existing rules and signatures in real time.
2.03	The IDS must allow users to manually create new rules and signatures in real time.
2.04	The IDS must allow users to create, in real time, new rules and signatures involving any of the following characteristics: • Communications protocol (e.g., TCP, UDP, IP, ICMP, SMTP, HTTP, FTP, Telnet, SNMP, RPC, DNS, etc.) • Operating system • Communications port • Source IP address • Source domain • Destination IP address • Destination domain • Quantity of individual traffic • Time of day or year
2.05	The rule set and signature database must be optimized for each sensor.

Criteria

2.07	The signature database must contain signatures for well-known and common attacks, including (but not limited to)	

- Denial-of-service attacks
- Ping sweeps
- SYN scans
- ACK scans
- Port scans
- UDP port probes
- Brute-force password-cracking attacks
- IP spoofing
- IP fragmentation attacks
- HTTP probes
- SNMP sweeps
- Known viruses and worms

The successful identification rate must meet the performance requirements specified for the IDS.

3	**Analysis and reporting**

3.01	The IDS should have the ability to generate alerts for the following events:

- Communication is lost between components of the IDS.
- The traffic load on a sensor exceeds IDS capacity.
- An active rule or signature is triggered by monitored traffic.

3.02	The IDS should have the ability to classify alerts as High, Medium, or Low.
3.03	The IDS should be able to escalate alerts as certain thresholds are reached.
3.04	The alert classification should be manually configurable in real time.
3.05	The IDS should be able to send alerts via

- On-screen messages to the management console
- E-mail
- Pager
- SNMPv3
- Syslog
- X Windows pop-up message
- Trouble Ticket

3.06	The IDS should be able to modify applicable firewall rule sets for a specific period of time.
3.07	The IDS can terminate sessions when a particular event occurs.

Table 8.1 *Continued*

Criteria	
3.09	The IDS can tailor response action according to the • Classification of alert • Type of attack • Target of attack • Time of day or year
3.15	Reports should be produced in a format compatible with existing client standards.
3.16	The IDS should be able to create reports based on any of the following: • Date and time • Generated alerts • Alerts or attacks • Rules or signatures • Communications protocol • Domain, IP address, or port of source or destination • Network segments • Target application(s) • An individual session
3.17	IDS reports must identify the following characteristics of any alerts: • Communications protocol • Domain, IP address, and port of source • Domain, IP address, and port of destination • Rule or signature violated • Type of attack (if possible) • Recommended fix(es), if any
3.22	The IDS should be able to log the following events: • Alerts • Traffic leading to alerts • Modifications or updates to the rule set and signature database for each sensor • The time at which communication between the management console and sensors is lost and/or restored • User-defined sessions
3.23	The IDS should be able to analyze the data from syslog.
3.24	The IDS must be capable of performing protocol analysis on monitored traffic.

Criteria

4	Integration and implementation
4.03	IDS maintenance should be minimal, taking less than two hours per week.
4.04	The IDS attack signature update should be obtainable via the Internet using HTTP or FTP.
4.05	The IDS should be able to obtain the attack signature updates without losing the current IDS configurations.
4.07	The IDS vendor must supply historical records covering the previous 12 months of a new rule set, attack signature generation, and product updates (including new patches and releases).
4.10	The IDS must be able to monitor the network while under average and peak traffic loads.
4.11	The IDS should be scalable to potential future traffic loads (gigabit network) and the number of network nodes from a central point of management.
4.13	The IDS must be compatible with existing and planned future technology infrastructure.
4.20	Communication between components (e.g., sensor and console) of the IDS must be encrypted.
4.22	The IDS must support multiple, simultaneous GUIs.

To check ourselves, we compared our list of requirements with the existing guidelines (again, such as NIST 800-31) to ensure that they were in line with standards and best practices.

8.4 MARKET RESEARCH

The IDS criteria we had developed gave us an understanding of the capabilities we were looking for in an IDS, thereby offering direction in how to perform market and literature research. The questions we began asking vendor representatives were, Can your IDS do this? and Can this capability be demonstrated in the pilot testing we plan to perform?

In addition to speaking with sales personnel (who naturally have something of a bias), we spoke with product users. Vendors provided references in the form of names of users, and whenever possible, we identified additional users from mailing lists and industry user groups for the IDS products being evaluated.[3] We used this research to score the available products; a partial listing showing our format for scoring appears in Table 8.2.

Table 8.2 Scoring Table

Criteria		Weight	Points	Score
1	**Performance**			
1.01	The IDS application should cause no network- or host-level performance degradation.			
1.02	The IDS must achieve the following success rates: **Load** **Success Rate**[a] Average 95% 80% of peak 80% Peak 75%			
1.03	The IDS should meet the performance requirements with the rule set and signature database tailored for this environment.			
1.04	An impact assessment (of both the network and the host) must be performed.			
1.05	The IDS should be able to monitor network traffic on 10Base-T Ethernet networks.			
1.06	The IDS should be able to monitor network traffic on 100Base-T Ethernet networks.			
1.07	The IDS must provide network-monitoring capability on TCP/IP and UDP/IP networks.			
1.09	The IDS must be able to capture and replay user-initiated TCP/IP sessions from authentication through termination.			
1.15	The IDS should be fault-tolerant; that is, it should not lose stored information if the host system crashes.			

a. *Success rate* here means the percentage of attacks that are correctly detected.

---

3. For instance, the Snort IDS has an extensive user community, http://www.snort.org.

The *weight* was the value of the specific requirement to the client. The *points* were a binary representation of the product's ability to meet the requirement (if the product could meet the requirement, it scored a 1; if not, it scored a 0.) The *score* was then simply a product of the weight and the points. Adding all of the individual requirement scores gave the total score for a specific vendor product. A separate scorecard was prepared for each IDS solution considered.

The interviews previously mentioned were not limited to IT staff; we also met with management to ascertain their budgetary concerns, as well as the level of customer support they were used to and would expect of an IDS vendor. The vendor's market share and installation base were also considered. Finally, any previous relationship the client might have had with the vendor was also evaluated because it could suggest a preexisting level of comfort or confidence in the vendor's commitment to customer service and continuing technical support. It might also indicate the discount that the client could expect.

Because of time constraints, only the top two IDS vendors were invited to come in for week-long pilot testing in order to see if they could meet the requirements in action. The pilot testing was performed on a network that we had configured to mirror the production environment. On this test network, we allocated IP address ranges for the IDS equipment as shown in Figure 8.2.

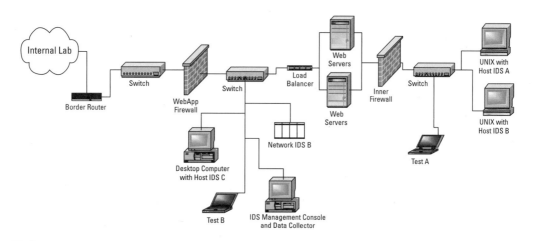

Figure 8.2 Test Network Topology with IDS and Testing Stations Deployed

8.5 PILOT TESTING

In addition to preparing a network, we needed to develop detailed test plans to make the best use of the one-week time period available. During this one week, not only did the testing need to be completed, but also the vendors needed time to tweak their systems so that they could repeat any test on which they performed poorly.

8.5.1 TEST PLANS

The test plans were designed with three simple goals in mind:

1. To verify that the IDS could perform as advertised
2. To assess the product's effectiveness against many known or expected attacks
3. To become familiar with the use and operation of the IDS

The attacks were prepared mostly from the perspective of external attackers because this was the primary source of risk against which the client wanted to defend. A partial listing of the test plan appears in Table 8.3.

The Weight, Points, and Score columns in Table 8.3 work in the same way as in Table 8.2. One point was awarded if the IDS demonstrably performed the specific test identified. A new set of weights was developed to grade the test results. As Table 8.3 shows, each of the individual requirements that we had developed (see Table 8.1) was further broken down to ensure that the IDS truly met the criteria in all cases.

The testing involved the use of numerous pieces of software. Cenzic's Hailstorm product was used to simulate attacks. This tool is capable of creating traffic that mimics numerous known attacks. Mercury Interactive's LoadRunner tool was used to simulate network traffic, at both the peak and the average levels. Manual techniques were used as well, such as attempting to Telnet into or open FTP sessions to hosts and directories at a higher privilege level and attempting to guess user passwords by brute force.

Table 8.3 Test Plan

Req. #	Requirement	Evaluation Criterion	Weight	Points	Score
1.01.1	Any network-level performance degradation specifically caused by the IDS application should be within acceptable levels, as defined by the client.	Performance-level degradation caused by the IDS			
1.01.2	Any host-level performance degradation specifically caused by the IDS application should be within acceptable levels, as defined by the client.	Performance-level degradation caused by the IDS			
1.02.1	The IDS must achieve a 95% success rate during average traffic load.	Success rate of the IDS in detecting attacks			
1.02.2	The IDS must achieve a 75% success rate during peak traffic load.	Success rate of the IDS in detecting attacks			
1.02.3	The IDS must be able to identify DoS attacks at average traffic load.	Ability of the IDS to identify DoS attacks			
1.02.4	The IDS must be able to identify DoS attacks at peak traffic load.	Ability of the IDS to identify DoS attacks			
1.02.14	The IDS must be able to identify port scans at average traffic load.	Ability of the IDS to identify DoS attacks			
1.02.15	The IDS must be able to identify port scans at peak traffic load.	Ability of the IDS to identify DoS attacks			
1.02.37	The IDS must be able to identify SNMP sweeps at average traffic load.	Ability of the IDS to identify DoS attacks			
1.02.38	The IDS must be able to identify SNMP sweeps at peak traffic load.	Ability of the IDS to identify DoS attacks			

The tests were run and scored. The preliminary scores were disclosed to the vendors, who were able to make any modifications they deemed necessary (while we were watching, and learning). Then the tests were run again, and final scores were tabulated. Final scoring took into account issues such as vendor support, market share, and product cost; and the final scores were not shared with the vendors. We handed our results (and the de facto recommendation based on the scoring) to the client for the final decision. Ultimately, it was OverSFS's call because OverSFS would be the one stuck with the decision.

8.6 IMPLEMENTATION ON PRODUCTION

We then designed the IDS solution, based on the declared winner, for the production network. The production network was quite similar to what we had in the test environment because the test environment was set up to mirror production. The network and host sensors, as well as the management console, were placed in the same position as in the test network.

We installed the IDS in the production environment, making sure that we didn't bring down any machines or stop, or in any way affect, normal business operations in the process. We also made sure that the configuration met the requirements we had just developed. We did not do a staged deployment of the IDS, contrary to common recommendations, because we had the benefit of having seen the vendor install and configure the IDS on the mirror test network. The IDS might not have been fully optimized, but some level of optimization had been achieved. Indeed, we were careful throughout the testing process to identify an optimal configuration to simplify the actual production-level implementation. We did, however, install the NIDS (network-based IDS) prior to the HIDS (host-based IDS), so this could be considered a two-stage installation process.

8.7 IMPLEMENTATION FOLLOW-UP

Now that the necessary intrusion detection system was in place (and in full compliance with the deadline), it actually had to be used to be useful. OverSFS was planning to create a team dedicated to 24/7 monitoring of the IDS. However, they did not initially have the manpower to put such a team in place. We developed minimal training for the security staff in monitoring, managing, and maintaining the IDS. This training was a half-day program dealing with the basics of operation and usage. It covered the GUI, the reporting tool, and how to develop signatures.

The minimal training was deemed sufficient for OverSFS because the testing period had been essentially a one-week crash course in the use and operation of the IDS. However, they wanted something that could offer guidance in the monitoring of the IDS and in helping to train future staff. So we developed an alert evaluation and escalation procedure for the IDS staff to use when monitoring the IDS alerts. This procedure was codified in a flowchart, which is shown in Figure 8.3.

The following explanatory notes go with the flowchart.

Step 2: Verify and Record Data

The potential data points include, but are not limited to, the following:

- Source IP address
- Destination IP address
- Source port
- Destination port
- Source MAC address
- Destination MAC address
- Protocol
- Time of event

After the initial alert, it is important to record and log all possible data.

Step 3: Research

Research into the incident can begin almost simultaneously with step 2. Table 8.4 lists some sites that provide helpful information; many IDSs do not provide links to additional information within the alert itself.

Step 4: Check for Related Alerts

Examples of related alerts include

- Similar traffic over the same ports between different source and/or destination hosts. (Source and destination host pairs are likely to be within the same source and destination subnet.)

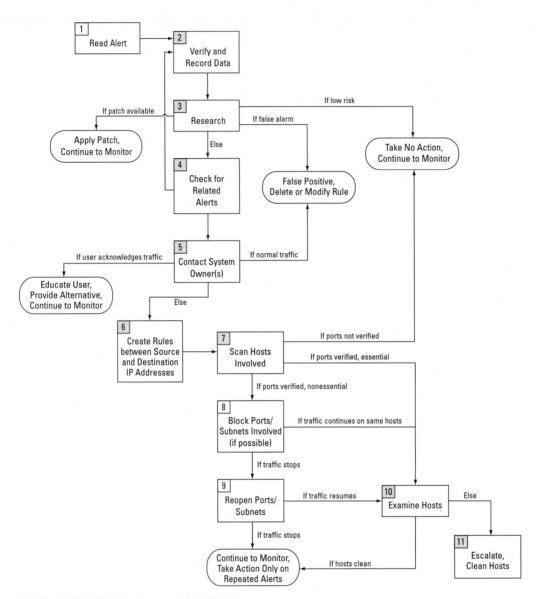

Figure 8.3 Flowchart of the IDS Alert Escalation Process

Table 8.4 Online Research Sites

Resource	URL
CVE (Common Vulnerabilities and Exposures)	http://www.cve.mitre.org
BugTraq	http://online.securityfocus.com/bid
arachnids	http://www.whitehats.com/ids
Port lists	
Internet Assigned Numbers Authority	http://www.iana.org
Internet Storm Center	http://www.incidents.org
Snort	http://www.snort.org

- Traffic between the same source and destination host over different port.
- Multiple alerts about the same traffic, or multiple alerts sharing the same characteristics—such as source and destination IP address, port, source port, destination port, or protocol. The more alerts there are that show similarities like this, the more urgent is the need to investigate them.

The purpose of checking for related alerts is to develop a picture of the overall scenario. Often a single alert tells only part of the story. Examining numerous alerts at the same time often reveals what is really taking place.

Step 5: Contact System Owners

After starting to draw a picture of what is occurring, we want to ascertain if there may be a known cause for the incident. Potentially useful questions include

- Have you recently started using any specific applications or programs, and if so what are they?
- Do you have any specific applications or programs that are not standard for the company?
- Are there any specific applications or programs that may be sending _____ traffic between _____ machines over port _____ ?

Step 6: Create Rules between Source and Destination IP Addresses

The rules we create in this step are designed to monitor traffic between source and destination hosts involved in order to see if the traffic remains consistent, if it becomes periodic (from a specific start time to a specific end time), if it occurs in bursts (i.e., randomly), or if it lasts only a short period of time. If the traffic is the result of a known security incident, it may be possible to implement rules to cut off the offending hosts from the network for a period of time and protect the rest of the network.

Step 7: Scan Hosts Involved

Scan hosts suspected to be infected in order to verify the infection, and also to verify that the hosts are vulnerable to the suspected attack in the first place.

Step 10: Examine Hosts

If the alerts return after the ports and subnets are reopened, it is likely time to clean, rebuild, or permanently remove the hosts from the network.

Step 11: Escalate, Clean Hosts

At this step, if you have found an infected host on your network, you must simultaneously inform the appropriate authority (at some companies, this can be the chief security officer, the director of IT security, or maybe the CIO) and clean the host. To clean an infected host you must delete the offending application or process, place it in quarantine, delete or (hopefully) repair any infected files, apply patches, and modify configuration settings to conform to security guidelines.

ROI for IDS

The authors freely admit and bemoan the fact that we do not possess the skill of selling. We simply are not good salesmen. But one thing that the protracted robust, jobless recovery of the early third millennium has taught us is that selling security software requires making and showing the prospective buyer a strong business case supporting the purchase. ROI calculations must become second nature.

Although in this particular case the need for developing the business case was not such a pressing concern, given the client's requirement. Showing an ROI is generally necessary.

To provide an ROI, there are two things we can use to build a case. First, it may be possible to consider the savings from a reduction in the number of security incidents (considering that having an IDS should stop some people from attempting to break in). Second, there may be a savings from a reduction in the length of time that a compromise goes undetected (considering that an IDS should alert you to the presence of a hacker), allowing earlier initiation of contingency procedures. Such an ROI argument is shown in Table 8.5.

Table 8.5 Potential Yearly Savings from an IDS

	Without IDS	With IDS
Cost of a security incident	$100,000 + $10,000 per day if unnoticed	
Number of security incidents	24	22
Average time before discovery (days)	5	4
Yearly cost	$2,450,000	$2,240,000
Yearly savings:		$210,000

We can take this estimate a step further and calculate the ROI over several years, as Table 8.6 shows.

Table 8.6 Potential Savings over Five Years from an IDS

Return on Investment					
	Year 1	Year 2	Year 3	Year 4	Year 5
Savings	$105,000	$157,500	$210,000	$210,000	$210,000
Costs	$185,000	$46,250	$37,000	$37,000	$37,000
ROI	−$80,000	$37,000	$173,000	$173,000	$173,000

The costs in Table 8.6 are all the costs associated with the purchase, installation, and use of an IDS. Included are not only the initial costs, but recurring costs as well, related to product maintenance and support. A long-term yearly cost of 20 percent of the initial cost is used in calculating this estimate (from year 3 on). In addition, the total yearly savings is estimated not to reach its full potential until year 3. As Table 8.6 shows, the savings in years 1 and 2 are calculated at 50 percent and 75 percent, respectively, of the total possible $210,000.

An effort to show a conservative ROI is illustrated in Table 8.7. In this conservative, long-term approach, an ROI of $476,000 with a net present value (NPV) of approximately $313,400 can be shown to the prospective client.

Table 8.7 Potential ROI from an IDS, in Aggregate Dollars Saved, and Its Net Present Value

	Sum of Money Saved over 5 Years	NPV of Money Saved over 5 Years
ROI	$476,000	$313,409

Naturally, these are strictly manufactured numbers for the sake of illustration. If one were to use this example as the basis of an ROI argument, actual numbers (or very close estimates) would be required throughout the calculation. If numbers are not available from your potential client, as is likely, figures for the industry in general may be available through an industry association. The yearly CSI/FBI Computer Crime and Security Survey also provides helpful data. And vendors can provide rough data for their product and support costs that can be used in the calculations.

8.8 LESSONS LEARNED

What we're about to say will sound obvious, but it needs to be said anyway. The more testing that can be performed prior to the purchase and installation of an intrusion detection system, or any other software or hardware product for that matter, the better. The level of testing performed in this case may be beyond the capability of most organizations; not all organizations will be lucky enough to have a test network that closely mirrors production. However, it is worth having vendors do more than just run through PowerPoint slides or their canned demos when you're trying to select the right product for your organization.

If possible, have the vendor install the product on your hardware and leave it with your system administrators for a period of time so that they can assess its effectiveness and compatibility with the organization's existing IT infrastructure. The more hands-on experience you can get with all the products you are considering prior to making the decision, the easier your decision will be. In addition, as seen in this case, the installation and configuration process on the production network will be much easier if you have had an opportunity to install, configure, and play with the product. This case study demonstrated that the test process is instrumental in setting the thresholds and customizing the rules for the IDS. The time saved in that process helps make up for the time and money spent doing the testing.

In addition, the test period is a great time to get hands-on training for the staff. What better way to learn about a product than to have it demonstrated and tested in your own environment with your own staff participating in the testing? Vendors may want to charge for the training they are providing, however, so this cost must be included in the overall cost of the product. The larger the company and the larger the potential sale, the more amenable vendors may be to throwing in a few days of ad hoc training as part of the sale.

Specifically for intrusion detection systems, developing and implementing a means of monitoring the IDS and evaluating and responding to events must be included as part of the overall buying process. An IDS with no one watching is not doing any good. An IDS with someone watching who doesn't know exactly how to handle an alert is not doing much better. An in-depth testing period will help a great deal, but even a half-day training session can offer a great deal of insight and experience to prepare an IDS analyst for the complexity of the job.

DISASTER ALL AROUND

The role of a security professional has been growing. Numerous additional, perhaps tangentially related, issues are now a part of the job and at a minimum demand that those in the security profession be knowledgeable in these areas. These issues include information privacy (especially given the alarming rise of identity theft), policy development, and disaster recovery.

In the case study presented here, a firm was caught off guard, and disaster struck before well-developed plans could be implemented. Some quick thinking and fast acting on the part of the IT staff allowed the firm to weather the storm and survive, but hopefully this case will underscore the need to be prepared for the unexpected disaster.

9.1 INTRODUCTION

Alanis, Inc., is an e-commerce organization providing insurance and real estate mortgage services to customers over the Internet. Its Web site allows customers to get information about various insurance policies, file claims, submit payments, and apply for mortgages. In addition, Alanis agents are able to complete all business processes required to develop and submit policies, as well as process claims, online. A typical day for Alanis involves financial transactions dealing in the millions of dollars. All of these transactions are carried out over the Internet and utilize sensitive client financial information, including policy information and credit card numbers. Confidentiality, integrity, and availability are important to Alanis; these features are considered by management to be major selling points of the company's online service.

Alanis, Inc., comprises 400 employees spread across various departments, as well as approximately 300 commission-based agents across the country who rely on the Web site to conduct business. The agents connect to the Web site using company-approved VPN clients, and the connections are all tunneled via IPSec. Again, security is a concern. Customers are able to connect to the site from their standard Web browser, and all transactions are performed over SSL. Cisco 3000 series concentrators are used for the purpose of routing all the VPN connection requests. Further, client authentication is handled through a RADIUS (Remote Authentication Dial-In User Service) authentication server.

Because Alanis is essentially an Internet company, its market presence is totally dependent on the strength of its IT infrastructure. The infrastructure has the usual communication links and networking equipment, including routers, firewalls, switches, an intrusion detection system, antivirus software, load balancers, Web servers, database servers, and so on. All the normal stuff. UNIX is the operating system running on all the mission-critical servers, and Windows 2000 is the operating system running on user desktops. Again, pretty standard stuff.

Cisco hardware is the standard for all networking equipment, and McAfee is the standard antivirus software running on all the systems. The freeware tool Snort is deployed at strategic locations within the overall infrastructure layout to provide intrusion detection capabilities. Data is backed up via storage area networks and network-attached storage. Data backup operations run on Sun tape libraries using VERITAS backup software. The basic network layout is shown in Figure 9.1.

As you can see, the company paid a certain amount of attention to its network architecture. The main data center of the organization is in Kansas, in a quiet midwestern town. The organization's branch offices are spread across the country and are responsible for different geographically disparate regions, including the Northwest, southern California, and the East Coast. Each branch office has its own set of critical infrastructure and operational assets, such as the data

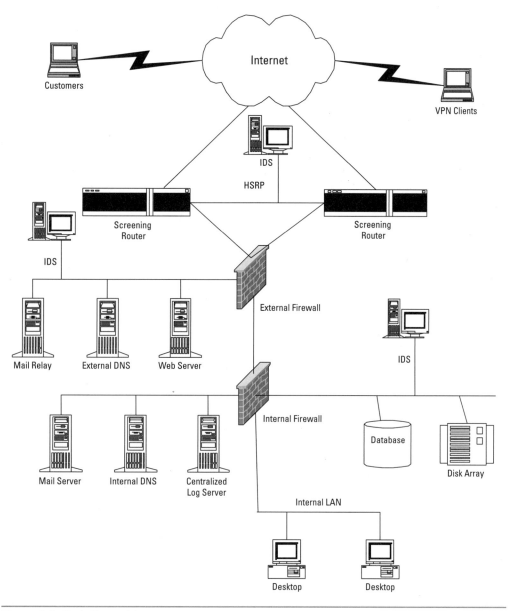

Figure 9.1 Basic Network Layout

backup server, mail server, DNS server, and other components necessary to handle operations.

The data backed up at each branch office pertains to the client information when a deal is in process or is still in the initial stages. Once the deal is finalized, all customer information is transferred to the main data center, and any further dealings are then carried out from that location. The mail server at each branch office acts as a local repository of the electronic mail that pertains to the employees and agents working from that particular office and/or region. The DNS server for a particular branch office operates as the primary domain controller for that office and is configured to be the secondary domain controller for the DNS server hosted at the main data center.

A distributed-system architecture connects each branch office to the main office. The workload is distributed accordingly between the main office and the branch offices to help minimize the effects of any minor interruptions in the operations. The branch offices also provide some level of data redundancy. Should one site become unavailable, the others can carry the load while the down site is restored.

However, the main data center in Kansas remains the most critical asset of the organization for the following reason: It hosts the company's public Web servers, database servers, DNS servers, mail servers, and other mission-critical application servers. The database servers store personally identifiable information, including credit card details, loan and installment figures, and Social Security numbers. Because this data is highly sensitive, Alanis decided to store the information in only one location to minimize its potential exposure. The company was working under the impression that the greater the number of places where this information resided, the greater the number of places that would have to be secured against cyber attack.

All the critical business operations, such as customer credit verifications, loan approvals, and financial transactions, are carried out from the main data center. The main data center also acts as a payment gateway establishing connections with merchant banks for payment authentication and processing. Further, the branch office data centers all connect to the main data center to access the information stored in the databases and to finalize transactions.

Therefore, the unhindered operation of the main data center is imperative to the continued business operation and success of the entire organization. Given this setup, management was well aware that the company could afford no more than very minimal system downtime. Though they took pride in their architecture, this single point of failure did emerge.

The location of the data center was originally selected to minimize exposure to potential natural disasters such as floods and earthquakes. Kansas is, however, prone to heavy snowfall that is potentially able to cause disruptions due to impassable roads and the inability of employees to get to the site. Snowfall could also cause disruptions to communications capabilities by physically bringing power and communications lines down. In one case 15 years before the incident in this case study, heavy snowfall had indeed caused statewide disruptions. In its 11-year history, however, Alanis, Inc., had not experienced a single weather-related interruption or systemwide network outage.

As a result, the organization had not developed a disaster recovery plan. With increasing business revenues and a growing customer base, however, the extreme reliance on the health of the infrastructure was being felt. In response, the chief security engineer, Paul Simon,[1] approached management with a proposal for developing a disaster recovery plan.

The plan that Simon presented highlighted the following elements as key requirements to be prepared to handle a disaster:

- The creation of a disaster recovery team
- A hot site from where to host the infrastructure during a disaster, should the main data center become unavailable
- Comprehensive risk analysis to be conducted by private consultants
- A ranked listing of the organization's most critical business functions
- An audit of the existing IT infrastructure
- Documentation of all critical assets, network configurations, and technical contacts

---

1. Our copy editor wisely urged us to resist the urge to call Paul "Al" in this case study.

A **hot site**, a backup site that can be taken over instantaneously to act as the primary site, from which to host the site during a disaster was absolutely necessary. Should anything happen to the main data center (the central hub on Alanis's network upon which the company conducted its entire business operations), there had to be an alternate site that would allow the company to continue operations. The risk analysis would help identify the core business functions that must be carried out, no matter what the circumstances.

The listing of Alanis's critical business functions would clearly identify which functions the firm would need to reestablish immediately, as well as the infrastructure components and other assets necessary to support and facilitate those functions. The audit of Alanis's critical assets would help identify the equipment the company already owned that could be moved around to set up an alternate data center if necessary. Having up-to-date and complete documentation of the entire network configuration and infrastructure would be valuable even beyond a potential disaster recovery situation.

However, the creation of a disaster recovery team was a central point of the plan. Simon suggested that, in the case of an emergency, a single entity within the company would need to be assigned the task of initiating and carrying out the emergency response and business continuity procedures to ensure minimum downtime and the safety of all personnel. The roles of each member of this entity had to be clearly spelled out and communicated to the group. Simon envisioned this entity to consist of existing staff members assigned to the group, with limited need for additional staff.

Management, however, found the plan to be too expensive in light of the current expansion plans and assigned it for consideration in the following fiscal year. Simon's persistence and further discussion on the topic led to the following temporary measures:

- Effective immediately, an off-site cold storage location would be identified, and all backed-up data would be transported to the off-site location on a daily basis at a predetermined time.

- The procedures for identifying an effective hot-site vendor would be initiated, and where possible, service-level agreements (SLAs) would be negotiated with the intent to have a hot-site SLA agreement in place during the next fiscal year.

- Using the off-site cold storage vendor as a potential hot-site vendor would be considered.

- A detailed report would be developed highlighting all the major potential disasters, their effects on normal business operations, and the strategies required to mitigate those effects.

This was certainly progress. By beginning the process of identifying a hot-site vendor, management had at least acknowledged that one would be necessary, and would be retained if the right agreement could be reached.

9.2 Disaster Strikes

At 12:30 AM on the third weekend of November, seven months from the date management had met to decide on a scaled-down disaster recovery approach, a short circuit at the main electrical panel resulted in a fire at Alanis's main data center. By 3:30 AM the fire had been brought under control by the firefighters who responded to the alarm; however, the main data center was reduced to debris. All communications links were cut off. Suddenly Alanis, Inc., had no main data center and no Web infrastructure. Business had come to a sudden standstill. Alanis, Inc., is an Internet e-commerce company; it does not have a paper process for handling business transactions. If it can't be done over the Web, it just can't be done. Thus, on this fateful November day the worst fears of Paul Simon, not to mention the rest of the company, had been realized.

In the absence of a formal disaster recovery plan, the security personnel on duty during the incident were at a complete loss for what to do. They tried to contact the CTO and the CEO, who were both fast asleep and thus did not respond to the calls. And neither of them replied to voice messages. After waiting about an hour in the hope of getting a return call and some direction, one of the security personnel drove to the CTO's residence to wake him up and inform him of the fire in person. It was 1:40 AM by the time he spoke with the CTO. By 1:45 AM the CTO had contacted the CEO and Chief Security Engineer Paul Simon, and had told Simon to initiate disaster recovery procedures.

Of course, the firm had no procedures in place, so Simon would have to fly by the seat of his pants (pajamas, given the time of day). By 2:45 AM, Simon and several members of the management team were on-site, but there was still no clear plan of action; in fact, it was too late at this point to do much about the fire. The fire-fighters had sealed off any access to what was left of the building and were busy trying to contain and put out the blaze.

Simon began calling members of his security team to fill them in on the night's events, and he asked each of them to report to the incident site—that is, what had been the main data center itself—for instructions about what to do. Then he began to assess the extent of the damage caused by the fire (something more detailed than simply "near complete loss of all IT infrastructure and assets at the main data center"). Salvaging operations were put into place as team members and the company's employees began to arrive. Local authorities were contacted, and steps were taken to salvage whatever equipment could be salvaged. Perhaps some CAT5 cables could be found. And, indeed, whether or not a fire had leveled the building, insurance carriers would demand all due diligence in attempting to save equipment or verify that it was lost or damaged beyond any functional use.

An assessment team was then formed, led by Paul Simon himself, to take on the responsibility of assessing the full extent of the damage. Simon established as the highest priority to chart a game plan for the recovery operations as quickly and effectively as possible and to communicate this plan to all relevant parties.

If an organization has a plan in place the day a disaster strikes, restoration of business functions can begin immediately and in accordance with the plan because personnel have clear-cut instructions on what to do and how to do it. But, in the absence of any such plan, as in Alanis's case, the first step had to be to jot down these instructions so that all groups and individuals working toward the recovery operations could coordinate their activities.

Documentation was also crucial in light of the fact that Alanis's insurance carrier would require a full and accurate account of all activities and recovery efforts.

One member of the team was specifically assigned this responsibility. In addition, the following specific activities were identified for the team:

- Documenting the extent of damage to the organization's resources, with special emphasis on critical assets.
- Salvaging any equipment that was left relatively undamaged, or at all usable, and making necessary shipping arrangements to a temporary facility.
- Working with the public relations department to develop how to respond (and how not to respond) to press, media, investor, employee, and customer inquiries.
- Establishing a central information center with the necessary toll-free numbers where concerned parties (employees and their relatives, customers, investors, and so on) could receive information regarding the event, the safety of personnel, recovery operations, and the future viability of the firm.
- Contacting additional workers and assigning them duties as needed. One of the immediate requirements was to identify additional temporary workspace, since the Kansas site was no longer available.

A second team of personnel was assembled and assigned the task of identifying the immediate steps required to get the organization back online. This team was called the recovery operations team and, again, was headed by Paul Simon himself. The following tasks were identified:

- Restoring Internet access.
- Assessing and identifying the requirements that needed to be met for the resumption of all critical organizational functions.
- Gathering contact information for all of Alanis's IT vendors and insurance carriers. There might be a chance of receiving, on temporary loan, replacement infrastructure components (routers, firewalls, and the like) to help the company reconstruct its infrastructure.
- Identifying and short-listing all vendors who would be able to provide the required infrastructure on very short notice.
- Contacting the team leads at the various branch offices to brief them about the incident and to ask them to be on standby should a necessity arise.
- Identifying a new permanent location for a primary data center.

Fortunately, Paul Simon had contacts with a few hot-site vendors with whom he now decided to speak. He was particularly interested in one vendor, Nirvana, Inc., because he had had four rounds of discussions with them prior to the current disaster and was comfortable with their services and capabilities. He contacted Nirvana and gave them details about the incident and Alanis's immediate requirements. Nirvana soon submitted a proposal to meet these requirements, which Alanis's management accepted and approved. The legalities of a contract were to be worked out by the legal departments of both organizations, but given the emergency nature of the situation, personnel of the two companies began work immediately on setting up the hot site. The following requirements were to be met by Nirvana:

- Establishing high-speed Internet access with dedicated communication lines within 24 hours
- Providing basic network infrastructure equipment, including routers, firewalls, switches, load balancers, Web servers, database servers, desktop computers, and other equipment as necessary to restore Alanis's Internet services
- Providing recovery personnel to assist the engineers from Alanis with all recovery operations
- Providing basic transportation to assist in moving whatever equipment could be salvaged, as well as any necessary personnel, to the hot site

Fortunately for Alanis, some of its vendor partners were able to lend equipment to the company for emergency use, and its insurance company approved such loans before formal claims were filed or processed. In addition, Alanis had a few other things going for it. Because regular system backups had been done, the company's data was approximately three hours old at the time of the disaster—fairly recent data, all things considered. Therefore, if general operations could be reestablished, they might not be very far behind.

Alanis also had a standard load set for its desktops, Web servers, e-mail servers, and other critical servers. (A **load set** consists of the operating system, applications, and all configurations on a machine. At Alanis, these were documented and common across multiple machines of the same purpose and type.) Paul Simon's biggest concern was that they might have to to redesign the network without knowing where to look for network configurations and system code. Scrounging among the IT staff, the company was able to capture portions of network configurations, diagrams, and other helpful information. Filling in the blanks required nonstop network design by Nirvana, Alanis, and Alanis's vendor partners.

Nearly 54 hours after the fire, Alanis had a hot site at its disposal with the minimum infrastructure needed to restore partial Internet presence at least. The recovery operation was started with Paul Simon informing the contact person at the hot site that the members from his team would be arriving to start work there. The vendor then activated the hot site by activating the communications links providing Internet access. After completing the necessary testing, the vendor then configured the networking equipment with basic configurations and loaded the systems with operating systems to mirror, as closely as possible, what Alanis was using. The following further actions were also carried out:

- All incoming telephone calls were routed to the central information center at the corporate office.
- In consultation with Paul Simon, the necessary arrangements for resuming all the critical requirements, including loading the servers and desktops with operating systems and configuring them with Alanis's standard load set, were made.
- All necessary arrangements to receive personnel from Alanis at the hot site were made.
- Dedicated transportation facilities were readied.

Desktops, servers, and hardware were configured as closely as possible to what Alanis had been using before the fire. (Given the reengineering that went into this effort, Simon had a sneaking suspicion that they might have actually improved their processes, but that is another matter.) The fact that Alanis had a standard load set for various machines was a very big advantage and a very big aid in the recovery operation because the recovery operation was being carried out in such an unfamiliar environment.

Transportation facilities were all pressed into service, and the equipment was moved from the various locations to the hot site. Human resources, legal, and media relations personnel were kept quite busy dealing with employees and their families, customers, investors, financial analysts, and the media who were concerned about the viability of the company both in the short term and the long term, as well as the safety and health of those who might have been on duty at the time of the fire. The finance personnel were handling all financial matters, and a dedicated line was provided to Paul Simon so that he could contact the CFO whenever necessary.

Sixteen hours after Nirvana had activated the hot site, Alanis was back online with its critical services again operational. Alanis personnel were now operating from Nirvana's location, and Alanis's field agents were again able to process critical claims over the Web. Another two hours later, further testing was completed and the remaining functions were deemed to be in operation as desired. Alanis, Inc., was back online 72 hours after the fire had destroyed its main Kansas office.

Where was the CEO in all of this? Alanis management had immediately fired the CEO after the disaster struck because they recognized his lack of foresight in visualizing a critical aspect of running a company that was so heavily dependent on its IT infrastructure. (Although the official firing did not go into effect until two months later, in order to avoid additional chaos during recovery from the incident, the CEO was immediately removed from the decision-making loop.) Management did not believe the argument presented by the CEO that a plan was being worked out and the company was in consultation with different vendors. They insisted that a plan should have been in place and the staff should have been trained on such vital aspects of running an IT-dependent operation. Although management acknowledged that there had been a lack of funding for the project when the subject had come up in the board meeting earlier in the year, they felt that a disaster recovery plan should have been integral to running operations and that such a plan should have been developed at the very outset of launching the operations.

9.3 Analyzing the Incident

It is often said that we learn more from mistakes and failures than from successes. Well, in this case, Alanis, Inc., certainly did its best to provide a great deal to be learned!

9.3.1 THE NEGATIVES

The biggest problem in the Alanis incident, perhaps a bit obvious, was the lack of a disaster recovery plan. This meant that when the disaster struck, the personnel on duty didn't know what to do. The company was severely unprepared for dealing with the fire. The lack of preparedness was evident by the fact that they were developing plans on the spot and that, while the fire was taking place, the staff on duty did not know how to respond. Critical time was lost.

On-duty personnel had no idea whom to contact immediately. Calls made to the CTO and CEO went unanswered, and after waiting for an hour, security personnel finally decided to drive out to wake up the CTO. One complete hour was lost in waiting. This delay could easily have been avoided if Alanis had had a notification procedure in place. The following additional personnel could also have been contacted—the infrastructure manager, the IT operations manager, and the chief security engineer—but none were contacted by the on-duty personnel. That being said, the security personnel should have made the decision to drive to the CTO's residence without waiting; after all, it was an emergency. By the time the chief security engineer reported in at the disaster site, he was over 2 hours late. This lost time could have been very well used to inform all the team members about the incident and instruct them to report to the incident site.

When Paul Simon finally did arrive, his first task was to document the recovery operation. This step was absolutely necessary because recovery personnel needed instructions on what to do and how to do it. However, the need to go through this process could easily have been avoided if a disaster recovery plan had been in place and had been communicated to all parties involved. The documentation took hours before Simon could circulate written instructions, during which time other personnel were, unfortunately, doing nothing constructive toward the overall goal.

A deeper look into the incident reveals a few additional issues.

The organization's decision to gradually move toward developing a disaster recovery plan came late (and it wound up costing the CEO his job). The step toward having a disaster recovery plan should have accompanied management's decision to use the Internet as the primary means of running all its business operations. The lack of such forethought was cited as one of the reasons for dismissing the CEO.

Even realizing that Alanis's business operations are all concentrated at a single point, making the system vulnerable to a single point of failure, management decided to delay formalizing a disaster recovery plan by one year. Clearly management was taking a chance that a disaster would not occur. Unfortunately, the fire made it abundantly clear that sound planning means also preparing for the worst-case scenario.

Further, Paul Simon and his team shouldered an unfairly large proportion of the responsibilities, leading to an inefficient use of personnel and division of labor. The sharing of responsibilities lacked discipline. The two teams formed—the assessment team and the recovery operations team—were both being led by Simon himself. This meant that he was running the show single-handedly, even though he could have easily enlisted the help of either the infrastructure manager or the IT operations manager to lead one of the teams. Overworking the chief security engineer in this way seriously compromised the quality of recovery operations.

Another significant issue was the lack of a central repository for network configurations. The lack of a central documentation server had led the team of engineers at Alanis to save copies of configurations on their laptops. Besides the fact that these copies did not prove to constitute a complete repository of network architecture documentation, saving the company's system information on laptops was, in itself, a serious security threat. It can't be safe to have the configuration of the primary Internet firewall walking around on someone's laptop. Laptops are mobile and are prone to theft and misplacement. In addition, allowing such information to be kept on laptops violated most industry standards with respect to protecting internal network architecture and configurations.

Paul Simon had brought the matter to the attention of the CTO on some previous occasions, and it was agreed that the issue would be given due attention when the disaster recovery plan was developed. In other words, the "we'll get to that later" reply indicated that the matter was not being taken seriously, and a central repository was not developed.

In the meantime, the partial solution was all that Alanis had to work with in the days after the fire. But network configurations, Web server codes, database programs, and other large-scale implementations are all developed over a period of time and slowly tuned to perfection (or close) in an effort to reduce network vulnerabilities and improve performance. They can't easily or practically be redeveloped overnight.

Alanis was fortunate that Paul Simon had already begun talking with a hot-site vendor (Nirvana) at the time the fire hit, but more than that, Alanis was fortunate that Simon was available and working on the day of the disaster. Given that the incident occurred on a weekend, it was certainly possible that he wouldn't have been available on that day. On the other hand, his physical presence would not have been essential if he had made notes of his meeting with the hot-site vendors and had shared those meeting notes with his staff.

All of these issues of unpreparedness caused Alanis to be out of operation for 72 hours. Because on average the company conducts over 3 million dollars of business a day, being out of business for three days meant a loss of revenue of potentially over 9 million dollars. And this figure does not even take into account the revenue loss represented by losses of equipment and various other assets.

9.3.2 THE POSITIVES

Despite all the problems, things were not all bad. Given that the company had no formal recovery plan, the manner and speed with which it was able to get back online was exemplary. After this disaster, Alanis could very well have faced closure and very heavy financial losses, but such losses did not materialize. A few steps had been taken to assist in disaster recovery, and these small steps ultimately saved the company.

1. The company had decided to have cold (off-site) storage, where data was being backed up every day. This meant that in the event of a disaster, Alanis would have had all the data on which its business operations so heavily depended. Though this was still far from what should have been done, it meant that nearly all of Alanis's data was intact at the time of the disaster.

2. The company had decided to identify a hot-site vendor as part of preparations for developing a full-scale disaster recovery plan in the future. This enabled the chief security engineer to initiate contacts and engage himself in serious discussions with hot-site vendors. This bit of homework came in handy because when the fire happened, Alanis was able to contract with a vendor (Nirvana, Inc.) to provide a hot site on very short notice.

3. In an independent initiative by the chief security engineer, some team members at Alanis had been trained to deal with disasters. However, only members of the network and systems groups had been included in this training, when really the initiative should have extended to the whole organization. (Successful disaster recovery requires the participation of members from all departments within the organization and is not limited to members of the IT department). Nevertheless, having at least a few, well-prepared employees was critical in the effort to quickly identify all the information and steps that Alanis had to take at that critical juncture.

9.4 THE SOLUTION

After things settled down, Alanis's chief security engineer, Paul Simon, presented the following soup-to-nuts business continuity strategy covering both short-term and long-term issues that the firm needed to address. The strategy included tasks for numerous departments of the firm and was approved by management.

9.4.1 IT RISK ASSESSMENT

Simon's report suggested an immediate, full-scale risk assessment of IT operations (which was now approved). However, the assessment was being performed internally. Simon formed a risk management team with members from IT as well as the company's various business units. Involvement by each department was necessary to ensure that the perspectives of all units were represented.

Several options for risk analysis were suggested: effective risk analysis, qualitative risk analysis, value analysis, and facilitated risk analysis. Facilitated risk analysis was chosen because its comprehensive philosophy of taking into account the risks to each system, application, and unit on an individual basis satisfied the needs of the organization.

The risk assessment would include a business impact analysis (which was now scheduled to be done yearly) to determine the financial, customer, and regulatory/compliance impact of failures of mission-critical information systems on the viability of the organization's core business processes. The business impact analysis was charged with identifying two critical thresholds for the firm with respect to IT systems downtime: *acceptable* and *maximum*.

Acceptable downtime is the period of time during which IT systems can be unavailable before any significant impact is felt to the critical business units. **Maximum downtime** is the maximum amount of time that unavailability of the IT systems can be tolerated. These two thresholds are based on the following considerations:

- **Productivity.** Productivity would certainly suffer without the availability of IT systems, and management wanted to determine, to the extent possible, the costs, the point at which they would start losing money, and the point at which they would no longer be able to afford having no IT systems running.

- **Health and safety.** At what point would the health and safety of the employees be threatened? This information would be used to determine when to send employees home in the case of an emergency.

- **Customer satisfaction.** Customer satisfaction was very important to Alanis's management in the wake of this disaster, so they decided to monitor customer satisfaction through regular (and voluntary) surveys. One main point on which the firm wanted feedback was how customers would react to a given amount of operational downtime.

- **Embarrassment.** Related to maintaining customer satisfaction was management's desire to minimize any embarrassment to Alanis, especially stemming from its IT environment, which, again, was the lifeblood of the organization.

9.4.2 AGENCY TASKS

Changing the way the firm operated to protect it better from such events was not limited to the IT department. Numerous departments within Alanis were assigned specific disaster recovery tasks.

9.4.2.1 Legal

Alanis's lawyers were expected to identify all legal liability issues in the event of an incident, including assisting in developing a process to identify which information could and should be released and which information must not be released to various parties, including employees, their families, shareholders, investors, media, and law enforcement and emergency response personnel. Further, the legal department was given the authority to handle communication between the firm and various law enforcement agencies related to any cyber incidents, both during and after the actual incident.

9.4.2.2 Finance

Management wanted the finance department to determine, in actual figures, the total cost impact of an incident, given the firm's cash flow and cost of operations. They also wanted proposals for modifying current operations to be able to increase cash reserves and insurance holdings that could be used to offset the loss of cash flow and the need for emergency funds during such events.

9.4.2.3 Public Relations

The public relations (PR) department was assigned the task of assisting the legal department in developing a process to classify information for release. (Naturally, few organizations can allow full disclosure.) Another task for PR was to act as a primary liaison between the organization and all non-law-enforcement organizations. Once information was approved for release, the PR department was also expected to take the lead in deciding *how* to let information be publicized or disclosed. They chose to develop an interactive training session to convey the new information release process to all employees and staff. The goal was to specifically ensure staff that they would be well informed themselves during an incident, but to help them know what to say and what not to say regarding the incident to outside parties and the media.

Further, an action plan was to be developed to keep the organization's embarrassment levels, in the event of cyber incidents, to a minimum. The critical component was to "stay ahead of the news cycle" by immediately reporting on any and all mitigation steps taken by the company even before relating the details of the actual incident. Presenting information about the incident in this way would cast the firm in a positive, proactive light before allowing the image of the disaster to be associated with the firm.

9.4.2.4 Human Resources

The assigned responsibility of the human resources (HR) department was to identify the resources necessary to handle the internal employee issues that would certainly arise following an incident. HR was free to develop the skills internally or to ensure that any needed skills were available through contract agreements with parties experienced in crisis management and counseling. Working with the company's health insurance carrier, HR was able to identify and develop a relationship with a local crisis management center to provide the necessary, certified psychologist—experienced with workplace issues—for two days a week for several weeks after such an incident, as well as on an on-call basis.

These services were added to the firm's health insurance, which did increase the employees' premiums, but the additional costs were deemed worthwhile. In fact, it was the first time that an increase in premiums was not opposed by employees.

9.4.2.5 Information Technology

IT was assigned the task of coordinating overall development of the disaster recovery plan, including planning for both short-term recovery and long-term recovery. A short-term recovery strategy was to resume work from an alternate location (the hot site). A long-term recovery strategy included ways to resume business operations at the primary site, acknowledging that this would involve potentially significant reconstruction. Assessments were carried out to compare the costs of reconstruction with the costs of simply finding a new primary site.

The assessment and selection of a new primary site had the team considering issues such as the distance of the site from the hot site, and the resources available at the potential site. The team chose a new primary site that was as far away as possible from the hot site but allowed them to use the same workforce. Clearly the firm wanted to avoid the situation of a single disaster hitting both locations but also realized that its employees would have to be able to reach either site to report to work.

In addition to the new site, the IT department identified the need for a comprehensive "Security Policy and Procedures" document to give every employee and staff member a clear picture of, primarily, exactly what the organization is trying to protect, what each individual's role in protecting the firm's IT assets is, and what to do and/or whom to contact in case of an incident or suspected incident.

Further, Alanis decided to implement data mirroring as a solution to speed recovery time. To ensure reliable data mirroring, the organization decided to invest in high-speed fiber-optic circuits between their primary and secondary data centers. Mirroring eliminated the need to retrieve the backup tapes from off-site storage and reload the data. In other words, future recovery operations could potentially be instantaneous because a "current" copy of the data would already be loaded on the secondary systems.

9.5 LESSONS LEARNED

The success of a disaster recovery operation is not known until after a disaster has occurred, at which time an organization is either congratulated or castigated for having or not having an effective disaster recovery plan. But rarely are the success stories clear at the outset, largely because there is no visible return on investment (ROI).

One of the paradoxes of disaster recovery methodology is that although it is judicious to make limited investments, sometimes a strong commitment is what leads to success. One way to reduce the severity of this dilemma is to make the organization flexible. What this means essentially is that a member of each department should be chosen to be part of a core team of individuals who could be trained in the essential functionalities of disaster recovery. The team would be composed of individuals from across the organization so that an understanding of each of the company's individual business processes would be brought to the table.

This team of individuals during normal times could perform their regular duties, but in times of disaster they would switch hats and perform the essential duties of recovery. Of course there are a few exceptions; for example, the team would have to assist in plan development and testing exercises that would take place during normal, predisaster business hours. And this is where organizational flexibility and commitment to the cause comes into the picture. The greater the organizational flexibility and commitment, the lower the cost incurred in putting together a total disaster recovery plan.

Alanis, Inc., lacked such commitment and flexibility. As a result, the staff was not ready to deal with disasters. If a disaster recovery team had been in place at Alanis when the fire at its main data center broke out, the organization might not have had to suffer the losses it did—and the CEO might still have his job.

SECURITY IS THE BEST POLICY

Chances are you thought a security professional wouldn't need to bother with any of those pesky writing skills, huh? Well, unfortunately (or fortunately, depending on your perspective), that's not necessarily true. Sometimes helping a client develop a security policy involves at least as much understanding of current regulations, business practices, and writing skills as it does technology.

This case study details the effort to develop a security policy document for an organization that felt it needed to have and follow such a document in order to be able to enforce standards with regard to employee use of the firm's IT resources. The firm had started to restrict certain types of activities and network usage that it had until recently unofficially permitted. Without a policy in place, however, it was felt that such restrictions would not be possible. A security policy was needed to formalize these new restrictions.

10.1 INTRODUCTION

Security professionals are usually assigned the task of taking steps to ensure that the network is safe. In the simplest terms, that's the job description. It is not true, however, that all they are called upon to do is of a technical nature. A major part of protecting networks is ensuring that legitimate users—those with access to the network and sometimes called *insiders*—do not abuse network resources. But what exactly does "abusing network resources" mean?

Is it abuse to send so many e-mails that they clog up the network? How about selling the domain administrator's password to the highest bidder? Or opening a port with a high number (because you don't think anyone will notice) so that you can visit restricted Web sites and play multiplayer role-playing games; is that abuse? What about setting up a Kazaa server and distributing music, videos, games, and so on free of charge to any fellow employee or interested Internet surfer?

The intuitive answer to all of these questions is yes, as you probably thought. And in general, we can say that any action that potentially increases the risks to the network is abuse and should be stopped (and punished—or would that go too far?).

However, these are extreme cases, so the answers are easy. What about an employee who views a nonpornographic but "adult stories" Web site on his lunch break? Or an employee who stores 10GB of her own, purchased music on her company-owned 60GB hard drive, just to play quietly at work in her office? Or an employee who forgets to update his antivirus DAT file on a daily or weekly basis?

These cases may not be so easy to evaluate. In fact, however, these are far more likely to occur and on a much more regular basis than the first set of cases we described. Therefore, there has to be a mechanism for knowing or deciding whether a specific action is abuse that must be stopped.

The mechanism that allows for identifying "abuses" is the **security policy**. In addition to identifying what constitutes abuse, this document defines the minimum-security posture that the organization will maintain to protect its IT resources from internal as well as external sources of compromise. And here's where we get into the technical issues that we have grown to associate with information security.

Many people are skeptical of security policies. They recognize that a policy may have some virtues, but no policy—not even a great policy—locks down a firewall, monitors an IDS, or patches critical servers. A common view is that all a policy does is occupy the IT and security staff's time—time that could otherwise be spent fighting real fires.

Certainly developing a security policy takes a certain amount—possibly a great deal—of time, depending on the size and complexity of the organization. You don't just develop a security policy to use as a tool to punish and prosecute your own employees (though it can serve that purpose for certain Stalinesque types); there is a more general reason to have a policy: It sets the tone for how seriously an organization takes its security—and therefore, how seriously it views protecting its assets.

A security policy is critical to helping people understand the security component in the day-to-day business decisions they make, and this benefit, in the long run, will help the overall organization be more secure. Still not convinced? Well, let's take a look at the legal perspective.

It is difficult to hold an employee accountable for a specific action if no policy says they can't take that action. When no policy is in place, if an employee or several employees actually perform harmful actions, they can argue against their liability by saying that the firm did not state that such actions were prohibited or even known to be harmful. And guess where the liability then resides. Yes, with the employer. Weigh these potential costs (money, reputation) against the costs of developing a policy (man-hours for writing and training), and the potential ROI is apparent.

Consider this analogous example: If an organization does not have a stated sexual harassment policy in place that all employees have to be aware of and formally agree to, then if an incident occurs or a pattern of harassment develops, the offending party could say that he or she (rightfully) didn't know that such behavior was against company policy. And in such a case, the company could be found liable for creating a workplace environment that fosters, permits, or even allows such behavior.

To defend against such an allegation, employers—almost across the board—demand that all employees and staff formally sign a document saying that they are aware of, have been trained on, agree to, and will abide by a strong sexual harassment policy (no harassment permitted). From a legal perspective, security issues present a similar scenario. (This is not to imply, however, that the same emotional and personal issues are involved.)

The Process

Whereas the case study presented in this chapter details an instance in which the overall process for developing a security policy was used, this sidebar discusses the process itself. Note that the process identified here for developing a security policy can serve as a general starting point. Certainly there will be differences across different organizations and sectors (e.g., commercial, government, education), and we will do our best to identify them as we go along.

The process to develop an overall security policy for an organization starts with identifying who will write the policy. You may think that the security staff are the best candidates. They should be involved, but theirs should not be the only voice. It is a good idea to select a team representing a cross section of the organization, with individuals from different divisions or business units and at different levels within the firm (management, middle managers, staff, field operators, and so on).

The idea is to have a group of people who collectively have a firsthand view of all of the organization's business. Often the policy is written to safeguard and protect the primary business unit but neglects the needs of other units. Although certainly it is important to protect the company's core operations, the needs of all divisions of the company should also be addressed.

Teamwork

Because the policy is written by a team, it is very important that the members of the team have good chemistry and function well together. It is tough to come to a consensus if the team doesn't work well. One factor to consider in determining the makeup of this team is that it should ideally consist of individuals who not only have the necessary talent, but are dedicated to the process and committed to working together. Size is also important. Although the size of the group will depend in part on the size of the organization and the scope of the security policy being developed, generally the best size ranges from four to ten people. Any fewer might not be able to bring into focus a full understanding of the firm's activities and background. Any more might be too many, hampering constructive teamwork.

Although having to work in a group can add to the complexity and difficulties (and possibly frustrations) of writing a security policy, there is a specific reason to create policy through a team effort: It is very rare for any one individual to have a keen understanding of the business processes, culture, attitudes, and capabilities of an entire organization. The larger the organization, the truer this statement is.

A case in point is Apex, the firm that will be discussed in this chapter. Apex's director of security wanted to use the policy to force the use of a desktop firewall on all of the firm's user desktops and servers. From a security perspective, this seemed like a wonderful, relatively cost-effective means of adding another layer of defense to the network. However, a representative from the user population voiced concern that the firewall might restrict access to critical resources, file servers, application servers, or Web-based, personal e-mail. The applications group wanted time to test various desktop firewalls to find one that would not adversely affect current operations. The tech support group said that the potential headache of equipping all users with a desktop firewall, developing common configurations, and answering the numerous additional help desk calls would be simply too great an endeavor in the current quarter or year and should be postponed until the next technology refresh cycle.

The security officer did not anticipate these concerns and certainly should not be expected to develop a security policy without knowing about such concerns. (The group was able to agree to a policy statement that encouraged use of a personal firewall as a technical direction for the company but did not mandate it.)

Kickoff Meeting

After team members have been selected, the process starts with a kickoff meeting. An effective start to such meetings is an icebreaker to help people get to know each other. There is one icebreaker that can accomplish this while starting the group on the path of developing a security policy. The first order of business is to have all members individually define what the organization is to them (in terms of its business operations, not on an emotional level). Then the group members compare these descriptions, not only to get a comprehensive definition, but also to gain an understanding of how other members of the task force view the organization.

The kickoff meeting is also a good place to set the expectations, schedule, and deliverables for the group. In addition, members of the group may not all agree on the need for a policy or on the format and intent of a policy. A bit of education may be necessary.

The organizers of the kickoff meeting (or any other meeting for that matter) need to keep in mind that many, many people think of these meetings as a waste of time. Therefore, you will need to keep these meetings focused to maximize their effectiveness. You may have to do a little bit of motivating as well; if people come in with a negative mind-set, it is all the more difficult to get the process off to a good start.

Identifying the Starting Point

Pen has to meet paper somewhere (or in today's world, fingers meet keyboards), so eventually you will have to identify a starting point for this effort. One suggestion is to identify the critical areas for the firm, as well as what may be the easiest policies to write. The issues that form a cross section of critical areas and easiest policies are always what we attack first. Management may simply identify the organization's most critical areas, as well as the desired initial starting point for developing a policy.

Looking for a starting point for a security policy begs the question of the format of the overall security policy document. A security policy can be a single document, consisting of many individual policy statements. (Table 10.1 shows a table of contents for a sample security policy.) The policy can be written in stages; we don't need to write all of it at once. The more critical (and/or easiest) statements can be developed and published initially, and the others can be completed in one or more later passes.

Table 10.1 Sample Security Policy Table of Contents

Foreword
Executive Summary
Security Policy
       Introduction
       Organization
       Definitions
    Data Handling Policy
       Data Sensitivity Policy
       Document Disposal Policy
    User Account Management Policy
       Password Management Policy
       Acceptable-Use Policy
    Access Control Policy
    Network Security Policy
    Incident Monitoring and Reporting Policy
    Configuration Management Policy
Appendix A: Glossary of Terms
Appendix B: Memorandum of Understanding
Appendix C: Incident Response Form

How do you know what may be the easiest part of the policy to write? One way to determine this is to research existing policy statements or documents to see which of them seem well-reasoned and applicable to your organization. Such policy statements may offer a starting point. Table 10.2 contains a list of sites that have template policy statements that are worth a look.

Table 10.2 Research Resources for Security Policy Statements

Resource	URL
SANS Institute: The SANS Security Policy Project	http://www.sans.org/resources/policies
National Institute of Standards and Technology: Federal Policy Requirements	http://csrc.nist.gov/policies
Internet Software Marketing Ltd.: WindowSecurity.com	http://secinf.net/ipolicye.html
American National Standards Institute: ISO 17799 ("Information Technology—Code of Practice for Information Security Management") (for purchase)	http://webstore.ansi.org
State of Texas Department of Information Resources: Security Policy Templates	http://www.dir.state.tx.us/security/policies/templates.htm

Whatever the case, it is important to establish a reasonable number of policies that can be written and developed at one time. This is not just a matter of manpower on the policy writing/developing side; only so many policies can be reviewed and approved by management at one time, let alone implemented, publicized, and enforced.

Essentially we adopt the philosophy that you don't have to wait for the entire policy to be finished before you start putting it into effect. It seems pointless to us to make some issues wait, like stopping the use of Kazaa, while you wrangle over other issues. Others, however, will take a different approach.

Research

We hope you didn't think this writing assignment would require no research. It doesn't seem like you can go anywhere these days without having to look things up. And with the Internet, it has become terribly easy to do that.

Once you know which policy documents you'll be developing first, the team can identify potential template or starting-point security policies, if they haven't done so already, and compare notes. One good way to do this is to trade research among team members for a sanity check and to verify that some identified material will be valuable for the organization.

In addition to searching for templates on the Web, looking within the organization is important as well. Interviews with members of the organization's IT staff, management, end users, and sometimes business and extranet partners is helpful for assessing current business practices, how security can be improved, and the level of resistance to the adoption of new policies.

Writing

The templates or material you can find will certainly help. But once you have found some templates, you will have to tailor them to your organization, and this is where the different perspectives of the team will be the most useful. At the policy level, it is important that the team agree on its goal. The writing can then be assigned to a team member and reviewed by the overall group.

For example, the writing of a password policy statement can be relatively straightforward once the password policy itself has been decided. Should there be a minimum of six characters or eight? Should a history of five passwords be maintained, or ten? Should the same policy apply to all applications, or will different applications have different policies? Who will make and review these decisions as technology changes?

Once the answers to these and other questions have been generated, the policy can be developed (and, in fact, taken mostly from available templates).

The policy statement may not be the only thing that has to be developed, however. At times, standards and procedures will have to be written as well. **Standards** are documents that support the policies, and **procedures** generally cover the implementation details. The relationships among policies, standards, and procedures are best illustrated by examples, as in Table 10.3.

Table 10.3 Definitions of Security Policies, Standards, and Procedures

Document	Description	Example
Policy	The law	All users must be authorized and authenticated before gaining access to IT resources.
Standard	How to comply with the law	User authentication should be implemented through passwords.
Procedure	What exactly we're doing	The password scheme should be implemented through operating system controls.

Once the policy is written, we can turn our attention to the standards, again resting heavily on our research. The procedures can follow essentially a cookbook format to detail, step-by-step, how user actions conforming with the policies are performed.

A good process for developing procedures is to carefully conduct the actions for which procedures are necessary and note all of the steps involved (at a granular, click-stream level). These are then the procedures. It often helps to have a second person perform the same actions by following the written procedures to make sure that no steps have been skipped or assumed in writing the directions.

An organization does not always choose to develop all the levels of a security policy—policies, standards, and procedures—at one time. Organizations may want to develop all their policies and then work on the supporting standards and procedures. Or they may develop a few policies and the supporting standards and procedures all at the same time before moving to the next set of policies.

The Review Process

Because very little is written perfectly the first time, there will be a review process. There are three kinds of reviews, each with its own benefits:

1. Quality (user) review
2. Peer review
3. Management review

The quality review involves sharing the policy with a group of end users to get their feedback on the clarity and potential ease of implementation of the policy statement. There's little benefit in a policy that will be too tough for people to follow. The interviewees that we will talk about in the case study are a good group of this purpose. The peer review involves sharing the policy with peers who are familiar with security and can comment on the substance of the material. A good potential group are security personnel at another, perhaps similar organization—one subject to the same regulations. The quality and peer reviews can be performed simultaneously.

After these mostly optional reviews, the policies must be reviewed by management, and the policy development team hopes to get management's approval at this time. More likely, though, the team will get feedback, and once that feedback has been incorporated, the policies can be passed. Every organization will have a different process and timeline for reviewing and approving policies. In some organizations, such as universities and governments, policies can be approved at a rate of only one per month (other governments will marvel at such efficiency).

Publishing the Policy

Sufficient lead time should be given to allow the organization to learn about and adapt to the changes. The amount of lead time necessary will depend on the size and culture of the organization and should be balanced against the urgency of the need for the security change.

For example, a university, typically slow to change, while being an "open-door" environment anyway, may be given a full college semester or year in lead time. On the other hand, a small, high-growth firm, as was prevalent in the dot-com era may require only a matter of days or even hours.

In addition, if a security policy is being implemented in response to a specific event, such as warnings of the release date of the latest Sobig or Mydoom virus or the threat of an imminent denial-of-service attack, then measures may need to be implemented almost without notice. Such cases are more likely for individual security measures than for overall policies, however.

Keeping Current

Once the policy has been made known to all—that is, when it is essentially *live*—don't make the mistake of thinking that the job is done. The policy must keep up with changing technology, network resource usage patterns, and even the organization's objectives and mission. A schedule for reviewing the policy on a regular basis is needed. Naturally, it is best to ride on the coattails of existing review schedules. A yearly or periodic audit might be a good time to review the policies. Regularly scheduled business process reviews are another good time to reevaluate the policy.

In addition to assessing the appropriateness of the policy, the review can be used to assess how well the policy is doing when measured against user complaints and violation citations.

Areas showing a high number of violations may indicate that the security measures are too strict or complicated for the workforce, or there is something that runs counter to that policy. You may want to develop a workaround or modify the business process involved.

In addition, certain measures may be falling short of their intended goals and need to be strengthened. One indicator of the success of a security measure is the frequency of security incidents (infections, data corruption, and so on). If such incidents occur with the same frequency that they did before the policy was put in place, an alternate solution may be required. Specifically, it may be time to bring the group back to the drawing board to redesign an effective solution.

10.2 THE COMPANY

This case study will discuss the efforts to develop a security policy for Apex Dental, a Midwest dental care insurance provider.

Apex Dental is a medium-sized dental insurance company with a staff of 200 at headquarters, and another 40 in the data center across town. Apex submits claims for 1,800 dental offices and provides insurance for 1,200 companies. There are over 400,000 beneficiaries in nine states. Apex partners with three HMOs to offer dental coverage as part of a single health-care package.

In general, dentists submit claims directly to Apex, which then sends the dentist payment for a portion of the bill, and the dentist invoices the patient for the remainder. For out-of-town emergencies or treatment by nonparticipating dentists, patients submit claims directly to Apex. Apex invoices participating companies for amounts that are based on negotiated or standard fees on a monthly basis, and it receives monthly remittances from its HMO partners.

Apex converted several years ago to a mostly Sun-based data center, and all user workstations except for those of some developers, are Microsoft Windows–based machines. Apex uses two dedicated T3 connections that connect to separate SONET (Synchronous Optical Network) rings at separate switching offices to connect its office and data center. These are normally load-balanced, but they can provide failover options if one is cut. Similarly, the data center has two T3 connections to two ISPs via the same two central offices. The network has the usual assortment of Cisco routers and firewalls, with a DMZ for the two Web servers, an external DNS, and mail relay.

Although most of the claims processors work at headquarters, the company has been experimenting with telecommuting alternatives for claims processors, which will allow it to expand without more office space, while at the same time meeting commute reduction mandates. Each claims processor who works at home is provided with a computer, a DSL line, and a phone line. The company has also been quietly exploring the option of outsourcing some routine claims-processing functions to a company in Bangalore, India.

Apex still invoices customer companies on paper, but it accepts direct deposits from customers and makes direct deposits to provider's accounts. Customer companies and provider dentists can use a secure portal for most interactions, such as changing lists of insured patients and submitting claims.

The only union-represented workers in the company are the cleaning staff hired by the building owners, and the construction contractors brought in on a contract basis for electrical and telecommunications moves, additions, and changes. The building security guards are hired by Apex from a guard service, but they are not unionized. None of these workers have authorized access to company systems except for the guards, who have access to a Web-based identification system that they use to verify employees and visitors and to check scheduled visits and events. Each guard has a unique ID and password to access the ID system. The guards also have full access to the buildings, though all access to sensitive areas such as media storage, network closets, and the computer room is logged with a card and a PIN, as well as by security cameras. The contract with the security company allows Apex to dismiss a guard without notice.

10.3 THE CALL

One day, Ken Rickter, director of IT security for Apex Dental, called us seeking assistance in developing a security policy. We set a meeting for the following morning to discuss the issue.

Upon our arrival, we were greeted by Rickter and Marla Patel, legal council for Apex. They explained that they currently had no security policy, or even an acceptable-use policy, in place and wanted to develop such policies right away. They wanted to protect Apex against any potential prosecution or lawsuits related to illegal music and video file sharing—which they knew was happening on their network.

We explained that in order to help them develop an overall security policy that would meet their specific goals, we would need to see any corporate policies that were in place, such as the corporate mission statement. A firm should be consistent in its policies, whether corporate or security-specific; having a copy of this policy would help us maintain consistent substance, tone, and format for the policies we would develop.

From here, we proceeded to gain an understanding of the firm's current IT environment. This process involves our favorite of activities: the Interview! We had the opportunity during the next couple of weeks to interview staff to learn about the inner workings of the organization's infrastructure, as well as about end users' basic computing habits.

10.3.1 THE INTERVIEWS

We wanted to make sure we got a broad view of Apex's operation by interviewing the whole spectrum of people who had a stake in the security policy—from executives to end users to IT personnel to clerical staff—as well as others who might have useful perspectives, such as contractors and customers. Our primary point of contact was Ken Rickter, so we worked with him to develop the list of those we would like to talk to. Besides helping us create the list, Rickter was invaluable in arranging the meetings and briefing other management personnel to make sure they understood that this was not an audit or investigation of their department, and that the effort had the full support of executive management.

We asked a standard set of questions of everyone we interviewed, centered mainly around good computing practices—for example, password management, security awareness, and knowledge of threats such as viruses and human engineering. We also asked all interviewees about their specific jobs, and about how they used the computers and networks and handled their data. A few specific questions are included in Table 10.4.

Table 10.4 Sample Interview Questions

Interviewee	Questions
End user	Do you log off, power off, or just leave your machine on when you go to lunch or leave for the day? Do you know what other people do?
	Do you write your passwords down? Do you know of others who do?
	Do you feel you are following any/all of the basic security measures communicated to you by management/IT?
System administrator	How are firewalls managed?
	How is antivirus software managed?
Management	Is security training a part of the planned budget?
	How strongly do you feel you support the IT department in developing and implementing security strategies?

We ask about how antivirus software is managed because at one of my first jobs, users were responsible for updating the virus definitions on their own machines. I never did. I don't know how old my DAT file may have been, but back then I just didn't understand the need or have the patience for it. Better to be lucky than smart, I guess.

We took the following notes from our interviews.

Sally Morris, IT Operations Manager. Ms. Morris has overall responsibility for operations of the systems and networks, and her staff consists of mainly young employees with tech school or military education in IT. The staff range from very sharp employees who are intensely curious and always exploring new ways to use the systems, to clock punchers who do their jobs and are perfectly happy on swing shift. Her staff, while responsible for operating the systems, often have little information about the networks and systems, and what little they do have is often out-of-date. Often they are given little or no notice of changes or new deployments, and sometimes they have to "wing it" when strange things happen to systems at 2:00 AM. Sally is fairly sure that there are no security issues; otherwise someone would have told her about them. Bob on swing shift has set up the backups and knows how to run them. They're run each night and taken off-site the next afternoon, where they're kept in a locked storage room with the spare laser toner cartridges at Apex's other office. Bob says that the backups are running smoothly with no significant error messages, so Sally is confident they're in good shape for disaster planning.

> **ASIDE:** You will probably want to know for sure if the backups are working properly and are reliable. A simple check on even a monthly or quarterly schedule can be sufficient.

Matt Smith, Applications Programming Supervisor. Mr. Smith has been running the applications development organization for years, and he has overseen the migration of the legacy applications from the mainframe to mostly customized versions of Web-based off-the-shelf vertical packages for the insurance industry. He says they're running fairly well now, after some initial issues with the new systems. The vendors were coming out with new versions and patches to their applications and middleware almost daily, and system stability was a problem until they got a handle on configuration management to carefully test and deploy changes. They're now following a policy of upgrading software only if there's a real business need, such as a new feature they must have, and then only on a strict quarterly schedule for enhancements. Otherwise, version changes to the application front ends and middleware are allowed only for critical bug fixes or if they're getting so old that the vendor won't support them. Matt is a bit concerned about the talk of new security policies and wants to make sure that they don't hinder his group's schedule. The release schedule is very strict, and they're in testing to ensure that this quarter's new release is validated to meet all the users' requirements. Since all the data is stored in an Oracle database and accessed through a Web front end that hides the database from the user, Matt says there shouldn't be any security issues with the applications that his staff is developing.

Bill DeJung, Network Architect. Mr. DeJung is very proud of the robust network that he has built for Apex. With the redundant WAN (wide area network) connections from the data center to the office and to the ISPs, he has engineered some very good reliability into the network. Within the data center, much of the network has redundant paths to eliminate single points of failure. The telecommuting program for claims processors is going well; each one uses a company-supplied DSL connection with a fixed IP address that is allowed through the firewall to access the claims-processing system. The claims-processing system is within the data center's network, and it uses SSL (Secure Sockets Layer), so all communications are encrypted. Because the users all have fixed IP addresses and the communications are encrypted, Bill explained, all he had to do was write access control lists (ACLs) on the firewall to allow those IP addresses access to the claims system from the Internet, and everything is secure without having to go to an IPSec VPN. We had to cut short our interview because Bill had just gotten an MSN instant message from a friend at Cisco who had an answer for him on a routing problem he had been having.

ASIDE: If you are wondering why MSN was allowed on the network—well, it wasn't. Instant messaging was one of the things that Apex wanted to discourage and stamp out with its new policy.

Sandy Watson, Data Entry Operator. Ms. Watson works with a group of six other data entry operators who handle entry of most of the routine forms that Apex receives from customer companies, providers, and patients. Most of the entry is text entered into preset forms, but the forms also include scanned copies of X rays, photos, and diagrams of work sent in by providers to document claims. These operators are a close group, and at lunch they laugh about some of the unusual patient names and records that they've seen. Several photocopies of patient claims (with names and patient IDs removed) containing pictures of exceptionally appalling teeth are posted next to the small icebox in their work area "to help us with our diets," Sandy joked. Sandy's proud that she's the one who usually fills in for Leona, the supervisor, when Leona is sick or on vacation, and she has Leona's password so that she can check Leona's e-mail and approve data corrections. Sandy did indicate that the group has heard rumors that the work they do might be outsourced, and she says that morale has been an issue there, but Leona tells them she hasn't heard anything about it.

10.3.2 EVALUATING THE INTERVIEWS

Our interviews gave us a feel for how Apex's business works, and they revealed several threats that needed to be addressed in the security policies. IT operations seemed to have numerous cases in which individuals had access to sensitive information with no oversight, and lack of coordination with other organizations on changes that could expose the company to unnecessary risks. The applications group did not seem to appreciate the risks of unpatched systems or security holes in their own software. The network group had left some possibly significant holes open by having no control over remote access and by allowing instant messaging into the network. The data entry group had difficulty understanding authentication and concepts of data privacy that could cause Apex to run afoul of HIPAA[1] regulations.

---

1. *HIPAA* stands for the Health Insurance Portability and Accountability Act of 1996.

10.3.3 THE INITIAL WRITING

From this interview process, we were able to identify the following areas where we should focus our attention initially in our attempt to develop security policy statements:

- Password management policy
- Acceptable-use policy
- Data classification policy
- Access control policy

Together with a mission statement for the overall security policy document, these specific policies would be our initial focus. At this point we did some research to identify potential templates that we could use as a starting point for writing. The difficulty in writing a policy is tailoring it to fit your specific environment, culture, usage patterns, and needs. You can't simply find something on the Internet and use it. The level of customization and original writing will depend in large part on how unique the organization's situation is with respect to the topic under discussion.

10.3.3.1 Password Policy

Because there was no standard for the use or handling of passwords throughout the organization, we developed a password policy. Password details such as lifetime and history were covered, but additional details, such as composition and length were left to the individual application.

The password policy also took into account the length of password that users would be comfortable with. We didn't want to create a system in which the new security policy made employees uncomfortable. Some changes would certainly take place, but we didn't want push too hard all at once.

10.3.3.2 Acceptable-Use Policy

The acceptable-use template available from the SANS Security Policy Project site (see Table 10.2) served as an initial draft, to which we added statements banning instant messaging and the downloading and sharing of music, video, and movies over the Apex network.

10.3.3.3 Data Classification Policy

One of the issues raised during the interviews was the lack of a data classification scheme. All data was simply considered "important" or "sensitive," and no levels of sensitivity had been established. We worked with Apex management to develop the following classification scheme:

- **Public information**. Information that would have to be approved by management for public dissemination, such as information on the company Web site or SEC filings.

- **Company private information**. The default classification for routine internal information such as e-mail that could be disclosed to others, such as business partners, if appropriate.

- **Company confidential information**. Sensitive information, such as personnel information, financial records, and competitive analyses, that should be controlled and disclosed only to those with a need to know. Specific information about business relationships with providers would mostly fall into this area.

- **Personally identifiable information**. This is the data of most concern to a health care organization, including any data that contains personal information about patients, such as treatments, Social Security numbers, addresses, and phone numbers. This data needs to be treated with high security precautions, and handling and storage must meet regulatory (e.g., HIPAA) requirements. All access and modification of this data must be auditable, and the data is generally stored in an encrypted format.

Every system must be reviewed and approved by the security group for handling of all company information to ensure that it provides necessary protections. There's no equivalent of clearances for personnel at Apex Dental, so, instead, a user access control mechanism must be put in place to ensure that users have access to only the appropriate information and systems.

10.3.3.4 Access Control Policy

On the basis of Bill DeJung's suggestion that ACLs could improve overall network security, a policy was developed mandating their use. Application and system owners were made responsible for designing the lists, and administrators were assigned the responsibility of implementing and enforcing them.

Another identified hole was the lack of clarity about who had access to which resources and who was responsible for approving levels of access. To remedy this shortfall, the access control policy specified that there had to be an auditable process for requesting and approving access in which an employee would complete a paper or electronic form officially requesting access. The request would be routed to the employee's manager, who would approve or reject it and forward it to the relevant system administrator, who would actually grant the appropriate access rights.

Once the drafts had been modified, we delivered them to Apex management for their review, comments, and (hopefully) approval.

10.3.4 THE REVIEW STAGE

To review the policy, we defined a pilot group consisting mostly of interviewees, but also of some employees who had not previously been aware of this effort, as well as new hires, who were included for the fresh perspective on the security policy that they might be able to offer because of their very brief history with the firm at that point.

We explained the policy to the pilot group and asked them to abide by it (wherever applicable) during the following two weeks. Although we didn't enforce the policy, after the two weeks we conducted a focus group and asked the users what they thought of the policy—particularly how easy it was to follow, how understandable it was, and naturally, whether they had actually followed it. The results of the focus group, especially user suggestions, were considered and incorporated into the policy, and modified versions were forwarded to Ken Rickter to present to management.

Given that Apex had called us in, they were eager to act on the policy, so it was approved with only minor modifications. The focus groups really helped assure management that the employees would be accepting of the new policy. They did have their internal legal department review the policy, however, to ensure that the wording did not offend, overpromise, or overcommit.

10.4 YOU HAVE A POLICY . . . NOW WHAT?

After sipping the champagne of success to celebrate having a fully sanctioned policy, we met with our client to discuss the current status. The first thing Mr. Rickter asked when we arrived was, "What exactly do I have here, and what do I do with it?" (This really is the question you should ask if you've been in a position to outsource development of a security policy to a consulting firm.) We explained that the hope was that this document would be a road map leading to a safer computing environment that would offer protection of the organization's most mission-critical applications and would be targeted at the most likely means of attack.

> **ASIDE:** It is not that we ignore "less likely" types of attacks, but we take the basic risk mitigation approach of addressing the most common attacks first.

We also explained that the next step was to implement the policy. In the implementation stage, the intention to implement the policy needs to be formally announced, along with its implementation date, the place where it is available (such as an intranet site), and any scheduled orientation sessions. Some would call this the truly hard part—pushing policy out to users and getting them to comply—and in time to avoid the RIAA's fury. (We joke, but we certainly wouldn't want something to take a big chunk out of our profits.)

At this point the policy development team split into two groups. One group went on to conduct security awareness sessions to inform all employees and staff of the new policy and encourage full compliance; the other returned to developing the next set of policies.

The second group of policies included both basic policies and emerging technologies. The firm did not want to get caught behind on a technology issue again, as in the case of illegal music file sharing. For example, Apex wanted to expand its telecommuting to all employees and was considering a remote-access VPN, but they wanted to have a VPN policy in place before pushing out the technology. (See how policies can be used to help shape the rollout of technology?)

In addition to developing more policies, Apex would have to review existing policies at some point to make sure they were still applicable. The company's internal business processes were reviewed every six months, and it was decided that the security policies would be reviewed on a similar schedule.

10.4.1 Policy Awareness

Before the policy was announced to the entire firm, an orientation session was organized to communicate the policy to those within the firm who might be called upon to respond to employees' concerns, including managers, human resources personnel, and benefits personnel. Once these key individuals were aware of the coming changes, the rest of the organization could be told.

Orientation sessions are an important part of rolling out a new security policy, because there will certainly be questions about the new policy (the most common of which is, "Why do we have to do this?"), and these sessions are an opportunity to respond to questions and allay fears. Essentially, these orientation sessions are Q&A sessions. In anticipation of some employee concerns, a brief FAQ was added to the announcement memo sent to employees (a sample memo follows) to address what might be the most common questions or points of concern. Once this session had been developed, it was incorporated into the orientation process for new hires, to allow them to hit the ground knowing the firm's security policy.

Of course, one more piece of the puzzle needs to be addressed: enforcement. The firm must be committed to enforcing the policy once it is in effect. One suggestion that we made for enforcement was to implement a modification of the "three strikes" rule. In this enforcement paradigm, everyone gets two warnings, and no real punishments or sanctions are issued until the third offense (strike). This is just one type of enforcement rule that can work. The most important issue here is really the organization's commitment to enforcing the policy.

FROM: Management / Security Office
TO: All Employees and Staff
DATE: August 12, 2004

RE: New, Organization-Wide Information Security Policy

Apex Dental has developed a new, organization-wide information security policy to address the changing security concerns that we face on a daily basis.

The policy will take affect on January 03, 2005. The following orientation sessions have been scheduled to discuss the new policy and answer any questions or concerns that you may have.

  12:00PM May 1, 2004   Conference Room 1
  1:00PM   June 20, 2004   Conference Room 1

Because your compliance with the new policies is critical to their success, we appreciate your attendance at one of these sessions. Lunch will be provided.

Sincerely,

Shirley Jones
Security Officer

HIPAA

SECURITY BY REGULATION

The Health Insurance Portability and Accountability Act (HIPAA) of 1996 provides regulations pertaining to the security and privacy of protected health information (PHI) within **covered entities** (health care providers, insurance companies, claims processors, and others). The regulations also standardize health care transactions and code sets, but we will concentrate on only the security and privacy implications.

The security regulations outline controls that need to be in place to protect health information electronically. The privacy regulations focus on the privacy of PHI and create a broad standard that due care must be taken to protect all PHI, whether in electronic, hard copy, or other form. The privacy rule has security implications because it stipulates that organizations must take reasonable and appropriate measures to protect PHI.

The entities to which this rule applies (referred to as *covered entities*)—generally organizations that store, transmit, process, or otherwise handle protected health information—struggle to identify gaps between their existing security practices and those required by HIPAA. This case describes a technical vulnerability analysis that was performed to help with specifically this issue, as well as to make formal recommendations to bridge those gaps. It does not go into depth concerning the HIPAA regulation, but focuses more on HIPAA as the impetus for this review and on some of the issues that the organization involved had to deal with in its drive toward compliance.

HIPAA is specific to the health care industry; however, similar legislation has been passed for other industries, including the Gramm-Leach-Bliley Act (GLBA) for the financial industry, the Family Educational Rights and Privacy Act (FERPA) for educational institutions, and the Sarbanes-Oxley Act for publicly traded companies. Regulations continue to be passed that expand the security practices that organizations must put in place to protect confidential data.

11.1 INTRODUCTION

The Health Insurance Portability and Accountability Act (HIPAA) of 1996 security regulations (45 CFR Part 42) are federal regulations that require administrative, technical, and physical controls over electronic protected health information (PHI). The rule

> require[s] that each covered entity engaged in the electronic maintenance or transmission of health information pertaining to individuals assess potential risks and vulnerabilities to such information in its possession in electronic form, and develop, implement, and maintain appropriate security measures to protect that information. Importantly, these measures would be required to be documented and kept current.

The security rule does not take effect until April 21, 2005. The privacy rule (45 CFR Parts 160 and 164), however, went into effect in April 2003 and has security implications. Section 164.530I(1) of the privacy rule implies HIPAA security: "A covered entity must have in place appropriate administrative, technical, and physical safeguards to protect the privacy of protected health information."

The security regulation has many elements, some of which are "required," such as a risk analysis, and some of which are "addressable," such as workforce clearance procedures. An **addressable element** is an element that an organization needs to assess (through the overall risk assessment) to determine if it is reasonable. If it is reasonable, it must be implemented; if not, an explanation of why it is not reasonable for the particular organization must be documented and an alternative control must be implemented. Tables 11.1 through 11.3 list the security standards and the required and addressable implementation specifications.

Table 11.1 HIPAA Security Standards: Administrative Safeguards[a]

Standards	Sections	Implementation Specifications (R)=Required, (A)=Addressable	
Security Management Process	164.308(a)(1)	Risk Analysis	(R)
		Risk Management	(R)
		Sanction Policy	(R)
		Information System Activity Review	(R)
Assigned Security Responsibility	164.308(a)(2)		(R)
Workforce Security	164.308(a)(3)	Authorization and/or Supervision	(A)
		Workforce Clearance Procedure	(A)
		Termination Procedures	(A)
Information Access Management	164.308(a)(4)	Isolating Health care Clearinghouse Function	(R)
		Access Authorization	(A)
		Access Establishment and Modification	(A)
Security Awareness and Training	164.308(a)(5)	Security Reminders	(A)
		Protection from Malicious Software	(A)
		Log-in Monitoring	(A)
		Password Management	(A)
Security Incident Procedures	164.308(a)(6)	Response and Reporting	(R)
Contingency Plan	164.308(a)(7)	Data Backup Plan	(R)
		Disaster Recovery Plan	(R)
		Emergency Mode Operation Plan	(R)
		Testing and Revision Procedure	(A)
		Application and Data Criticality Analysis	(A)
Evaluation	164.308(a)(8)		(R)
Business Associate Contracts and Other Arrangement	164.308(b)(1)	Written Contract or Other Arrangement	(R)

a. Source: Health Insurance Portability and Accountability Act (1996), Appendix A to Subpart C of Part 164.

Table 11.2 HIPAA Security Standards: Physical Safeguards[a]

Standards	Sections	Implementation Specifications (R)=Required, (A)=Addressable	
Facility Access Controls	164.310(a)(1)	Contingency Operations	(A)
		Facility Security Plan	(A)
		Access Control and Validation Procedures	(A)
		Maintenance Records	(A)
Workstation Use	164.310(b)		(R)
Workstation Security	164.310(c)		(R)
Device and Media Controls	164.310(d)(1)	Disposal	(R)
		Media Re-use	(R)
		Accountability	(A)
		Data Backup and Storage	(A)

a. Source: Health Insurance Portability and Accountability Act (1996), Appendix A to Subpart C of Part 164.

Table 11.3 HIPAA Security Standards: Technical Safeguards[a]

Standards	Sections	Implementation Specifications (R)=Required, (A)=Addressable	
Access Control	164.312(a)(1)	Unique User Identification	(R)
		Emergency Access Procedure	(R)
		Automatic Logoff	(A)
		Encryption and Decryption	(A)
Audit Controls	164.312(b)		(R)
Integrity	164.312(c)(1)	Mechanism to Authenticate Electronic Protected Health Information	(A)
Person or Entry Authentication	164.312(d)		(R)
Transmission Security	164.312(e)(1)	Integrity Controls	(A)
		Encryption	(A)

a. Source: Health Insurance Portability and Accountability Act (1996), Appendix A to Subpart C of Part 164.

In one particular engagement, the client sought our assistance in performing a technical vulnerability assessment of key technologies in its organization as part of the required risk analysis. The goal of vulnerability analysis is to identify vulnerabilities or weaknesses in the system that, when combined with a threat (such as a dishonest employee), creates a threat-vulnerability pair that results in risk to the organization. Hopefully this condition can be mitigated to a level at which the remaining risk (residual risk) is acceptable to the organization. Ideally the organization will be able to eliminate the vulnerability altogether.

To begin the process in the case study in this chapter, we reviewed the inventory of the client's technology assets. This inventory was a key step in analyzing risk because the client needed to know what items it had to protect and where those items were located. Next we used checklists and questionnaires to assess the administrative controls and to get an idea of the technical controls that were in place. Then we performed detailed technical testing to assess the effectiveness of those controls and identify vulnerabilities within the technologies.

The review covered mainly two technical areas: the external perimeter and internal systems. Each of these areas could be a case study in itself; we will discuss the highlights of each and how they fit together. In the external review, we scanned for external vulnerabilities, reviewed the firewall and router configurations and the network architecture, and performed a war dialing (attempting to identify weak modems that could be exploited). A lot of this is basic external security analysis. During the internal review we performed an internal vulnerability assessment of a sample of platforms, databases, and applications.

11.2 THE ASSESSMENT

We started the review by gaining an understanding of the organization and associated risks (threats, type of information handled, and so on). We interviewed key personnel within management, as well as technical staff and end users. (Yes, the interview is a critical part of, it seems, every job.) We also reviewed any existing network documentation. The goal was to understand where PHI might exist and what systems were the highest risks.

11.2.1 THE CLIENT

The client, BWell Clinics, manages and operates a chain of small medical clinics, serving over 400,000 patients a year and providing both outpatient and limited inpatient care. The company keeps patient records and tracks patients—much as hospitals do. The company's clinics are located in the same geographical region, and their IT infrastructure is managed centrally through a corporate headquarters. As Figure 11.1 shows, BWell has a standard campus environment featuring essentially a flat network with one primary and one secondary connection to the Internet. The clinics access the Internet through the corporate router, as Figure 11.2 shows.

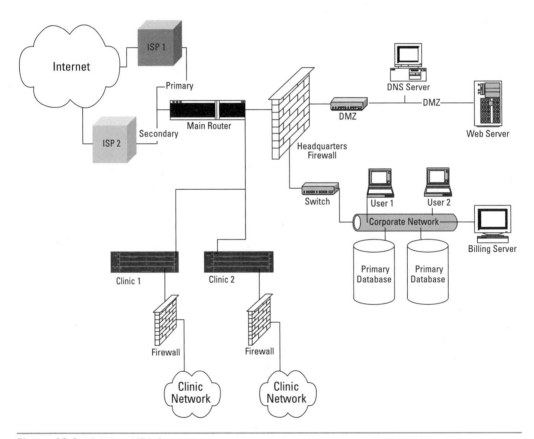

Figure 11.1 High-Level IT Infrastructure

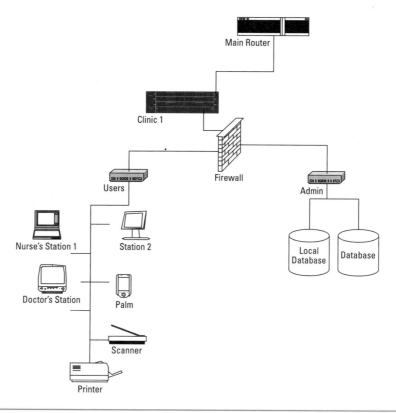

Figure 11.2 Clinic Network

11.2.2 THE EXTERNAL REVIEW

After learning the layout of the infrastructure, we proceeded with the external testing. We started by scanning for external vulnerabilities. We obtained the IP address ranges from the client and engaged in a discovery process to confirm the range by performing whois queries on the client's IP block over the American Registry for Internet Numbers (arin.net) and the SamSpade tool, and we attempted to identify additional entry points or IP address ranges that might be available. We also identified publicly available information on the client's Web site, through Google searches, and in news articles, and we read through the client's 10-K forms in the Securities and Exchange Commission's (SEC's) EDGAR (Electronic Data Gathering, Analysis, and Retrieval) database.

Two different vulnerability scanners—ISS Internet Scanner and Nessus—were used to test the network. This combination of scanners represents both commercially available tools (ISS is considered a leader in the market) and open-source tools (Nessus is considered one of the better freeware scanners available). Each scanner tests the target system for hundreds of known vulnerabilities. We also conducted a complete 65,535-port scan on interesting hosts, to identify additional services that may have been open. Using a banner grabber, we obtained the banner and identified the version of the service running. We then conducted research to identify additional possible vulnerabilities that the scanners might have missed.

In some cases, we were able to access remote log-in screens, such as the one shown in Figure 11.3. We did not attempt to gain access, however, because in order to keep costs down, the client had selected vulnerability scanning over penetration testing.

Next we reviewed the firewall and router configurations. This step is essential to an external review because some vulnerabilities or exposures could be missed through just external scanning. By reviewing the firewall, we are able to see exactly which protocols are allowed through into the DMZ and internal network. We can see what systems an attacker would be able to access on the internal network if she compromised a DMZ system. By reviewing the services allowed between the internal network and the DMZ, we are able to assess the associated risk better.

We identified some high-risk rules in BWell's firewall rule set—rules that allowed services into the environment that were not necessary. For instance, SMTP (port 25) was allowed directly into the internal network to several hosts. As a result, attackers were able to launch exploits at those systems over port 25.

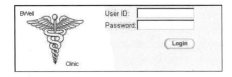

Figure 11.3 Captured Log-in Screen

By implementing a mail relay in the DMZ, BWell was able to control SMTP access better and provide virus scanning and content filtering before the traffic entered the internal network.

In addition, some Web servers were maintained by divisions within the company. These servers did not reside in the DMZ and were not configured by the IT staff. An IT representative within the business unit was responsible for maintaining the server. Our scanning identified numerous holes on these Web servers. Patches were missing, and the system had not been hardened. The organization was thus quite exposed: Not only were its systems vulnerable, but they were located directly on the internal network. If an attacker were to compromise one of these Web servers, she would have a clear path to attack other internal resources that contained PHI.

Our recommendations for dealing with these problems were to move all externally accessible servers into the DMZ, to centralize IT security, and to develop baseline standards outlining the minimum controls that needed to be in place on all servers. These standards could be used across the organization and could serve as a baseline for a monitoring and compliance program.

The router is another essential control point that is often overlooked. The router can provide excellent screening capability through the use of ACLs. In addition, the router can serve as an early warning system through proper logging and alerts. The router can also become a chink in the armor that is often overlooked by an organization because it is not viewed as an essential part of perimeter security (in fact, a router is often not even considered a security device). An attacker that can compromise a router may gain valuable information about the network, modify routes, divert traffic, capture traffic, or cause a denial of service.

We reviewed the router to make sure it was configured in accordance with industry leading practices. Our leading-practice documents were built on standards from organizations such as the vendor, SANS, CIS (Center for Internet Security), and others. CIS (http://www.cisecurity.org) provides excellent baseline standards and tools for reviewing routers that can be used as a model for evaluation. We identified additional controls, such as securing SNMP, using SSH instead of Telnet, filtering ICMP, and other services.

To identify rogue modems and assess the security of known modems, we war-dialed a range of the organization's phone numbers. We obtained 10,000 num-bers and dialed them using PhoneSweep. This tool programmatically dials each number, attempting to identify a carrier. We identified several carriers. We pro-vided this list to BWell and compared it to the BWell's list of authorized modems. The client identified the unknown modems and attempted to discover where each was located and the responsible party.

BWell used vendors to help maintain some systems and applications. The ven-dors were given dial-up access via modem and used a generic account. The account and password were rarely changed, and the password did not follow normal guidelines for composition, expiration, and so on. These old and likely insecure vendor passwords over dial-up vendor accounts created significant risk to BWell. The vendor could experience turnover, and a departed employee would still have all the information necessary to break into BWell's system: modem phone number, account name, and password, as well as some knowledge of the internal network. In addition, the HIPAA regulations require a unique identifier for all users, and shared accounts such as the vendor account violate this principle.

11.2.3 THE INTERNAL REVIEW

Our goals for the internal review were similar. As part of the vulnerability assessment, we wanted to see if an attacker would be able to access PHI. To do this we performed a limited internal penetration test. This test simulated two scenarios. In the first scenario we connected to the network with no access other than a network connection. In the second scenario we simulated a normal user that might want to gain unauthorized access to systems or data. Again, the penetration test was a snapshot that may have missed critical vulnerabilities in other areas. Therefore we performed host-based testing on a sample of systems in the environment—AS/400, Novell, Windows NT, and AIX. (AS/400 has since been renamed *iSeries*, but the name *AS/400* is still commonly used.) These exam-ples represented all the major operating systems and platforms within BWell's internal environment.

During the internal penetration test, we set up in an unoccupied room. We plugged in our laptops and began to see what was available. Our first task was to map the network. From our Windows laptops, we began by using net commands to identify NT systems. Using the command net view /domain, the team was able to view all domains on the network. After discovering the different domains, we used Nltest, an NT resource kit tool, to locate the multiple domains with a PDC (primary domain controller) and three BDCs (backup domain controllers) per domain.

Once the domain controllers and other target systems were identified, we attempted to get more information about these systems by identifying sensitive resource information. We then performed a null session, a net use connection to the IPC$ share on each server with no user name and password. The **IPC$ share** (IPC stands for Interprocess Communication) is a default share that Windows NT uses for NT communications. The process of connecting to the IPC$ share as an anonymous user is called a **null connection**. We then used tools available with the NT resource kit and DumpSec to identify local users and user information, last log-in time, account status (active/disabled), the last time the password was changed, local administrators, and global administrators.

The Restrict Anonymous registry key could be set to limit the information that we would have been able to obtain, but in this case it had not. We then identified the local administrator accounts on each system; inherently these accounts cannot be locked out unless the passprop.exe resource kit utility is enabled. We attempted to deduce the administrator password three times by making educated guesses and used DumpSec to determine if the account had been locked out. We noted that the account had not been locked out and then utilized more intrusive tools to attempt to access the account by brute force. The brute-force tool, Net-BIOS Auditing Tool (NAT), ran for three days and, using several password lists, finally cracked the administrator's password.

In actuality, we did not even need to use brute force to do damage. We were able to identify NT shares on several servers that allowed access to the Everyone group. On these shares we found sensitive PHI. The HIPAA regulations require that only the minimum access necessary be allowed, and therefore having PHI available on open shares (shares open to everyone) was a problem. This was partly a technology problem, but more so a security awareness problem. Users were not aware of the need to set share permissions to prevent unauthorized personnel from accessing the data.

Next we targeted Novell. We used Novell client software to view the Novell trees, contexts, and servers. We were able to identify two Novell trees, the contexts associated with each tree, and the servers and resources associated with each context without having to authenticate into the tree. The next step was to create anonymous attachments to servers identified as Novell servers. We did this by utilizing a tool called *snlist* (which stands for *Serial Number List*). Anonymous attachments are possible because an attachment and log-in are not interdependent.

After we attached to multiple Novell servers, the team's next step was to view each file server, as well as the associated groups and users. We were able to do this by identifying each server to which we had attached, setting each server (one at a time) as the primary server, and running the command-line tool Bindin against the primary server. Executing the `bindin u` command identified the users on the server; and executing the `bindin g` command identified each group and its members. Next we used another command-line tool, Chknull, to identify users with null and easily guessed passwords. We identified accounts with blank passwords and accounts with passwords that were identical to the user name. We used these user names and passwords to access servers containing PHI data. Strong password controls and intruder lockout would have helped combat this vulnerability.

For the platforms, we selected a sample of servers from the environment. We selected several of each server type—NT, 2000, HP-UX, AS/400. Our goal was to assess the server configuration against industry leading practices based on information from sources such as vendor documentation, white papers, and organizations like SANS, NIST, and CIS. To accomplish this goal, we used Symantec's Enterprise Security Manager (ESM), a commercial tool; interviews; and manual reviews.

ESM uses a three-tier agent-manager-console architecture to assess the security of the target operating system. The **agent** is loaded onto the system by a system administrator. The **manager** resides on a separate system and collects and analyzes the data from the agent. Using the **console**, a reviewer can review the data and reports, as well as configure test policies. ESM performs hundreds of checks in areas such as account policy, permissions, and system settings. Using a policy editor, the user can edit a policy for each type of OS that specifies the actual checks to be performed. In addition to using ESM, we used scripts to check the account policy and the password policy and to gather user information, registry settings, and file permissions. The scripts were used predominantly on machines that did not support an ESM agent.

During the host review we found several problems. First, configurations were not consistent. Security settings were different between OS types, as well as within OS types. For instance, settings on Windows 2000 systems differed from server to server, specifically in their auditing, password policies, and user settings (e.g., account lockout was enabled in some cases but not others). Further, the account policy on Novell was different from that deployed in the Windows 2000 environment.

In addition to the settings being different, in many instances they were weak. Many key security settings, such as password policy, account lockout, auditing, and system hardening, were not in place or were improperly configured. Although not a direct violation of the HIPAA security regulations, the weak settings put the organization at risk of not properly securing PHI.

These OS problems can be attributed to several sources. First, different groups within the organization maintained the systems, and the different groups' styles and performance varied. BWell did not have baseline standards or standardized operating procedures that spanned all divisions of the company. Baseline standards would have defined the minimum security settings necessary on each platform and would have helped close many of the holes identified. Further, a compliance-monitoring program would have dramatically reduced the number of findings. Compliance monitoring would "audit" against the defined baseline standards and note deviations and noncompliance so that the organization could take action to close the hole before it became a problem.

Databases often contain PHI and need to be secured properly to protect it. BWell used several databases—Oracle, SQL, and Sybase. To review the security of these databases, we interviewed database administrators (DBAs) concerning standard database configuration. Unfortunately there was no standard configuration.

We then used ISS Database Scanner to get an idea of how well the databases were secured. ISS Database Scanner has penetration testing modules that attempt to break into the database, as well as modules that review the database from a DBA's point of view. In using this tool, we worked with the DBAs to get their perspective. The scanner tested each database for hundreds of security settings related to passwords, auditing, permissions, views, encryption, and others. A modified version of Security Level 5 (see Figure 11.4) was used to perform the testing.

In general, we found the same types of problems as we had noted in the OS review. The configurations were inconsistent, and many of them were weak. Minimum baseline standards and compliance monitoring could help close many of the holes.

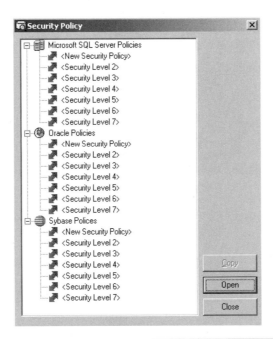

Figure 11.4 ISS Database Scanner Policy Security Levels

BWell used many applications that contained PHI. We reviewed a sample of them for key security settings, such as auditing, password controls, encryption, backup and recovery, timeouts, and access controls. We accomplished this inspection by reviewing documentation, analyzing the application, and interviewing administrators. For most applications, the existing controls were adequate. Some had a few accounts that did not use unique identifiers. Many accounts had weak passwords, and the application had no mechanism for enforcing complex passwords.

The application usually had audit and logging capability, but either that capability was not enabled or it was enabled but not reviewed. Logging and auditing are very important under the HIPAA regulations. Any organization should develop a standard for logging and auditing that indicates what types of events will be audited and logged, how the logs will be reviewed, where the logs will be stored, and who will be responsible for the logs. Log retention is also important. Often logs are overwritten and not backed up or retained. Logs are essential in helping to identify potential incidents and problems, as well as for evidence and response when an incident does occur.

We noted several other areas of risk during our review as well, but we were unable to address them because of time and scope limitations. BWell was preparing to install a wireless LAN. The WLAN would extend the perimeter of the organization and introduce significant risk if not properly secured.

PDAs and other handheld devices were being used for authorized applications, as well as by personnel just to hold information. In addition, several individuals were carrying USB data keys. Often this data contained PHI. PDAs are difficult to secure properly, and at this time many health care organizations do not even take them into consideration when assessing security risks.

E-mail with outside entities is also difficult to secure. Such e-mail could contain PHI, which would be susceptible to sniffing. There are numerous other areas of risk as well, which only a proper risk assessment would identify. In addition, the technical environment changes at blazing speed. Therefore the risk assessment needs to be reviewed and redone often (we would suggest every six months) to identify new exposures resulting from the latest technological advances.

11.3 ANALYSIS

In our findings, we were able to cite numerous holes in BWell's system, such as weak passwords and unnecessary services running on multiple servers, in addition to the items already mentioned. The organization's systems and networks had many holes and weaknesses that exposed PHI to potential compromise. Most of these holes can be attributed to a lack of defined standards and security program: no defined responsibility, lack of standards and awareness, and lack of compliance monitoring. If the organization had standards, at least administrators would know what was expected when initially configuring or performing maintenance on the server. A compliance-monitoring program would find many of the holes that system administrators had inadvertently let slip by.

Policies and procedures set the tone. Without effective policies and procedures, it is difficult for an organization to protect PHI and critical resources. Also the HIPAA regulations require documented policies and procedures.

Awareness is a challenge in and of itself—from the perspectives of both the administrator and the end user. All users, which in this situation include nurses, doctors, IT staff, administrative staff, and all employees of the company, need to know what they have to do to help protect PHI. Their contribution to the overall goal will range from selecting strong passwords, to recognizing, resisting, and reporting social engineering attempts, as well as other potential security incidents. Administrators need to know what part they play in protecting PHI, as well as how to do it. Often administrators know how to make systems work and perform well, but not how to secure them properly.

The key to compliance with the HIPAA security regulations and to properly protecting information assets lies with the risk assessment (RA). The RA determines how the organization should respond and comply with the addressable elements of the regulations. (Tables 11.1 through 11.3 provide an overview of the elements of the HIPAA security regulation stating whether each element is required or addressable.) The RA also identifies the highest-risk areas, upon which the organization should concentrate its resources.

The HIPAA security regulations do not specify the RA methodology to use, and many methodologies exist. Numerous resources—such as NIPC (National Infrastructure Protection Center), NIST (National Institute of Standards and Technology), and others—provide risk assessment methodologies and documentation. Whatever methodology the organization chooses should identify threats, controls, and risk levels. In addition, it should aid the organization in determining how it will comply with the addressable elements of the HIPAA security regulations.

11.4 CONSEQUENCES

In this case we were called in to assist a company in response to the anticipated implementation of a specific government regulation (HIPAA), rather than in response to a known cyber incident. Therefore, the consequences that we describe here are the potential consequences of failing to comply with the regulations (and incurring the wrath of regulators) and the possibly more severe consequence of having PHI compromised by unauthorized individuals (e.g., hackers).

Essentially, patient data was at risk. BWell was not in compliance with the anticipated HIPAA security regulations. Attaining compliance would mean creating an infrastructure that could develop and maintain organization-wide security standards. The first step would be to establish a security office (or department) with organization-wide authority and responsibility.

11.5 THE SOLUTION

BWell formed a committee to address the issues identified in our final report. Many of the recommendations were implemented. Specifically, a security officer position was created, initially with a staff of four, all drawn from internal resources. Formal risk assessments were conducted on a regular basis to identify vulnerabilities within key systems. The risk assessments were also used as a mechanism to perform compliance monitoring before more-formal methods were established.

BWell started to develop standard builds for their back-end machines, with plans to migrate all end user machines to a standard, secure build during the next technology upgrade cycle. They also started the development of a security awareness program. This program, a combination of instructor-led and online training, was rolled out in conjunction with HIPAA privacy-training initiatives.

11.6 CONCLUSION

The HIPAA regulations were the impetus for the review of BWell's system. More and more regulations similar to HIPAA mandate security practices; examples include the GLB Act, FERA, the Sarbanes-Oxley Act, NERC/FERC[1] guidelines, California's SB1386 financial privacy law, and organizational requirements such as Visa, Mastercard, and other credit card standards. The basic steps of this review, findings, and recommendations apply to many organizations. Sound security practices, policies, and procedures are the foundation of a solid security program. Any organization within the health care industry and other industries that collect, process, maintain, or generate sensitive data—for example, financial, legal, and educational services—should start adopting sound security programs that will help address elements of any security regulations, as well as decrease the organization's risk profile.

---

1. NERC stands for North American Electric Reliability Council; FERC stands for Federal Energy Regulatory Commission.

PART IV
OLD SCHOOL

A WAR-DIALING ATTACK

It's quite easy to forget or overlook the fact that the revolution in information technology began in the telecomm sector (no matter what former VPs may say about their role in creating the Internet). So naturally, telecomm would be home to some of the initial kinds of what we now refer to as *cyber security incidents*.

This case study illustrates the level of effort required to launch such attacks. (As you read this chapter, bear in mind that launching attacks becomes easier all the time and the attacks simultaneously become more effective.) We also discuss how the attacker was caught and what the victim thought about prosecuting the hacker.

Although the attack discussed in this chapter is quite old, war dialing is still a viable means of attack today. The interesting thing about war dialing as a whole is that because of the general concern about compromises at the network level, it's easy to forget about vulnerabilities on slow, old dial-up systems.

As a case in point, many mainframes are still connected to modems with default user names and passwords that can be found on well-circulated lists that continue to be accurate. These can be called *tried-and-true targets*.

12.1 WAR DIALING

War dialing is the automated act of dialing phone numbers in search of a modem or dial-up phone connection that allows the caller to gain access either directly or via an authentication challenge, such as a user name/password scheme. Often routers, mainframes, back-end systems, and even user desktops are connected to a listening modem that allows remote connections, possibly from unknown users and (though rare these days) with no authentication challenge at all. More items than you may think can be connected to telephone lines. In addition to those mentioned already, voice mail systems, PBXs (private branch exchanges), air conditioning systems, security systems, and other facility control programs can be connected for the purpose of allowing remote access, monitoring, and control of these devices.

Although this mode of attack may not be as popular as it once was, the vulnerability to war dialing continues to this day. The prevalence of rogue (unauthorized) modems smuggled into workplaces by employees and connected to their desktops has not abated. Employees use rogue modems for a couple of reasons: On the legitimate side, they may want to work from home or other remote locations and use the modem, along with remote-control software (e.g., pcAnywhere, Timbukto, VNC) to facilitate their pursuit of this level of productivity. With the growth of virtual private network (VPN) solutions, however, such connections are becoming less popular.

On the not so legitimate side, many people are under the misconception that if they are not connected to the Internet through the office LAN, or Ethernet, connection, and instead use their own modems, their employer will not be able track their Internet surfing habits. This is usually not true, however, because the recording may be taking place on the host system itself, and not just at the router or backbone switch. A system may track personal use by recording the cookies stored on the host, or by recording the Web browser history file. So using your own modem may not protect you from workplace monitoring (Big Brother?) at the office.

Whatever the reason for using a modem, the desktop modem is one of the more recent targets of war-dialing attacks. In addition to personal desktop modems, some modems are intentionally left connected to back-end machines (e.g., mainframes) for vendor support. Such a modem enables the vendor to dial in to the system to perform diagnostics and fix the system without making a costly site visit. Often these modems are accessed via generic user accounts with weak passwords. The passwords are generally known by multiple personnel on the vendor side and are changed infrequently. For example, it is highly unlikely that vendor passwords will be changed when vendor employees turn over. A terminated vendor employee could still have access to the company's system.

In addition, vendors tend to use the same default password on all installations. (In fact there are even default user name/password lists available on the Internet.) Therefore, if an attacker cracks one vendor account password, he may see the same account on your system and use the same password to gain access. Often these vendor accounts have no lockout features, so they are susceptible to brute-force attack. These accounts are generally left this insecure because they are not expected to be connected for long periods of time. They are supposed to be connected only at scheduled periods and only long enough to allow service.

Even with both the desktop modem and the vendor account as targets, however, the mainframe is still a prime conquest. The following case study describes one of the most successful break-ins we have been fortunate enough to witness. (Of course, the "fortune" aspect of the situation was lost on the victim.) The only reason we are relating this story is that although the target has now taken the necessary precautions—countermeasures—and is no longer susceptible to such attacks, untold other companies may still be vulnerable.

12.2 THE ATTACK

Some years ago, a hacker was trying out his new modem with a war-dialing application called XPOT (short for eXtended Phone Operations Tool), aimed at finding some unattended modems at a (any) company, with the purpose of "exploring his skills," as well as, undoubtedly, eventually making some profit from the discovered access point.

XPOT is now quite old and may be difficult to find. Many more popular tools have been based on this early war dialer, however. At the time, the hacker was

> **ASIDE:** We certainly hope that the hacker has since "grown up" to realize that such behavior is inappropriate—not to mention against the law—and is *not* recommended to any party.

using a state-of-the-art 486DX PC computer, with 32MB of RAM and almost 1GB of hard-disk space. And of course, his pride and joy was a new 19.2 Kbps modem. (Although some parts of the country are still limited to 26 to 31.2 Kbps, the speeds cited in this study, more than anything else, will date this particular incident.)

Using XPOT, the hacker launched a war-dialing attack against several hundred phone numbers, being careful not to have the numbers dialed in numeric sequence. The telephone numbers were simply taken from the phone book. The hacker was really just looking to see what he would hit.

Random Schmandom

It is important to dial numbers randomly. For many, many years, telephone companies have implemented mechanisms to trigger an alert when many sequential numbers are dialed rapidly, because this is a mark of an ongoing war-dialing attack. Apparently the authorities and phone companies have been wise to the threat of war dialing for some time. Therefore, random ordering of the numbers is critical, as we will see later.

Because XPOT is quite old and is not readily available today, we will not explain the detailed process of configuring the tool. Rather, we will highlight the important issues in configuring and setting any war-dialing tool. The foremost issue is to make sure that the numbers are not dialed sequentially, but are randomized to guard against identification by the phone companies. You can also set the outgoing phone lines to block caller ID if you want to try to hide your phone number.

It is also important to have appropriate spacing between the numbers being dialed. The time between successive calls and the call timeout settings determine the pace of the war-dialing effort. The issue here is optimization. Consulting engagements are often performed under a strict timeline, so you will want to maximize the time you have and set these numbers low. However, setting them low leads to additional noise and may cause the dialer to miss some systems that do not pick up quickly. In an ideal world, we would call a few systems, see how long it takes them to pick up, and then set the timeout interval; but this rarely happens, and usually we just estimate a single setting for all systems. The choice is between speed and coverage. Choose wisely. Of course, those on the dark side don't usually have strict timelines, so they can afford to be conservative, spreading the dialing over consecutive days.

In addition, it is important to save the results (the list of numbers through which access may be possible, such as those connected to modems).

In this case several numbers were answered by listening modems. One of those numbers demanded particular attention. The remote modem picked up the carrier line, and after a few attempts—with a very good application that runs the Telephony Application Programming Interface (TAPI), the software programming standard that enables telephony applications and protocols, including Xmodem, Ymodem or Zmodem, and Procomm Plus on numerous platforms—the remote end of the connection displayed a command prompt.

The hacker then attempted to log in by brute force, hoping to find a default (or at least easily guessed) user name and password that were active. He had come across a few default user name/password lists in his time and was going to put them to use. After a few tries, the hacker was indeed able to discover a valid user name, ALPHASPROUTS, because the error for a failed log-in identified where the mistake lay. In all but one instance, the attacker received the error message "User not valid," but in that particular case he received the message "Password incorrect, please try again."

Naturally, this name has been changed to protect the innocent; we will confess that the discovered user name was a system default that had not been changed when the system was installed. The next step was to discover the matching password. One might think that perhaps the back half of the user name/password authentication challenge would make it hard to break into the system. However, the hacker in this case must not have had to make too many attempts to discover the password. If he began with a few of the more common guesses—such as the ever popular PASSWORD, the user name itself, and the user name backwards—the hacker may have had to make only three attempts.

As in many default installations, the default password did indeed work. The user name/password pair ALPHASPROUTS/STUORPSAHPLA turned out to be valid, granting access with administrative rights to the remote computer.

At this point the hacker had gained administrative rights on a remote host over a dial-up connection to a modem. However, he did not know exactly what the remote host was or what purpose it served. Getting this information was the next step.

The hacker determined that the modem belonged to a credit union by matching the telephone number to a range of numbers that belonged to that credit union. He simply scanned the phone book and found numbers close in sequence to the identified phone number. Because it was likely that the credit union had a range of numbers, if the numbers surrounding this one belonged to a certain organization, this number likely belonged to that organization as well.

The machine was a mainframe, as was apparent in the log-in screen because it contained a banner that identified itself (make and model). This was the jackpot; you could almost here the casino bells going off in the hacker's head.

The basic connection was as illustrated in Figure 12.1, which shows an external modem on the victim's side simply to underscore its presence. In reality, the mainframe had an internal modem. The hacker, however, was using an external modem.

After determining that he had located a mainfraime, the hacker played it smart; to avoid arousing suspicion, he did not connect for long periods of time. During the next few days, his connections to the modem lasted shorter and shorter amounts of time. The purpose of these "visits" to the mainframe seemed to be to get updates on the mainframe's operating system, which, after a couple of dial-up connections, was determined to be OS/400—again through interpretation of the log-in screen. Most mainframes run on IBM operating systems, so this was not a terribly difficult guess.

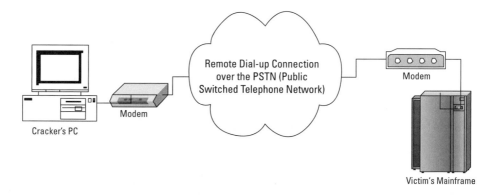

Figure 12.1 Remote Dial-up Connection

By browsing around during the periods of time he was connected, the hacker gradually began to understand the internal working of the mainframe, but the going was slow because this hacker was not already familiar with IBM mainframe architecture. In fact, we learned later that this was his first time ever working on or even seeing a mainframe up close and personal.

Nevertheless, he persevered and did what any good, resourceful hacker would do: He went to what was at the time a popular BBS (bulletin board system) and found some friends with more experience who shared documentation on how to get around in a mainframe OS. After a couple of days of reading and practicing, he managed to traverse the file structure and understand what was an application and what was a simple file.

During these explorations in the remote computer, the hacker determined how to pull up the mainframe equivalent of a process list and determine the most accessed or used application. This information itself can be a great source of intrigue, as you might expect, because if many people are using an application, it is likely to have some value. So, upon finding the most commonly accessed application, the hacker launched that application; and there indeed was the transaction program that the credit union staff used to move money to and from customers' accounts. You can now imagine the Vegas lights in the hacker's eyes.

At this point the hacker began to attempt to take advantage of this major security hole in the credit union's system—and this was the point at which he changed from a hacker to a **cracker**, an individual who attempts to compromise a network for profit. (This is why Figure 12.1 says "Cracker's PC" rather than "Hacker's PC".)

> **ASIDE:** Many people would call the individual a *cracker* as soon as he gained unauthorized access to the credit union's system. That is, as soon as someone broke the law, he would be considered a cracker. The fact that you are not profiting from breaking into someone else's system does not make it all right to break in.

The cracker opened an account with the credit union and, from time to time, transferred small amounts of money from several hundreds of other accounts into his own. To avoid detection, the cracker kept the amounts small. We learned later that he transferred sums sufficient to cover his own phone and computer equipment expenses.

Things went on like this for a couple of months as the cracker gained greater insight into how the application worked. As long as no one at the credit union changed the password or altered the dial-up access system, and the cracker didn't become too greedy, he figured he could continue doing what he was doing for quite some time. After all, the expenses he needed to cover were not very substantial—in his opinion.

However, the day finally came when dial-up attempts to the mainframe with the user name/password pair ALPHASPROUTS/STUORPSAHPLA kept being refused. After failing to gain access enough times, it dawned on the cracker that the log-in information had been changed, and his heart rate began to rise and palms became moist as he realized that someone had figured out what was going on and now he might be in trouble. The modem had finally been used once too many times and had been disconnected from that number.

So the cracker began another war-dialing attack on a separate range of numbers, but the sweat on the hands and the racing heartbeat made him sloppy. The cracker made a major mistake, forgetting one crucial setting: The telephone numbers in this second war-dialing attack were dialed sequentially because the hacker forgot to set the war dialer to dial the numbers randomly. Very early in this war-dialing attempt, the cracker noticed that he wasn't receiving a response from any number. He couldn't find anything—not a modem, fax machine, answering machine, or anything else.

Even the "small" amounts of money that the cracker had been transferring into his account had been discovered by the credit union's auditors. They informed the IT and computer crime staff, as well as the legal department, and together they traced the discrepancies back to the transfers made from certain accounts into a particular (the cracker's) account from a mainframe by the default (ALPHASPROUTS) user. With this information, the credit union went to the police, who alerted the phone company to be on the lookout for anyone (and specifically this individual) potentially performing a war dial (which the phone company was already doing).

The hunt for the cracker was on. All parties were just waiting for him to slip up. After the appropriate investigation, and because the cracker was performing a sequential war dial and using number masquerading, the police got their man.

Number masquerading is, essentially, blocking caller ID. Caller ID was not a popular option at the time of this case, but XTOP had this option. Nonetheless, you can't hide the source phone number from the phone company. Today you can set the outgoing line to block caller ID, but the phone company will still know who the caller is.

Beyond a Reasonable Doubt

One point we'd like to make clear is that the police didn't just arrest the hacker because it was his account into which money was being transferred. Just the fact that money is being transferred into a particular person's account doesn't automatically make that person the guilty party. Crackers may transfer money from several (victims') accounts into another user's account for a period of time, trying to stay off of anyone's radar. And then they might move a great deal of money into that account and either electronically move that money from those accounts to an offshore credit union (one of those that truly values privacy), or physically withdraw the money by social engineering (after all, the cracker has all the account information and may only need to create a false ID), or force the individual to withdraw the money and hand it over. Such an arrangement has the advantage of potentially deflecting suspicion from the true cracker by framing the victim instead.

At this point the credit union had a choice to make. Should they pursue prosecution of the cracker? They certainly had the evidence, and the individual had been caught red-handed. However, because this incident occurred early in the days of cyber crime, the credit union chose instead to force the individual to explain in detail to the credit union's IT staff what he had done and how he had done it. They made this decision in the hope of getting the cracker's full cooperation in assisting them with securing their network, especially at dial-up access points. Of course, the cracker was also required to return all the monies he had transferred (i.e., the money was *reappropriated*)—and his only choice was to do this or face prosecution. If he did not comply or if he ever attempted to break in again, the penitentiary would be his new address.

You might imagine the cracker's relief at the credit union's decision. He kept up his end of the agreement and even shared a few security pointers on issues unrelated to dial-up access points. Specifically, he recommended first that the credit union implement a call-screening feature at its PBX, so that incoming calls would originate from known telephone numbers, and second, that the dial-up access be modified so that instead of reaching the mainframe, remote users would initially access another system that perhaps would be a bit more hardened and could act almost as a proxy (or sort of a buffer) for the mainframe.

At the time, this was the best possible solution. Don't forget that this whole thing happened years ago. Today there is a bit more that an organization can do to protect itself against war-dialing attacks. We will discuss these additional measures in Section 12.3.

12.3 Lessons Learned

In today's environment, a few countermeasures are available to help prevent the situation we have just described. These are not necessarily mutually exclusive and may be coupled together. We consider several of these potential countermeasures in Sections 12.3.1 through 12.3.6.

12.3.1 Restricting Access

Modems are used to break into systems because of their ability to connect to devices remotely, often over the Internet. In today's interconnected environment, the number of such connections is only likely to increase; therefore, identifying ways to keep out unwanted and untrusted users will become only more critical.

12.3.1.1 Source Phone Number

One countermeasure that might work, but might also remove a certain bit of convenience and therefore requires a degree of dedication from all parties involved, is to restrict dial-up access only from specific phone numbers (or IP addresses) for all modems connected to mainframes, routers, back-end servers, and other critical devices. Generally these modems are available only for vendors to perform maintenance or software upgrades; therefore, access can be limited to a certain set of phone numbers. The consequence is that the vendor service representative or customer support agent will not be able to service the machine from remote locations, but will have to be at the home office with a predefined phone number.

A slightly less restrictive version of this defense is to have customer service representatives call in advance either to specify the incoming phone number/IP address or to specifically request the phone line to be connected at a certain time. However, these protective measures rely on constant human involvement and leave open the potential for a social engineering attack (such as the one that will be described in Chapter 13).

12.3.1.2 Dial-Back

Another potential precaution is the dial-back option that has long been available but has never attained widespread usage. In **dial-back**, once a call has come into a modem, the user has been authenticated, and a source telephone number has been determined, the modem will disconnect the line and dial the source phone number to establish the channel. One failing of this approach, however, is the availability of call forwarding, which can allow a hacker to call from a legitimate number and then forward the return call to almost anywhere in the world.

12.3.1.3 Multifactor Authentication

For modems that are part of a remote dial-up telephone system or are accessed by telecommuters or a mobile workforce, in which case the source phone numbers cannot be restricted or dial-back may not be an option (such as from a hotel room), the security measure that should be considered is the use of a **multifactor**

authentication scheme, such as SecurID. Such schemes create, essentially, a one-time password. Users can log in with a familiar user name/password scheme, but the password is difficult to obtain or pilfer because it changes every minute and is valid only once.

The multiple factors are generally (1) something you know, (2) something you have, and (3) something you are. The **something you know** is a string of alpha-numeric digits (like a regular password), the **something you have** is a string of numeric digits that are read from a credit card–sized random number generator (called a *token*; this is the component that changes every minute), and the **something you are** is a biometric reading, such as a fingerprint or a retinal scan.

Two-factor authentication schemes, such as SecurID, have become popular, especially for remote users. As biometric devices become less expensive and more effective, and as user acceptance grows, especially for unobtrusive readers such as keyboard fingerprint scanners, three-factor authentication schemes may become commonplace.

Multifactor authentication makes it more difficult for potential intruders to break into remote systems by sheer brute force.

12.3.2 IMPLEMENTING USER PRIVILEGES

Because remote dial-up is essentially an access channel, many of the safeguards used for access control will apply here to help restrict the attacker from accessing critical applications and the information they hold. Such safeguards include restricting access on the basis of the user, role, or group level. User privileges, including authentication and authorization, can be implemented through RADIUS or TACACS+[1] servers. These systems integrate well with the SecurID two-factor authentication scheme described in Section 12.3.1.

---

1. TACACS+ is an authentication protocol that grew out of the original TACACS (Terminal Access Controller Access Control System) protocol but is not compatible with any previous versions of TACACS.

12.3.3 Maintaining Logs

Remote-access attempts, both successful and failed, should be logged, as well as the access to and use of sensitive applications (at least the critical commands, such as those responsible for transferring money from one account into another). Logs of access attempts can be recorded and fed to a log analysis tool to determine if a brute-force break-in has been attempted. This reactive approach can be teamed with proactively blocking access temporarily after the appropriate number of failed log-in attempts over a short period of time. In this way, even if an attacker makes only a few attempts at a time, there will be a way to trace this activity.

Although this countermeasure may not eliminate unauthorized access to applications and the pilfering of their data, recording access and potentially sensitive actions creates a trail, which can assist in tracking and identifying the offending user.

12.3.4 Creating a Demilitarized Zone

As mentioned earlier, there is little need to allow direct access to the mainframe. It is possible, and preferable, to create a demilitarized zone (DMZ) into which users enter through remote access, often through a VPN. Once in the DMZ, users can log into sensitive applications, whether they're on mainframes or servers. The DMZ offers an opportunity to separate critical applications and data from direct telephone access and thereby offers some protection against war dialing. Naturally, you will need to implement access and user authorization controls internal to the network to stop someone who has dialed in from getting to those applications, but having a DMZ certainly offers more protection than if the modem leads intruders directly into the mainframe, server, or application of interest.

Of course, it is possible to be hacked even with all of these countermeasures in place, but it would take additional time.

12.3.5 Installing Digital Lines

Modems must be connected to analog lines to work. They cannot work when connected to digital lines. This is a very good reason to put digital lines in your office space. Digital lines should reduce the incidence of rogue modems. We say "reduce" instead of "eliminate" because there are digital-to-analog converters that allow a modem to be connected and dial out over digital lines, but fortunately these have not become very popular yet. Digital lines are still an effective defense because the requirement of a digital-to-analog converter in addition to the modem itself does raise the cost of using a rogue modem.

12.3.6 PLACING CONTROLS ON VENDOR ACCOUNTS

In Section 12.1 we discussed briefly the issue of having default vendor accounts left active. There are ways to address this issue, not the least of which is simply to change all the default accounts and implement strong passwords, with different (nonstandard) user names. Passwords should be changed periodically as well. Just because a password is not expected to be used heavily does not mean that it should have a longer lifetime. In addition, logical access to these accounts should be in place only on demand. In other words, these modems should be connected for access by the vendor only when requested by the vendor for only the specific length of time requested.

A Low-Tech Path into the High-Tech World

When was the last time you scored some free food at a restaurant by sweet-talking the waiter or waitress? How often have you extracted some "extra" information from someone by giving him that extra glass of a vintage Merlot? These scenarios are examples of social engineering. If hacking can be defined as gaining access to network resources and/or data to which you don't have rights, then in the computer world social engineering can be considered hacking by any nontechnical means at your disposal.

In today's high-tech world, we seem almost entirely focused on technical means of compromising networks (and most focused on viruses and worms), but as long as humans are involved in running or managing computers in any way, there will be ways to get those humans to allow you access to resources that are supposed to be off-limits. This case study discusses a popular method of social engineering and covers a few countermeasures that can be put in place to defend against such attacks.

The case will make the point that social engineering continues in the present and should be addressed by all organizations. One additional point to consider is that although the more common hacking is becoming easier and easier because of the increasing sophistication of available hacking scripts (which allow more and more people to engage in hacking), social engineering involves no technology, and therefore absolutely anyone can engage in social engineering.

> **ASIDE:** There is a perception within the security industry that several of the "really good" hackers are actually better at social engineering (hacking the wetware) than at technical hacking (hitting the gear).

13.1 INTRODUCTION

Many news reports have held that hacking is becoming more and more *easy* because of the proliferation of hacking scripts, how-to hacking Web sites, and security books (such as this one). However, although the technical-knowledge barrier to compromising an IT infrastructure may have come down over the years, the low-tech method of compromising networks remains as prevalent and as challenging as it has always been.

Through a process called **social engineering**, attackers are able, often with little more than a friendly conversation, to gather the information they need to gain access to systems, steal network resources, and walk away with the sensitive data they want. Social engineering is one of the oldest methods of compromising a target, and although it receives less media attention than other forms of cyber attack do, such as denial of service or Web site defacements, it has remained a threat that companies must address.

One of the reasons social engineering does not receive the attention it deserves is that as our society becomes more and more technical- and IT-friendly, it becomes easier to lose sight of nontech methodologies. In addition, because social engineering is designed to bypass the technology and security mechanisms in place, it may be difficult for an organization even to know that an incident has occurred—that someone who shouldn't have access does, and that someone who shouldn't be able to read certain information can.

These attacks are launched against average employees, anyone the attacker feels she can talk into volunteering a bit too much network and security information. The average employee, or network user, knows a lot more about the IT infrastructure of his company than he might at first imagine. Some of the information that he knows or can reasonably acquire is shown in Table 13.1.

Table 13.1 Information Potentially Available to Users

Host IP address	IP address structure
Host MAC address	Services running on network
DNS information	Security measures in place
DHCP information	Name of information security officer
Host netmask	Name of CTO/CIO
Routing information (route table)	Workplace routine
Gateway address	Printer setting
Host name	Antivirus status
Host-naming convention	

Sometimes the information listed in Table 13.1 may be all that is necessary to compromise a network. Information in the hands of the wrong person can be terribly dangerous. Naturally, capturing or changing a user's password is still the main prize. Toward this end, customer service and help desk personnel are often targeted in schemes to have one or many user passwords changed.

There are many ways to perform social engineering successfully. Every social hacker has a favorite routine. The key is simply to request and get the information you want without raising any suspicion about your motives. We will discuss an incident in which an attacker was able to change an individual user's account password, and then use that account for his own nefarious purposes. In addition, we will discuss processes that can be put in place to protect against such attacks.

> **ASIDE:** Let's be clear that we're certainly not advocating social engineering. This case study isn't a policy statement in favor of this or any other such tactics. The purpose here is to educate the reader about this threat and to help illustrate how one can be protected from such an attack.

13.2 Doing Your Homework

During the Internet day-trading boom, many people in all walks of life saw riches in the roulette wheel that is publicly traded stocks. It was the mood of the day that someone could make a fortune by starting with just a few thousand dollars. It's not surprising that hackers, at least one in particular, shared such visions of grandeur. Instead of investing his own money, however, this individual dared to dream of even higher returns by utilizing the seed capital of other investors—whether they knew of their investment in his efforts or not.

The hacker in question set out to research potential online trading sites but was not necessarily motivated by which site offered the best research tools or real-time stock quotes. Instead, he was interested in learning the transaction-handling process and in finding out which firms offered the best, and worst, security in terms of handling customer data. His research included reading the relevant media reviews, surfing the competing online stock-trading firms' Web sites, and calling different companies' sales departments simply to ask about the overall process of buying stocks over the Internet and the technology that the company brought to the table.

In such questioning, the hacker was able to gather the information he needed regarding the company's processes as far as handling transactions and communicating with its customers, and he settled on one stock-trading firm in particular. We'll call it Stockmoney.com. The business process of Stockmoney.com can be summarized as follows: Once an account is created and money has been deposited, stocks can be traded at will. The user supplies a user name and password at log-in to access the site. The user is also required to enter the password again at the time of executing a trade. Whenever a trade is executed, both an e-mail and a letter are sent to the customer confirming the transaction.

The electronic and physical mailing addresses are specified by the customer at the time of account setup and can be changed online at any time. If these addresses are changed, a confirmation is sent to both the new and the old physical and/or electronic addresses—unless the user instructs the trading firm in writing not to send confirmation to the old address, because she has already moved, changed jobs, or no longer has access to the account and will not be able to receive such confirmation.

This exception, the hacker felt, would be the loophole that would allow him to use an unsuspecting user's account without that person's knowledge for at least some period of time—and long enough to hit the jackpot.

13.3 THE HACK

The hacker opened an account for himself at Stockmoney.com (with the minimum amount of money necessary) to become comfortable with the company's system, Web interface, and processes. After using the site for a while and going through the process of making a few trades, he was ready to go.

Social engineering is a con game. All you have to do is build a rapport with the target individual, and you can get all you need from that person. In this case the hacker's first goal was to find a valid user account. With that, he would change the user's contact information and simultaneously send in a signed letter (purportedly from the target user) saying not to send confirmation to the old address. This letter would give the hacker a window of opportunity—of unknown length—to make all the trades that his victim's money would allow.

The hacker started looking for a user account among people whose basic contact information he would be able to get, such as fellow employees at work. Within that group, he would at least have access to users' basic contact information through the company's records and employee directory. He started having discussions about the stock market around the office, hoping someone would let it slip out that they also used Stockmoney.com. From there, he would try to draw the user name out of that person. In addition to searching for fellow Stockmoney.com users at work, he looked in other venues where he knew people, such as his church's congregation and his health club.

The hacker was able to find three individuals who had accounts with Stockmoney.com, and he obtained their user names by complaining about the user name he had received. He claimed that the user name he wanted, smartpicker, was unavailable because someone already had it, so he had had to settle for smartpic05. In this process he was able to elicit the user names from his three colleagues, as shown in Table 13.2.

Table 13.2 Captured User Names

trader0719
jarmstrong
n0wrngtrade

He selected the user name of an individual, n0wrngtrade, who had indicated by comments in conversations that he was not an active trader (and thus would offer the hacker potentially the longest active window), and he initiated his plan.

The first thing to do was to update n0wrngtrade's contact information. He faxed in the information and mailed the notification requesting that no more letters be sent to the old address because that information was no longer valid. He called customer service at Stockmoney.com to give them the new address, inform them of the fax, and apprise them that a hard copy was coming in the mail as well. This phone call also allowed him to gauge whether he would be able to successfully fool the customer service reps into believing him to be n0wrngtrade. Knowing that user's personal information (address, phone, and so on) from company records certainly came in handy.

Now for the hard part: calling customer service as the account holder and having the password changed. The hacker conducted this attack against numerous user accounts and made several such calls, so we will not relate here a word-for-word recitation of any individual phone conversation. However, we will address the primary issues involved. In the portions of conversation that we will recount, "Jim" is Stockmoney.com's customer service rep.

Prior to the call, the hacker had to develop a believable and effective story. The story should establish the reason for the call, as well as what you're requesting (here a password change) as the most logical course of action. The hacker's story was that his account password wasn't working and needed to be reset. The story he crafted was that he had failed to access the account multiple times from different computers at different times with the correct and carefully entered password. He had sent an e-mail to customer service and had been informed in an official e-mail reply that calling customer service for a password reset would likely solve the problem.

The story must be concise; it should not take a lot of words to relate. Here's an example:

> JIM: *Hello, this is customer support. My name is Jim. How can I help you?*
>
> HACKER: *I'm having trouble with my account. My password doesn't work. I sent a message to support and was told in an e-mail from Charles Smith that having my password reset would solve the problem.*
>
> JIM: *I'm sorry you're having trouble with the account. Let me take a look at it.*
>
> HACKER: *OK.*

While using his own account, the hacker did in fact e-mail customer service claiming password problems and found that he received a standard e-mail reply signed by the head of the customer service department saying that calling the tech support help desk during its hours of operation and seeking a password reset could indeed solve this and a range of other problems. If what the hacker had received was indeed the standard reply e-mail, Jim would probably be willing to believe that such communication had taken place. Lies should always be mixed with strands of the truth.

Once you have made your request, you have to be prepared for some resistance— for example:

> JIM: *Thank you for holding, sir. I looked at your account, and I don't see anything wrong with it. What is it telling you when you can't log in?*
>
> HACKER: *I'm getting the message "Access denied, please contact customer support for assistance."*
>
> JIM: *Are you trying to log in from a new machine? Maybe you have cookies turned off?*
>
> HACKER: *No, I'm using the same computer that I've always used, and cookies are not being blocked. I've actually tried from home, work, and even my library, but it doesn't work. And I have used the account from home and work before. I've been all over the place trying to get into the account because I need to move some stock.*

The goal here is to remain polite but start to sound a little annoyed with the customer service rep. Sounding annoyed tells him that you're serious about having your request honored, but it is important not to make him so angry that he won't help you. You also want to give the customer service rep an easy out. Customer service, help desk, and telephone support personnel are evaluated, in part, on the number of customer calls they can successfully resolve without having to escalate. You want to make changing your password the easiest thing for him to do. When that happens, the job is done.

However, before immediately resetting the password, Jim wanted to run through all of the system checks at his disposal.

JIM: *Let me try one more thing. Please hold.*

HACKER: *Uh, OK.*

JIM: *Thanks for holding. I don't see anything wrong with the account. You should be able to access it fine.*

HACKER: *But I can't. My password isn't working. I know I'm typing my password correctly because I get into my e-mail account with the same password. It's just not working here, and that's probably why it needs to be changed.*

JIM: *I can change your password, but I don't see anything wrong with the account, so I don't know if that will help or if anything will change.*

HACKER: *Well, that's what the e-mail from customer service said—that resetting the password might help—and that's why I'm calling. Obviously this must have happened before, and maybe often, if this is one of the recommended solutions for this problem.*

JIM: *Can you verify your identity by giving me your address, please?*

Again the hacker must stand his ground armed with facts. It is hard to convey tone of voice in written words; we'll say simply that the tone of voice and phone persona you use must be catered to your personality as well as that of the individual to whom you're speaking. Some individuals are intimidated by a shouter, and some will casually leave the shouter on hold until they return from their coffee break. Choose carefully.

Jim's last question is a classic stalling technique. Asking for information about the problem (e.g., "What error message are you getting?") and requesting verification of the user ID are common tactics that customer service reps use to buy time while seeming to be working on the problem toward the caller's desired end. In most cases, there is little choice but to answer the questions. Sometimes, however, these questions can be deflected on grounds of their (lack of) merit—for example:

JIM: *Let me try to log in. Can you give me your password, as you are trying to enter it?*

HACKER: *Why?*

JIM: *So that I can try to log in to your account to see if it works.*

HACKER: *There's nothing wrong with the password. I know my password. I use it for my e-mail, and I have used it here as well. It just stopped working now. I don't see how giving you my password will help.*

JIM: *I just want to see the error.*

HACKER: *But I've already described the error. And we've already seen the path to follow. So I don't see how it will help. Even if it works for you, but not for me, I will still need the password reset so that I can get in.*

One thing that the trend of security awareness has done (we hope) is to give people more reverence for the secrecy of their password. Therefore, you certainly can feel confident refusing to give out your password if asked for it, whether over the phone or in person.

Another delay technique is the request for a Social Security number:

JIM: *Can you please give me your Social Security number?*

HACKER: *Why?*

JIM: *It's part of the process we go through when we change a password.*

HACKER: *You're going to change my password to the last four digits of my Social Security number, right? Isn't that the process? So why do you need to have the rest of my number? If I don't know it, I won't be able to log in, so how does giving you my Social Security number help, except that it gives you my number?*

In this case, Stockmoney.com's policy was to use the last four digits of the user's Social Security number as the default password—a bad idea in and of itself. However, this practice certainly creates grounds for not surrendering one's Social Security number. The caller will have to know at least the appropriate portion of the number if that is what will be used as the default password, and a case can be made, as shown here, that the caller need not be forced to surrender the entire number to prove he knows the last four digits. People are often hesitant to give out their Social Security numbers anyway.

Ultimately, the goal of the exercise is to hear the following:

JIM: *All right, I've changed your password to the last four digits of your Social Security number. You will be asked to change it as soon as you sign in again.*

Bingo!

HACKER: *Thank you.*
JIM: *Is there anything else I can help you with today?*
HACKER: *No, thank you.*

If we are able to survive any system testing and delay tactics by the customer service rep and to create a credible scenario in which our objective (resetting the password) is the simplest solution, this is certainly how the conversation should end.

After his conversation with Jim, the hacker had the password, and all letters and communications from Stockmoney.com would go to him instead of to the real account owner. This was his chance to hit it big. He made the stock trades he wanted—not only using the victim's money, but also taking as much as he could on margin. Only wanting to use the site for a short period of time (no more than one or two days to be safe), he sold when prices were high and ordered his money to be wired into a bank from which an associate would be able to withdraw it easily. (Naturally, he didn't take the chance of withdrawing the money himself.)

Exit Strategy

If the customer service rep doesn't bite on changing the password, you can't just hang up. Doing so might cause the rep to flag the activity on this account as a sign of potential attack (i.e., to place the account under observation). These days, firms are becoming more accustomed to being targets of social engineering and may be tracking requests for password changes and the like. Instead of just hanging up, you want to have an exit strategy. Allow the customer service rep to give you some suggestions to try before you hang up.

If you're going to try again, you probably want to try within the next hour or so, hoping to get a different customer service rep, and to call in before any flag has had time to propagate through the system. You have to be careful, though, because there's no telling how fast any suspicion about this account might spread through the system; it is often deemed safer to move on to the next account.

13.4 THE FALLOUT

In this case study the hacker was able to replicate the process just described on a few accounts, in each case trying not to speak to the same person at customer service because he was not comfortable with using different accents or changing his voice. Luckily, customer service personnel identify themselves when they answer the phone, so if someone he had already dealt with in the past answered, he just hung up and called again after a while. Naturally, when the rightful owners were unable to get into their own accounts and called in to have the password reset, Stockmoney.com began to take note of the disturbing pattern. After a few complaints, they noticed that someone had changed the contact information for several customers, had called in to get passwords reset, and then had begun to manipulate those accounts to his own benefit, stealing the funds.

Ultimately, Stockmoney.com had no choice but to compensate the account holders for any losses, because in effect they had granted an unauthorized user access to those accounts. The date of the address change served as a marker identifying the onset of the unauthorized activity. Repaying the losses meant replacing either the customers' stockholdings or the cash equivalents as of the established time of the address change (naturally, the victims chose the greater of the two values) and wiping out any amounts owned on margin, again for trades after the time of the address change.

Stockmoney.com had to eat the losses, though their business and cyber insurance would help with portions of the losses. Naturally, management became quite keen on improving methods for authenticating callers into customer service and tightening the password reset process. One step they took was to identify and terminate all the customer service representatives involved in the calls in this case. (This move was unfair, of course, because the reps had *mostly* just been following orders; they had not willfully participated in the crime.)

The users had lost a certain amount of faith in Stockmoney.com and online trading in general, as you might imagine, although having their accounts reset was certainly a relief. To encourage them to stay with Stockmoney.com, the company offered them free trades for a year and promised to monitor activity on their accounts more closely.

13.5 Lessons Learned

As we have seen, attacks such as the one described in this chapter can prove quite costly and should be guarded against. Companies need to address the risk of social engineering with much the same vigor that is applied against more-mainstream, technical attacks. Certainly, with just a telephone, a talented social hacker can steal more-critical information (and real money) from, and cause greater compromise to, an organization than a team of "script kiddies" armed with the latest Microsoft RPC buffer overflow exploit downloaded from the Internet.

One action that Stockmoney.com took after discovering this attack was to bring in a security consultant to identify countermeasures they could take to stop anything like it from happening again. The first thing the consultant did was to perform a top-to-bottom review of Stockmoney.com's call-handling and -tracking processes.

An immediate recommendation was to automate the password change process so that users would be allowed to change passwords themselves only if they entered the old password. When speaking to essentially a stranger, a caller (who is supposed to be an account holder) understandably might have concerns about handing over a password; customer service personnel do not know user passwords for very valid security reasons. Moving the password reset function from customer service to an automated process can close this loophole.

In an automated password reset process, users can be asked for a password, as well as for other identifying information, such as address, phone, and Social Security number (if applicable) without the fear of giving this information to an unknown person. In addition, an automated process can include a verification step based on an identifying question. The question can be anything—from something simple, such as, Where were you born? to something like, What is the atomic mass of Au? The point is that users choose the question and answer themselves, so the process gives the company some assurance that the person requesting the password change is really the customer. (Note that the answer to the selected question doesn't actually have to be correct. The company will only be matching the fields, not check someone's knowledge that the atomic mass of gold is 196.96655 amu.) An automated password change process has the additional benefit of saving money because it is well documented that a great deal of a help desk/tech support group's time is tied up in password resets.

Further, standard operating procedures for customer service/tech support should include provisions for verifying caller identity before performing critical operations such as resetting accounts, changing passwords, or giving out sensitive information. These guidelines, however, are already part of the standard arsenal. What is called for is a recommitment to effective security awareness training for all client service staff, especially individuals who are often targets of social engineering, including customer service and phone support personnel. The more the staff understand the need for security and comprehend the risks in the environment, the more willing they will be to go through the hurdles of enforcing strict security.

What is really needed is a mechanism that allows the organization to identify and track potential social engineering attacks. Customer service reps should be able to flag accounts of users when a suspicious event (such as a password change in close proximity to a change of address) occurs. Through such flags on user accounts, the security staff might be able to track and develop a profile of the attack that will ultimately lead to identifying the culprit. Such monitoring could also be used to warn other members who might fit the victim profile.

Specifically in the case discussed here, if three compromised user accounts belong to people who work at the same company, then other members who are employees of that company might be at risk, or the culprit might be another employee or someone else who is privy to the company's information.

Finally, social engineering should be included in regular security assessments, including using social engineering techniques as a part of any penetration testing or ethical hacking efforts. The reason is that although social engineering is indeed an age-old concept, techniques and processes are always changing.

PART V
COMPUTER FORENSICS

INDUSTRIAL ESPIONAGE

Stated simply, **industrial espionage** is stealing data from one company for the benefit of another. Long considered to be nothing more than a rumor, industrial espionage is now understood to be a serious threat against which corporations have to defend themselves.

This case study presents an instance of what turns out to have been industrial espionage—though it doesn't involve the more glamorous roles of secret agent-type spies and cloak-and-dagger rendezvous to exchange documents for cash. Nonetheless, the potential damages to the victim firm are real, as are the consequences for the guilty party.

The legal issues surrounding industrial espionage and the protection of intellectual property assets are also discussed. This discussion is meant to be a starting point rather than an ending point. Readers are advised to consult with legal counsel if they find themselves involved in an industrial espionage case.

14.1 SPIES ALL AROUND US

The following case study will discuss how corporate policy and procedures and computer forensic investigation can be used to prove guilt (or innocence) in situations involving industrial espionage.

Obtaining business or competitive intelligence through information in the public domain that has been classified "for public use" (or is "unclassified) is considered legal. Gaining information through a breach of confidentiality is *not* legal. The latter scenario is a case of industrial espionage, like the case presented here.

This chapter will focus on policies for protecting intellectual assets.

It was August 23, 2001. We received a call from Mandy Weaver, a manager of Department 123 at XYZ Genetic Research Labs, who told us of her suspicion that an employee had left Department 123 with confidential and sensitive information. The employee, Tiffany Hamil, had informed XYZ that she was joining ABC Genetic Research Labs, a competing firm. Hamil had been overheard in the office saying, "XYZ will lose significant accounts but will never know why, and will never be able to tie it back to me or you."

We requested a meeting with Department 123, along with the legal, human resources, audit, and security departments, in order to get the background on the case, establish a preliminary timeline, and obtain copies of relevant corporate policies and procedures. On the basis of these meetings, we established a preliminary timeline as follows:

August 8	Employee Tiffany Hamil submits resignation to XYZ, effective August 18.
August 16	XYZ's legal department discusses confidentiality requirements with Hamil.
August 18	Hamil's last day at XYZ.
August 19	Hamil's first day at ABC.
August 21	Mandy Weaver informs security department of the possibility that Hamil has left with confidential sensitive information.
August 23	XYZ's corporate security department calls us to ask for assistance.

After establishing this timeline, we met with various departments to get background and policies.

XYZ alleged that Hamil had taken confidential and proprietary research and development material, including formulas and lab notes. In addition, Hamil was alleged to have "appropriated" a complete price and customer listing from XYZ.

As indicated in the timeline, on August 16 Tiffany had been reminded by XYZ's legal counsel of the confidentiality and nondisclosure agreement that she had signed with XYZ when she accepted employment. Hamil's signature on this document might provide a legal remedy if she had violated any of her agreements.

In the employee nondisclosure agreement that Hamil had signed, she had agreed to terms similar to those outlined in the sidebar that follows. We recommend that you consult your legal counsel for a nondisclosure agreement appropriate for your situation.

XYZ Genetic Research Labs Employee Nondisclosure Agreement[1]

For good consideration, and in consideration of being employed by XYZ Genetic Research Labs, I, Tiffany Hamil, hereby agree to and acknowledge the following:

1. That during the course of my employment, there may be disclosed to me certain trade secrets of XYZ Genetic Research Labs, said trade secrets consisting of but not necessarily limited to

   (a) Technical information: Methods, processes, formulas, compositions, systems, techniques, inventions, patents, machines, computer programs, and research and development projects.

   (b) Business information: Customer lists, pricing data, sources of supply, financial data and marketing, production, or merchandising systems or plans.

2. That I shall not, during or at any time after the termination of my employment with XYZ Genetic Research Labs, use for myself or others, or disclose or divulge to others, including future employers, any trade secrets, confidential information, or any other proprietary data of XYZ Genetic Research Labs in violation of this agreement.

1. This agreement, with minor modification, is taken from the Internet Legal Resource Guide at http://www.ilrg.com/forms/non-disc.html.

3. That upon the termination of my employment from XYZ Genetic Research Labs

   (a) I shall return to XYZ Genetic Research Labs all documents and property, including but not necessarily limited to, drawings, blueprints, reports, manuals, correspondence, customer lists, computer programs, and all other materials, and all copies thereof, relating in any way to XYZ's business, or in any way obtained by me during the course of my employ. I further agree that I shall not retain copies, notes, or abstracts of the foregoing.

   (b) XYZ Genetic Research Labs may notify any future or prospective employer or third party of the existence of this agreement, and shall be entitled to full injunctive relief for any breach.

   (c) This agreement shall be binding upon me and my personal representatives and successors in interest, and shall inure to the benefit of XYZ Genetic Research Labs, its successors, and assigns.

XYZ Genetic Research Labs also had corporate policy backing them up. XYZ had a computer use policy that reminded employees that it was their duty to protect XYZ intellectual assets from unauthorized disclosure. XYZ would also be able to show that its employees were regularly reminded of the policy and that Hamil had in fact signed the policy and had been reminded about it often and not long before her departure.

Our first order of business was to secure the personal computer and any other equipment that Tiffany Hamil had used. Immediately upon securing the equipment, we tagged everything with a chain of custody (COC) form. Section 14.5 discusses the COC form and its importance in tracking evidence through a forensic investigation.

After securing the equipment, we put a hold on all electronic mail, Internet, and system logs that could have recorded any of Hamil's activity. It is important to check first that logging was enabled, and that activity had, in fact, been recorded. Although starting logs in the middle of an investigation can certainly be helpful, such logs may not be allowed as primary evidence in a court of law because they would not meet one of the guidelines regarding computer evidence admissibility—specifically the guideline stating that evidence must be generated in the "normal course of business" (see Section 14.6). Logs that are activated in the middle of an investigation are not considered part of the normal course of business.

It was now time to process the PC in question for evidence. Specific procedures and tools were required for this engagement. We prepared our forensic tool bag to include the software listed in Table 14.1 and the hardware listed in Table 14.2.

Table 14.1 Software Used for a Forensic Investigation

Forensic software from New Technologies, Inc.
Norton Utilities
Norton AntiVirus
TCP/IP boot disk with drivers and software for backup drive
DOS boot disk

Table 14.2 Hardware and Supplies Used for a Forensic Investigation

Handheld mini cassette recorder
Cassette tapes
Digital camera
Memory cards
Backup batteries for camera and recorder
Extra hard drives (2)
Computer repair toolkit with antistatic wrist strap
Diskettes (50) with labels
Evidence labels
Chain of custody forms
Masking tape
Markers

The ways in which the software were used will become apparent in the description of the case study. New Technologies, Inc. (NTI) produces a great many tools for computer forensic investigations. The use of several NTI tools will be discussed in this case study.

Of the hardware items listed, the cassette recorder and camera are for recording any notes and thoughts during the investigation and for taking pictures of the computers and devices to be investigated. Additional memory cards and backup batteries for these devices are important. The masking tape is used to mark wires and connection ends. The antistatic wrist strap is necessary because static electricity and computers don't function very well together. The evidence labels and chain of custody forms are absolutely necessary for preserving evidence for later use in a courtroom.

14.2 THE INVESTIGATION

As for conducting the investigation itself, the four A's of computer forensics guide the investigator's actions:

1. Acquire evidence
2. Authenticate the evidence
3. Analyze the evidence
4. Archive the evidence

We follow these guidelines throughout any investigation after the initial planning and consultation with the victim.

14.2.1 ACQUIRE EVIDENCE

All evidence needs to be acquired and secured in a manner that does not alter it in any way. We begin by documenting the configuration of the system, including any attached peripherals, as they were when we arrived. This documentation includes taking pictures of the system from all angles. We also attach masking tape to all cable ends and label it to identify what the cable is connected to. Marking the cables in this way will help if the the system is reconnected in the future.

The system may have been moved from its point of operation before we arrived. For example, the computer may have been located on a user's desktop, but upon that user's departure from the firm, it may have been moved into storage awaiting reassignment to another employee. Any such changes—again, made prior to our arrival—should also be documented.

After the preliminary documentation, you should always shut down the computer. In this case, the computer had already been shut down because Hamil had turned in her computer, and fortunately it had not yet been reassigned to another employee. It is important to shut down the computer in case destructive processes are running in the background. If a computer is on and you need to process it as evidence, first document what is on the screen before shutting it down. It is also recommended that you remove any network connectivity.

Because computer forensic investigations are generally performed in response to a possible crime or criminal event, it is imperative to establish and maintain the proper chain of custody (through the use of forms and evidence labels) for all devices seized. A separate chain of custody form must be filled out for each device and for each component—for example, hard drive—if it is removed from the system for investigation.

Secure the computer. If you are not in a good location where you have enough room, resources, or the privacy necessary to complete your review, the computer should be transported to a secure location. In this case study our client, XYZ Genetic Research Labs, was able to give us a lockable conference room that had the necessary space and the requisite environment.

Create a working backup of the original hard drive being investigated. The original hard drive is *never* altered or examined directly. The backup that is taken should be a mirror image or bit stream backup of the hard drive, not just a file-by-file backup. The backup tool you use is up to you. Remember that you cannot write any data to the original hard drive; therefore, make sure that the backup process does not accidentally alter the original in any way.

Unlike other special investigations, in this forensic review we were able to use a TCP/IP boot disk to create the mirror image. Note that use of such technology should be severely restricted because it is very difficult to accomplish. Other backup methodologies that can be used will be listed at the end of this section.

A **TCP/IP boot disk** is a boot disk that contains only the necessary drivers for the network interface cards (NICs) in a particular computer. We boot from the floppy drive (or possibly CD-ROM) of the machine under investigation with minimal drivers, just enough to establish a secure network connection to the network, as illustrated in Figure 14.1. We *never* boot again from the original hard drive. Booting from the hard drive would corrupt any possible evidence and ensure that any destructive program operating in the background would continue to operate.

After the disk has established a connection, we generally issue two NET USE commands. A NET USE command establishes a network connection to a server. The first NET USE is directed to the computer and folder that contained the software and to the backup options used to make the mirror image. The second is directed to the machine to which the backup will be sent. We can then take advantage of network speed and bandwidth.

We go through the same process after taking out the original hard drive and installing a copy. The first NET USE command is to the computer and folder that contain the software used to make the image. The second is to the backup machine to bring the original backup down through the RESTORE process.

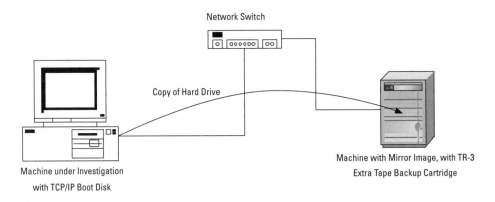

Figure 14.1 Setup of Data Copy

Different acquisition methods—involving different software, hardware, and processes—should be used to create a mirror backup depending on the situation and the target of the backup. Although not complete, the following list describes other methods of acquisition that we have used in the past or use now:

- **Tape drive acquisition**. Acquisition using a tape or Jaz drive connected to the computer under examination via a SCSI or parallel port.

- **Parallel port cable acquisition**. Acquisition using a parallel port lap-link cable between the computer under examination and the forensic computer that will acquire the image.

- **Network cable acquisition**. Acquisition using a crossover network cable between the computer under examination and the forensic computer that will acquire the image.

- **Disk-to-disk acquisition**. Acquisition using the hard drive from the computer under examination placed in the forensic computer.

- **FastBloc acquisition**. Acquisition using a hardware write-blocked device from Guidance Software attached to a forensic computer and the computer under examination. Such devices give you the ability to review or preview the evidence without contaminating it.

- **Road MASSter acquisition**. Acquisition using a portable forensic unit from Carinex. Such acquisition can proceed at high speed (over 1GB per minute). Everything needed is contained inside a special briefcase.

As mentioned earlier, you *never* want to boot from a suspect hard drive. Booting from a hard drive can cause you to alter and/or lose evidence. Before backing up the hard drive, we use the NTI (www.forensics-intl.com) utility GetTime to document the CMOS date and time on the computer under investigation:

```
A:> GETTIME
```

The results of the file will be saved on the diskette in the following format:

```
STM-MMDD.00X
```

where MM is the month, DD is the day, and X is the file occurrence number.

We compare this system date and time to the current (or actual) date and time on a watch and document any differences on paper, and then we edit GETTIME.DOC later in the investigation, noting the source of the actual date and time—for example, a Lance Hawk Timex wristwatch. GETTIME.DOC should then be edited and printed (but not on the suspect machine and printer). Here is a sample printout of GETTIME.DOC (not from the XYZ case):

```
Forensic System Status Documentation Tool  GETTIME.EXE Version 2.0
-----------------------------------------------------------------
Licensed to Lance Hawk
-----------------------------------------------------------------

        System Time set at 12:28:10
        System Date set at 02-18-2003
-----------------------------------------------------------------
Make a note as to what the actual time and date is and compare.

The actual time was observed to be _12:28:17_.  LPH initial

The actual date was observed to be _02-18-03_.  LPH initial

Source of the actual time and date _LPH Timex wristwatch_____.
```

In this file we also record the current time on the watch and document any differences. After using GetTime, we use PTable from NTI to document and analyze the hard-disk partitions. This analysis identifies the specific type of partitions, thereby suggesting which specific forensic software we should use. The PTable information should agree with the information that we get from the backup software used, which is the next step in authenticating the evidence.

Once again, you can use DOS redirection to document PTable:

```
A:\PTABLE > PTABLE.DOC
```

Here is some sample output from PTable (again not from the XYZ case):

```
    PTable version 1.5 -- Partition Table Analysis tool by NTI
        Build date Thu Nov 09 12:49:00pm 2000
```

```
The following Hard Disk partitions were found on this system:
    XBIOS                  |  Begining   |    Ending    |   Size in Kbytes
Vol     HD System          | Cyl Head Sec | Cyl Head Sec |(1 Kb = 1024 bytes)
Boot C: 80 FAT16 > 32Mb |   0   1   1 | 1021  63  63 |    2060320
Boot    81 DiskMgr DDO  |   0   0  10 | 1459 255  63 |   11773435
```

In this case PTable indicated that FAT16 (Windows 95 before release 2) was on the computer being investigated. Note that the second line of the output specifies DiskMgr, which is a program that was used to get around previous drive size limitations in FAT16 file systems. After ascertaining that the backup software has worked with the operating system as indicated by the PTable utility, we begin the backup process.

Here are some other systems you might see in the field:

- **FAT32** (for Windows 95 release 2, Windows 98, Windows ME, and Windows 2000)
- **NTFS** (for Windows NT, Windows 2000, and Windows XP)
- **VFAT** (for Windows 95 and Windows NT 3.5)
- **HPFS** (for OS/2 and Windows NT)

Remember, not all backup software can work with every operating system. Sometimes it takes a bit of effort to identify a good match. It is also important to make sure you have a stable and effective version of the backup software—one that you have experience with and are confident will work effectively. In the absence of confidence, get the latest version. Unfortunately, however, there is no substitute for experience.

If any diskettes are involved in the investigation, you should make a mirror image or bit stream backups of them as well. You can use the DOS DISKCOPY command with the /V (verification) switch. Note that whatever software you use to create the mirror image backup, it must have been tested in court and have withstood defense challenges. Contact the vendor for confirmation and proof.

14.2.2 AUTHENTICATE THE EVIDENCE

Once the original evidence has been copied, it is time to authenticate that the copy is an accurate reproduction of the original. It does no good to investigate a copy if it isn't an exact and precise copy. Original evidence is *never* directly examined. Original evidence is only copied, and in turn the copy is examined. Sometimes we make multiple copies in order to have a second backup available in case something happens to the one under investigation.

The CRCMd5 tool from NTI helps authenticate the evidence by producing a CRC checksum and an MD5 digest on both the original and the copy. Once produced, these values can be compared, and if they are identical, they constitute proof that the original and the copy are mirror images. This documentation needs to be stored in the same manner that evidence is stored. The **CRC checksum** and **MD5 digest** are mathematical values that we produce by running a one-way mathematical algorithm over the input (the original data and backup copy) that produces a mathematically unique output. By *unique* here, we mean that any two inputs that are different, in even a single character, will have different output values to a very high degree of certainty. Therefore, matching values essentially confirm that the data has not been compromised or altered during the copying process and can potentially be admitted as evidence.

To generate a CRC checksum and an MD5 digest for all files on drive `C:` and redirect the output as headerless text to the file `A:\CRCMD5.doc`, we would issue the following command:

```
A:\CRCMD5 C: /s >CRCMD5.DOC
```

Following is a sample listing created with CRCMd5. Note that only the root directory, `C:`, and the first subdirectory, `\DOS`, are listed. A full listing of a hard drive would be much longer. The `/s` option will list corresponding directories and subdirectories. The field `ATTR` is for file attributes such as `H` (hidden), `R` (read-only), `A` (archive), and `S` (system).

Sample Directory C:\

FILE NAME	LENGTH	DATE	ATTR	CRC-32	-----------MD5 DIGEST------------
===========	========	======	======	========	==================================
SUHDLOG.DAT	6451	05/05/01	HR	893c0a4c	5043dd2cb91f7cf5 d47e05b55c2ee057
SUHDLOG.BAK	19627	05/05/01	HR	c04c766a	6bfbb3b0ad3f65ba 73ea2dc5fca5abbc
COMMAND.DOS	54619	09/30/93	R	acd2e2f6	c98e0df201047722 fec01cfda0db3ce0
MSDOS.SYS	1646	05/05/01	HRS	85f4670a	aa145c54695534ad a649ebd87428068c
SUHDLOG.---	7738	10/23/96	HR	b0db49d3	ef44981ab1b9a3ab 942243215671e6c4
BOOTLOG.PRV	29183	05/11/01	AH	e7fafd55	dd73b113c8dfc74c 31923e6fb89e277b
CONFIG.OLD	109	10/23/96		ec283c0e	df90cdb4b7bf95d3 4b011fd0eae1c6df
AUTOEXEC.OLD	84	10/24/96		dbf90dcd	b4e3576a12571f3d 97f39a362f47d1bf
CONFIG.DOS	204	10/23/96		702ee315	591afd8239dd94b2 5b504ba21ae5d0a4
AUTOEXEC.002	147	05/06/01	A	84742f2f	d38ada016be17e18 32cd29dff27ee49d
PAGECNT.H	357	03/21/01	A	27f97f7	650c5170f87d9854 fe4d85340e001297
CONFIG.SYD	273	05/11/01	A	482677f0	3abe15000251a0dc 743c469ac7f6c129
DBLSPACE.INI	84	08/02/97	HRS	1c61d555	67b0b294b23e3255 3a389943e2a7199f
SETUPLOG.OLD	45647	05/05/01	H	5b8cf0f2	a784aa81542e3f58 dd251694bf62e1d9
SHOCKW~1.EXE	0	07/21/97		0	0000000000000000 0000000000000000
AUTOEXEC.001	139	04/20/98		6ac0fb38	84563fecd73180b6 112c1a77c1c369ac
MBRBAK.DM	512	05/04/98		cd970690	2967121506f394ea fc9a7a52649ce75e
AUTOEXEC.BAK	147	05/05/01	A	390c66a	7b3cb7dfce1ce4f3 5460f9f9e285d488
AUTOEXEC.BAT	147	05/06/01	A	84742f2f	d38ada016be17e18 32cd29dff27ee49d
MSDOS.DOS	38138	09/30/93	HRS	c05f942b	75959bc417c19135 b982f7959ee9c92a
MSDOS.BAK	1634	05/05/01	HRS	e0fd5720	489bd95374137f8f 6f0ac31d3f8a0114
IO.SYS	214836	08/24/96	HRS	ef1122a2	35c813f9f84e68f0 1b675cec3841b435
MSDOS.001	1634	05/05/01	HRS	e0fd5720	489bd95374137f8f 6f0ac31d3f8a0114
VERSIGN.P12	4390	06/01/99	A	a2f5bdaa	58ca2a10c69c3ea1 f1e1dd4b37f1830a
CONFIG.002	69	05/11/01	A	8045c988	e0b2f45c4fcc24d6 9bbee4401d50859e
AUTOEXEC.003	147	05/06/01	A	84742f2f	d38ada016be17e18 32cd29dff27ee49d
MSDOS.002	1646	05/05/01	HRS	85f4670a	aa145c54695534ad a649ebd87428068c
APCIPUB.CRT	803	06/01/99	A	854ffcea	694ccaf3ace11a1b 4bf0c6a826fe5f43
LOGO.SYS	129078	08/24/96	H	d0b0b399	534407f0fb482094 8e322aa7cf5e4990
SYSTEM.1ST	3090692	05/05/01	HRS	2e54a6bc	5bf804a8354a0c6d 9cc44dad90b9f445
FAX.DOC	69	06/03/00	A	d7d3ed34	492d4e5034d4a4e0 6e76d0928fd2dab7
TUBPATH.BAT	22	07/18/00	A	9862b95c	cfce16f3de43e403 0394cc2cbdc86c40
SCHDPLUS.INI	49	05/10/00	A	2774fe6b	6e820d2dc6f611e4 6d3e11ac3c79f5b1
AUTOEXEC.BIT	135	06/11/99	A	173cd57f	ae5d1889398a9c04 6a791ea769ee34ef
LOG.TXT	0	05/28/02	A	0	0000000000000000 0000000000000000
STUB.LOG	20592	11/05/01	A	c4151e53	a4d68c70c3b80ea7 330d30f78df7dd26

Directory C:\DOS

FILE NAME	LENGTH	DATE	ATTR	CRC-32	-----------MD5 DIGEST------------	
=========	======	====	====	======	=================================	
DRVSPACE.BIN	71287	07/11/95		46d9da28	2c38baabdd0bbe36	77eeb0f3841c2ed4
DBLSPACE.BAT	403	07/11/95		f4351167	9e5203f68b75adda	a024f1d2681b3eac
DEFRAG.BAT	339	07/11/95		b835a5e7	816c38b511e60efb	025888a53a54ad08
DRVSPACE.BAT	329	07/11/95		7495220d	7570d72a0e5d6cd4	5040fbc8c5ed1c07
DBLSPACE.BIN	71287	07/11/95		46d9da28	2c38baabdd0bbe36	77eeb0f3841c2ed4
DBLSPACE.SYS	15831	07/11/95		275747b6	d6c4c40caf932c45	fc264e09c800b915
DRVSPACE.SYS	15831	07/11/95		275747b6	d6c4c40caf932c45	fc264e09c800b915
SCANDISK.BAT	152	07/11/95		7bc0179c	9d6bd9bd69e039f2	b5afbbf424d934f4
EXPAND.EXE	16129	09/30/93		a09fcf14	917a703374f842a2	ab2cfdbb9454f9e4
OSETUP.EXE	160720	08/21/95		61369f4a	5d9031f28a8aee63	e335505155c51d12
OSETUP.INF	1820	11/26/95		b148e66	ae843a7ac45a8ed3	6ca6e813e091bb2b
MSD.PIF	967	05/25/97		ce53b3f3	ac7a150fd2420e36	09defb877dd89c0a
OSETUP.SYS	39	08/24/95		36ab9958	e8dd24773c2e804e	61d3f10734fc1e13
UNDELETE.PIF	967	12/02/96		2c94e232	20be2e556ef88e79	c0d52b6910b2348b
QBASIC.EXE	194309	09/30/93		4ead2021	f84f0bf74b830603	a29f77b11b9e4833
APPEND.EXE	10774	09/30/93		746f5417	487d985dc691564f	75ebacb4b757496d
DBLWIN.HLP	8597	09/30/93		549ad7fb	8e21a3f32ea7d5ed	35a68331269b3827
DISKCOMP.COM	10748	09/30/93		755975cf	7d44b8da2489675d	a0fd42a2f96986ea
DOSHELP.HLP	5667	09/30/93		ff56ae42	69c4969a52f121bf	fa227fa192db577c
DRIVER.SYS	5406	09/30/93		ede07ee0	7daa31644808b693	d9f3c6441193db77
FASTHELP.EXE	11481	09/30/93		97adaf5c	89ee3f94f207bd74	b2c16bd27e531b9f
FASTOPEN.EXE	12082	09/30/93		bc0da3ec	dce3ebff45016ff1	6416a1ceb631971c
GRAPHICS.COM	19742	09/30/93		ec264b82	33f61083be04f8e3	50a65c2b50d7e08d
HELP.COM	413	09/30/93		1b5ac11c	1caba11891a5d217	571a133be8bb8d02
HIMEM.SYS	29136	09/30/93		ded7aa9b	d96aaa22ca28b8d5	5570429e4e8617e7
INTERLNK.EXE	17197	09/30/93		a28591a7	871dad393adba453	7e763ad59302ab18
INTERSVR.EXE	37426	09/30/93		fd2d05a1	aa04841234ddb0aa	11529df3380f60cc
POWER.EXE	8052	09/30/93		d529a7ca	fc5cad5db544c4d4	bc55aeda598a0feb
VFINTD.386	5295	09/30/93		c2b4053d	4e3983e1c564548f	936c5c53a1cca58c
CHKSTATE.SYS	41600	09/30/93		3068202e	6548811e80d36d49	76052e05e31742ed
DBLSPACE.HLP	80724	09/30/93		aaea18f0	6ec26081adf4de8b	af290653b3ced234
DBLSPACE.INF	2620	09/30/93		93390092	aa25125463591c43	e7c5629f5d0b8766
LOADFIX.COM	1131	09/30/93		f18750e4	536460507b20ae0f	03d7bee8111028cf
MEMMAKER.EXE	119557	09/30/93		18a76de6	d11ca5b9e7de7c43	4b0812958e1081da
MEMMAKER.HLP	17237	09/30/93		55fbe1e9	2327811fca14b947	79328982d65cae65
MEMMAKER.INF	2911	09/30/93		f0ebded	f746b7e9546e1926	9a4cfa738d73634d
MSD.COM	867	09/30/93		906fbec	3faf9b29a9da858a	277d2efc755de974
MSD.EXE	158470	09/30/93		cea66e61	c0dfb48743671254	fe9cae9e2a121c47

```
QBASIC.HLP      130881 09/30/93     7f4661e3 4d0b9e7d5a07d717 23e725c2bb07fb82
REPLACE.EXE      20274 09/30/93     2504d5d0 698cebe154201ba8 ff0cf2c27055420d
HELP.HLP        296844 09/30/93     e71c82d2 d8819c8f1878f97f a2c3aa1b18d4730b
MONOUMB.386       8783 09/30/93     dda52144 0d33605d20095399 c95a571b603f8214
PRINT.EXE        15656 09/30/93     6296d9ca fc274a56dec9b54a be0ed7a0a66ee5d3
$WPM1D1F.DOC     32256 02/05/02 A   84e9c585 38a3db70a945119f bb62d685cf164c48
~HP3A37.TMP          0 04/03/02 A          0 0000000000000000 0000000000000000
~GL_0967.EXE      2560 01/27/99     268204cf 815372073da85b20 98a37ded84083c8a
```

Once we have the checksum and digest information for the C: drive, we can compare these values to those of the copy (which we calculate immediately after making the copy) and if the values match, we can assume that on the bit stream level they are identical.

> **ASIDE:** Remember to run CRCMd5 against all media seized and copies made!

Remove the original hard drive and label it with information as entered on the chain of custody form. Then secure the original hard drive. Depending on the acquisition method used (turn back a few pages for a description of methods), you will most likely be examining the hard-drive copy in a forensic computer or in one similar to the computer being investigated. You will need to be careful here so that you do not run into BIOS and hard-drive geometry issues.

Insert the mirrored hard drive into the forensic computer for further analysis. Then insert a DOS boot disk into the floppy drive. Run PTable and compare with the original. Note that the space occupied may differ because the hard-drive copy may not map to the exact size of the original. This difference should not affect the CRC checksums or MD5 digests, nor will it affect the examination of the evidence. Run CRCMd5 against the copy and compare as discussed earlier.

You can now label the original hard drive with information as entered on another chain of custody form. The hard drive must then be secured under lock and key. (See Figure 14.3 for a completed sample chain of custody form, and Figure 14.2 for a blank chain of custody form that you can use.)

14.2.3 ANALYZE THE EVIDENCE

Now that a full, accurate, and precise copy of the original has been created (and the original is stored securely), we can begin to analyze the hard-drive copy. Of all the forensic processing steps, this one will take the longest, with the total amount of time depending on the amount of analysis done and the size of the hard drive.

We will investigate the normal files, file slack, and unallocated space. **Normal files** are all the user-created, system configuration, and other files that are on the drive. **File slack** is space that consists of memory dumps as files are closed. Data dumped from memory is stored at the end of each normal file to which additional space was allocated but never used. To view what is in this space, you would need forensics software or a hex editor. NTI has a software tool, GetSlack, that allows you to capture all file slack to one physical file that can then be searched repeatedly with the NTI tools IPFilter, Filter_I, and TextSearch Plus. IPFilter searches for Web addresses, electronic mail addresses, graphics files, and zip (compressed) files. Filter_I filters out unuseful binary data and data not likely to be a word. TextSearch Plus searches for text only, but using GetSlack or Get-Free (discussed next), it has the ability to search slack and free (unallocated) space without previously capturing the slack and free space.

Unallocated space is the space occupied by erased or deleted files. Whenever a file is deleted in Windows or DOS, what is deleted is not the actual physical file, but the pointer to the file. That file's space in memory is now marked as "available," but until something is written over it, the data is still there. One can easily recover unallocated space with an undelete program or forensics software. NTI's GetFree tool allows you to capture all unallocated space to one physical file that can then be searched, again with IPFilter and Filter_1.

To search for text on a Windows 95 machine, we have always had the most success with NTI's TextSearch Plus tool.

First insert your DOS boot disk. After booting to the floppy drive, which is often the A: drive, insert the TextSearch Plus disk and enter the following command to execute the program:

```
A:\> txtsrchp
```

TextSearch Plus is an indexing tool that will search the identified files or file space for particular keywords or strings. You can search up to 120 words of up to 30 characters each. Each search word must be separated by a carriage return (pressing **Enter**). Complete details on the use of this tool appear in Chapter 16 (Cyber Extortion).

Clearly, successful use of this tool requires the correct selection of keywords. And the type of investigation performed will dictate the keywords to search for. In this case we would search for the words *confidential* (to get hits on documents that were stamped "Confidential") and *ABC* (for ABC Genetic Research Labs). One important note about TextSearch Plus is that the list of keywords is not saved. It is strongly recommended that you save the keywords in a file for purposes of documentation. The search will then be conducted, and results (hits on the keywords) will be printed out in their order of appearance within the normal files, unallocated space, and slack space.

The search in the XYZ case yielded the following results:

- **Résumé and cover letter of Tiffany Hamil sent to ABC Genetic Research Labs on July 7.** This is OK, in and of itself. Employees are allowed to use their current employer's network to send out their résumés.
- **Letter of acceptance of the ABC job from Tiffany Hamil dated July 23.** Again, the fact that she chose to join ABC and to inform them of her decision before speaking to her current employer about leaving is not proof of guilt. Most people do secure a new job before leaving their current position. However, this letter helps establish a likely window of opportunity. A **window of opportunity** in this context extends from the time a new job is contemplated to the time the job is accepted to the time an employee leaves the old job. All activity within that window of opportunity should be examined for possible compromise of the system.

An easy way to examine file activity is to sort all the files by the date attribute. NTI has a utility called FileList that creates a `.DBF` file of directory and file information. The information can then be brought into a Microsoft Excel spreadsheet (or any other program that reads `.DBF` files) to be analyzed in whatever way is desired. We generally sort on the file date attribute and examine all activity in the time that we deem to be the window of opportunity. We also review all logs and e-mail for activity during the window of opportunity.

This sort indicated that Hamil had accessed and transferred various Microsoft PowerPoint presentations to an e-mail address later determined to be her personal account. A review of these files by Mandy Weaver, Hamil's former boss, revealed various confidential files that Hamil did not need to have. These files contained information about XYZ's leading customer, which we will call Top Customer. We performed another TextSearch Plus search on *Top Customer*. This search turned up more confidential documentation on this client that Hamil had accessed during her window of opportunity. We discovered many documents in unallocated space, and using the Norton Utilities UnErase utility, we restored those documents to a floppy drive, reviewed them, and verified that they were confidential.

Because we had identified an e-mail address to which Hamil had been sending these confidential documents, we reviewed the backup tapes of the e-mail server for the previous three months for outbound e-mails to that address and discovered that Hamil had sent a customer database with names, contacts, and sales figures to that address as well.

With this information in hand, the legal department at XYZ Genetic Research Labs contacted ABC Genetic Research Labs, which, by law, had to stop Tiffany Hamil from working with Top Customer or using XYZ's confidential data. If ABC did not stop Hamil, they in turn could have been sued. Hamil was ordered to return all XYZ confidential data, including the Microsoft PowerPoint presentations and customer database.

But the damage was done. A competitor had gained insight into XYZ's operations, billing process, technology, and client list, as well as inside information about the company's relationship with its top customer.

14.2.4 ARCHIVE THE EVIDENCE

Although general computer forensic theory stops at three A's (acquire, authenticate, and analyze), we have included a fourth (archive) because having an accurate and complete archive, or record, of all evidence gathered, software used, and methodology followed will be both necessary and helpful if the case does indeed go to court.

You will need to make copies of all software used in the forensic review (including backup software and drivers, boot disks, all NTI software, and virus software) and store them securely (meaning that you need to create evidence labels and COC forms) along with the other evidence. Having a copy of the software is important in case you ever have to re-create the steps taken, in which case you will need the exact version of the software that you used, not an updated version of the software.

14.3 LESSONS LEARNED

Corporate policy and procedures are effective tools for dealing with many aspects of crime. But policies need to be in place before an incident. In this case, XYZ required employees to sign a nondisclosure agreement *and* reminded employees of the terms of that agreement prior to their release from service. The company's policy also dictated that employees had no right to privacy when it came to data residing on or passing through company-owned computers. XYZ reserved the right to review any of its employees' PCs and electronic mail.

All organizations need to have data classification standards and intellectual asset protection programs in place. These policy-based protections can then be coupled with log files that track and record access to critical data (by whom, when, and possibly any read/write/delete actions taken). Such information will be useful in tracking the distribution and spread of at least electronic versions of sensitive data.

Still, these situations can be very delicate, and seeking the advice of legal counsel, as well as help from a forensic analyst, is quite appropriate.

14.4 INTELLECTUAL ASSET PROTECTION

Every company should remind each of its employees on an ongoing basis that it is their duty to protect the company's intellectual assets from unauthorized disclosure.

As part of the hiring and termination process, employees who come in contact with intellectual assets need to have signed a statement acknowledging their responsibility in dealing with those assets. They need to declare that they will not disclose any confidential, sensitive, or proprietary information during or after their employment. Many employers also seek noncompete arrangements with their employees.

Companies must continue to remind current employees of their roles in securing corporate data, as well as their obligations to abide by the computer use and IT security policies that the firm has established. Any existing consequences or "failure to comply" penalties (which are strongly encouraged) must be explained to all employees.

Protecting your intellectual assets requires that you have a classification system for them. This is by no means an easy task! A simplistic scheme for classifying assets divides them into four categories: *public*, *internal*, *sensitive*, and *confidential*. The categories may be given different names, but a basic four-tier system is fairly common.

Public intellectual assets do not need much protection. The term *public* assumes that the information can be released to anyone in the public domain. Information in this category includes things like the content on the Web site address, the firm's marketing information, and press releases. The more people who see this information, the better. There is no need to have a lot of security around public data. Public data in anyone's hands would not or should not give an advantage to any party.

Internal intellectual assets need to be protected from the "outside." *Internal* means that the information should be kept in-house and should not be divulged to anyone outside the company, but it can be distributed to all company personnel. Such information is generally kept from contractors, third-party employees, or parties that have an external business relationship with the company. Employees should be aware that they may not take this information with them if they leave the firm. Internal assets require a minimal number of controls placed around them. Often a password policy with sufficient guidelines will do.

Sensitive data is reserved for specific groups within the company, and generally it is disclosed on a need-to-know basis. Sensitive data may include client information that can be shared with all employees working with that client, if even in a peripheral capacity. Sensitive data deserves a fair amount of protection—if not for the company, then certainly for the client.

Confidential intellectual assets need to be protected in the strongest way possible. Release of these assets could seriously damage or harm a company. Confidential subclassifications may include *secret* and *top secret*. Personnel and personal information may fall into this classification, as well as client account information, intellectual property, and details of the company's technology. Protection in this class will mean a combination of authentication mechanisms—from passwords to tokens to biometric devices. These are the *something you know* (password), *something you have* (token), and *something you are* (biometrics) that we talked about in Chapter 12 (see Section 12.3.1.3).

The amount of control placed on any asset should be commensurate with the risk associated with the loss of that asset.

14.4.1 ADDITIONAL INTELLECTUAL ASSET CONSIDERATIONS

Expanding on the preceding discussion on protecting intellectual assets are a few additional considerations:

- **Communication of trade secrets clause**. Unless expressly authorized, storing, sending, transmitting, or otherwise disseminating intellectual assets classified as internal, sensitive, or confidential should be strictly prohibited. E-mail communications would be included in this restriction.
- **Electronic mail**. Although e-mail is a part of communications, as noted above, separate policies are needed regarding the use of certain types of electronic mail, including policies that clearly cover each of the following topics:
  - E-mail disclaimers. Each e-mail message should have a disclaimer indicating that the e-mail is for only the intended recipient. Anyone else who comes into possession of such a message must destroy the message or forward it to a designated party.

- Privacy. The level of privacy that employees may reasonably expect (if indeed any privacy is granted), including when using e-mail, should be identified. The policy should specify that the company reserves the right to monitor or audit the use of e-mail at any time because it is a company asset and not a personal asset. There is no expectation of privacy; in fact, privacy rights are waived.
- The retention and archiving of electronic mail.
- When and when not to use electronic mail.
- Controls to be used when dealing with internal or confidential data.
- E-mail disposal. Any intellectual asset deemed internal, sensitive, or confidential must be disposed of in a safe manner. Intellectual asset data should not be thrown out with the regular garbage but needs to be disposed of properly (i.e., shredded).
- Forwarding electronic mail.
- Sending unsolicited electronic mail.
- Assuming another person's or machine's identity when sending electronic mail (also when using the Internet).

> **ASIDE:** Means of enforcing corporate policy are discussed in Chapter 10: Security is the Best Policy.

- **Nondisclosure agreements**. A nondisclosure agreement needs to be signed between an employee and the company when the employee is dealing with internal, sensitive, or confidential data. Nondisclosure agreements also need to be signed between an employee and a third party when any internal, sensitive, or confidential intellectual assets are being discussed.
- **Software license clauses**. This topic includes clauses covering the misuse of software and the copying of software.
- **Information disclosure procedure**. There may well come a time when information, even at the top secret level must be shared, perhaps by court order, or when the firm has been purchased or is in merger talks. The firm should have a well-identified procedure that it can follow to ensure that the right checks and balances are in place so that only the necessary information is

disclosed, and is disclosed with the full knowledge and authority of the firm's management.

14.5 CHAIN OF CUSTODY

Chain of custody is the legal concept whereby you need to be able to show to a court that the evidence presented was in your possession at all times from the time it was collected until the time it was presented to the court. Any gap in time could be enough reason to throw out the evidence presented.

Before any evidence is seized for investigation, it is recommended that pictures be taken of all media and hardware to be seized. Digital pictures are great because they can be electronically attached to the case documentation. Each item seized should have its own chain of custody form.

All media or hardware should be marked with a control number that is assigned by the computer forensics specialist. We assign control numbers using the following nomenclature:

YYYYNNN-DDDdd-TTBBBB

Here YYYYNNN is the case number, where YYYY is the year and NNN is the case number within that year; DDDdd is the date the evidence was seized, where DDD is the month and dd is the day (01–31); TT is the media type or hardware seized, where, for example,

- Personal computer = PC
- Hard drive = HD
- Router = RT
- Software on diskette = SD
- Software on CD = SC
- Memory card = MC

and BBBB is the media type or hardware number (0001–9999).

All items seized should be marked with a control number and logged into a chain of custody (COC) form (see Figure 14.2 for an example), which will also indicate a description of the seized item, its original location, the person seizing the evidence, the date and time the evidence was seized, any witness(es) to the seizure, and the purpose of the line item. (A sample completed COC form appears in Figure 14.3.) Unless the item changes location or custody, we enter "Establish COC" in the "Purpose" column.

CHAIN OF CUSTODY

Control Number:					
Item Description:					
Item Source Location:					
Name	Signature	Date & Time	Witness	Purpose	ITS

Figure 14.2 Blank Chain of Custody Form

CHAIN OF CUSTODY

Control Number: 2001055-AUG23-PC01					
Item Description: PC seized 8/23/01 from XYZ Genetic Research Labs. PC was turned off and had previously been used by XYZ Genetic Research Labs. PC was an IBM-compatible running Windows 95. No Passwords on PC.					
Item Source Location: 123 Sesame Street 3rd floor core 2					
Name	Signature	Date & Time	Witness	Purpose	ITS
Lance Hawk		8/23/01 8:51 PM EST	AMH	Establish COC	8/24/01 #5123
Lance Hawk		8/23/01 9:12 PM EST	AMH	Transfer to LH vault	8/24/01 #5123

Figure 14.3 Sample Completed Chain of Custody Form

Note that whenever evidence is moved to a new location, the transfer should be recorded on the COC form. If evidence is ever transferred in or out of a safe or a property room, the transfer must be documented. If we transfer an item to a different location, we indicate the transfer on the second line in the "Purpose" section. It is suggested that the computer forensic specialist maintain a copy of the COC form and that the original stay with the evidence. COC forms can easily be automated and digital pictures directly attached.

An automated incident tracking system (ITS) can be created without too much effort to track the evidence. That is what the "ITS" column is for on the COC form. If you do use an ITS, remember the words *backup* and *archive*. Under no circumstances do you want to lose all or any portion of your evidentiary records or tracking history because if you do, there goes the case.

14.6 FEDERAL GUIDELINES OF COMPUTER EVIDENCE ADMISSIBILITY

The following is a layperson's explanation of the U.S. Department of Justice federal guidelines for searching and seizing computers.[2] The following listing is in no way complete. You should consult your attorney or legal counsel regarding these rules and how they may apply to your particular situation. We do not pretend to be lawyers!

1. Evidence must be probative. The term *probative* means "beneficial." The evidence must be beneficial to proving your case. It must be directly related to the case under discussion. For example, suppose that, for an instant in the course of the forensic analysis, you discovered irrefutable proof of the existence of Santa Claus. Although such evidence might be interesting, it would have no bearing on the case whatsoever, and therefore would be of no *probative* value to the case. Such evidence would thus not be admissible (except of course in Children's Court).

2. You need proof that the records that you want to admit as evidence were produced in the normal course of business. This is why logs that were enabled in the middle of an investigation (see Section 14.1) may not be admitted into court. Any logs created during an investigation to follow or trap an attacker will not be acceptable by themselves as evidence. However, it may be possible for such logs to be added to other logs or records in order to corroborate other evidence.

3. The evidence must be authentic and real. It must be shown by an expert that the evidence is unaltered from its original state. The concepts of forensic evi-

---

2. These guidelines are published in a document titled "Searching and Seizing Computers and Obtaining Electronic Evidence in Criminal Investigations" (http://www.usdoj.gov/criminal/cybercrime/s&smanual2002.htm).

dence will be key determinants in accepting or discrediting the evidence. This is where the CRC checksum and MD5 digest (see Section 14.2.2) can be helpful.

4. The evidence must meet the "best evidence" rule. That is, the evidence must be the best copy available. The evidence does not have to be the original if it was taken under controlled circumstances and can be shown by an expert as having come from the original. (Again, the CRC checksum and MD5 digest play a role.) An example is the case of introducing a log from a file into evidence. Such a log can be introduced as evidence only if it has been properly acquired and authenticated and the original file can be made available for comparison.

EXECUTIVE FRAUD

The readers of this book will surely be aware of the recent outbreak of corporate fraud and accounting scandals within the executive ranks at major U.S. corporations. Enron, Tyco, AOL Time Warner, WorldCom (and these are real names now) are just the more well-known cases, and not by any means an exhaustive list. Well, we can say with some degree of satisfaction that computer security professionals do at least have a role to play in identifying, proving, and stopping this type of fraud.

This case study details the computer forensic procedures utilized to support a large-scale corporate fraud investigation aimed at many senior executives of an international company who were accused of fraudulently increasing corporate revenues in order to increase profits and subsequently their personal income.

Security professionals specializing in computer forensics and cyber crime investigations were asked to assist with the investigation. Computer forensics is a critical component of many corporate and law enforcement investigations. It is an excellent means of uncovering critical information and tracking the flow of information. However, computer forensic technicians must be knowledgeable in computer operating systems, system hardware, common business applications, and the function and design of hard drives. Because of these requirements, often—especially in larger companies—IT departments are responsible for providing computer forensic support to legal counsel or the internal audit director in support of an investigation.

We should define the term *computer forensics* here to make sure we're all speaking the same language. Computer forensics is most often thought of as involving the creation of a mirror image of a suspect's hard drive (and associated storage devices) and subsequent analysis of its logical file structure, unallocated file space, and file slack. This is a technical description of activities that a computer forensic professional may perform. In a larger sense, and as it is being used in this case study, **computer forensics** is the process of examining digital evidence for use in a criminal or other legal investigation.

15.1 INTRODUCTION: THE WHISTLE-BLOWER

A disgruntled employee at a large international company left a message on the company's fraud hot line indicating that he had information relating to fraudulent activities being conducted by many of the company's senior executives. Within hours the independent third party that managed the fraud hot line had contacted the disgruntled employee and the initial information was being gathered. Soon thereafter, the company's audit committee chairman was briefed on the initial allegation. Such allegations are not taken lightly in any case, but something about this caller and the information presented lent the accusation an extra bit of credibility, so a law firm was retained to conduct a full investigation.

Within 24 hours the law firm had its team of investigators in place. The initial efforts of the investigators were to meet with the disgruntled employee and collect any information relating to the fraud. The information gathered at this meeting suggested a fraud that could easily amount to millions of dollars.

The initial information identified several key executives in the company as potential conspirators in a plot to inflate corporate revenues in order to increase corporate profits and therefore the executives' annual salaries and bonuses. A lawyer representing the law firm hired to conduct the investigation assumed responsibility as the head of the investigation. A larger investigative team—consisting of more than 20 financial auditors, tax accountants, and corporate lawyers, as well as computer forensic professionals—was assembled.

Under the direction of counsel, three objectives were outlined for the investigative team.

1. To ascertain if any fraudulent activity had taken place.
2. To examine e-mails, internal communications, and the computer systems of all parties potentially involved, in an attempt to obtain proof and/or supporting documentation of the alleged fraud.
3. To identify the total financial extent of the alleged fraud—and ascertain how exactly the restatements, which certainly would follow, would be made.

This case study focuses on the second objective. We will operate under the assumption that the investigators determined that some amount of fraudulent activity had taken place. This is not a small assumption, and we make it here simply for brevity and to get to the heart of the case. We do not want to suggest, even in the current environment of corporate scandals, that allegations of fraud are immediately considered truth. Such allegations must be carefully investigated, and they certainly were in this case.

15.2 PREPARATION

The key to a successful computer forensic project is thorough preparation. Not only is preparation necessary for the most effective performance of the tasks at hand, but it is also critical for preserving any and all evidence for potential use in court. If there is even a hint that the evidence has been contaminated in any way, it cannot be used in efforts to prosecute the potentially guilty party.

> **ASIDE:** Though it's not what we want, we will suppress the names of the senior executives involved in this case.

At the outset of the investigation in this case, we attempted to learn as much as possible about the many "suspect" systems to be analyzed, including the following:

*   Size of the hard drive(s)
*   Type of each hard drive—for example, Integrated Drive Electronics (IDE), Small Computer System Interface (SCSI)

- Operating systems
- Associated storage peripherals—for example, external hard drive(s), CDs, tapes
- Number of system users and their names

> **ASIDE:** With any computer forensic examination you have both a suspect system and an analysis system. The **suspect system** is obviously the one that computer forensic analysis will be conducted *on*. The **analysis system** is the one that will be used to perform the analysis.

We worked with the client's IT assessment management team and obtained an inventory sheet that contained most of the information we needed. As you might imagine, they were very cooperative. Our primary concern was the size of the hard drives because we needed to prepare our analysis systems to ensure that we had the proper amount and type of hard drives for imaging the suspects' drives.

Once we were confident that we had the proper number and types of hard drives, we sanitized them and verified that they were in proper working order. Because we use the same analysis hard drives on multiple engagements, it is important for the drives to be wiped completely clean between engagements. Never should data from one job end up in the files of another job. If there is any doubt about the sanitization process, err on the side of caution and just buy brand-new drives. Actually, buying new drives is fairly common practice because whenever the investigation is being done as part of a criminal or legal action, the hard drive goes into evidence. We don't get these drives back, even after the case is over, because there may be an appeal down the road, for which the original evidence will need to be investigated.

A hard drive can be wiped clean in a variety of ways, such as through the Linux operating system's DD function or through commercially available software. The process involves writing a series of characters repeatedly over the entire hard drive and essentially "wiping" it clean of any data from a prior computer forensic analysis. This investigation required us to purchase several brand-new hard drives, but to take no chances, we wiped them clean as well. This added step ensured that no data would exist on our analysis drives until one of our team members placed it on the drive.

To use the Linux DD function to wipe a hard drive clean, you can utilize the following command:

```
# > dd if=/dev/urandom of=/dev/hda
```

where /dev/hda is the physical address of the analysis drive, and urandom is the built-in "random" number generator from Linux. This process should be repeated as many times as you desire. Many professionals sanitize their hard drives as many as three to nine times.

Upon examining the sanitized drive, you should see only a series of random characters throughout. No data should remain on the drive after this process is completed.

15.2.1 THE NATURE AND SOURCE OF THE ALLEGATION

One other essential preparation step was to work with the lead auditors and attorneys to ensure that all of our computer forensic technicians understood the nature and scope of the investigation and the purpose for conducting the computer forensics. Basically, we needed to ensure that everyone understood his or her own role and place within the overall team's goals.

We approached the task by holding facilitated meetings first thing every morning. Our meetings provided an opportunity for the computer forensic technicians and the financial investigators to share information.

The meetings also provided us the opportunity to collaborate as a team on identifying the type of information we should search for during the computer forensic examination. For this particular project, the financial investigators suggested that Excel spreadsheets, Word documents, PowerPoint presentations, and e-mail correspondence would be the most likely places where evidence of fraud would turn up, as well as being the best indicators of who had taken part in the fraud.

From information gathered at these meetings, we collaborated on developing a list of key search terms that we would use for string searches later in the computer forensic process. The terms we chose were determined by the type of information being sought for use in an accounting fraud case. A lot of the words we came up with are what would be considered typical for a case of accounting fraud; others were specific to the industry, company, and executives involved. When developing a list of search terms, you will almost always include the names of the people being investigated, as well as other pertinent parties, such as customers, vendors, and business partners—that is, the names of any relevant entity. Sample search terms that could be utilized in an accounting fraud case are shown in Table 15.1.

One use for search terms, especially when they are to be used to search through e-mail, is to check whether the suspects have been communicating with each other about the investigation, or the potential for an investigation if they are caught. (Such evidence would prove premeditation, negating the "I didn't know it was against the rules" defense.) This is why the words *investigate* and *investigation* are included in the list of search terms.

One thing we should mention is that we collaborated with the lawyers and accountants on the development of search terms. Certainly we wanted the financial investigators' input on the kinds of evidence to look for specific to their industry. But this is not to suggest that they were controlling the forensic investigation. If there was any doubt about whether a term should be included or not included, we included it. The seriousness of the matter (and, we'd like to think, the professionalism of those involved allowed the situation to remain collaborative and not competitive).

Table 15.1 Possible Search Terms for Accounting-Fraud Cases

allowance	growth	overstatement
audit	incentive	per our discussion
beginning balance	income	prepaid
bonus	in connection	receivable
confirm	internal	repay
deduction	investigate	total
earned	investigation	year-end

15.3 EVIDENCE COLLECTION AND CHAIN OF CUSTODY

A critical part of any computer forensic investigation is ensuring proper evidence collection and proper maintenance of the chain of custody of the evidence collected. **Positive control** is the phrase most often used to describe the standard of care taken in the handling of potential evidentiary material (e.g., suspect computer systems, hard drives, and any backup copies). You need to be sure that you can identify the who, what, when, where, how, and why of each piece of evidence or material that you collect during the investigation:

- **Who.** Who handled the evidence?
- **What.** What procedures were performed on the evidence?
- **When.** When was the evidence collected and/or transferred to another party?
- **Where.** Where was the evidence collected and stored?
- **How.** How was the evidence collected and stored?
- **Why.** For what purpose was the evidence collected?

If evidence must change hands multiple times, you may have a very long list of information to keep track of here.

At the beginning of the investigation in this case study we identified approximately 20 systems that required computer forensic analysis. Working with the client's IT department, however, we learned that the computers belonging to the people being investigated had recently been refreshed, and the old computers were still at the client site. That meant that we had to maintain positive control over approximately 40 computer systems.

The auditors on the team had already procured temporary office space near the client location to serve as the headquarters of the investigation. Because the investigative team members came from multiple firms, we needed a convenient space in which to work, and we certainly needed to be close to the client. The office space included a couple of offices that could serve as interview rooms, as well as a large conference room that would be the primary workspace. Before the team moved into that conference room, we had a locksmith install a new lock on the conference room door. (We joked that the owner of the facility might not be too happy that we were changing their locks, but the case warranted such action.) Only three keys to this door were produced, and all of them were marked "Do Not Copy." The keys were given to two of our investigators and the lead attorney. We all agreed to return the keys to the property owner at the end of the engagement.

The lead attorney expressed a lack of confidence in having the team's work papers secured by a simple door lock. The latch on the lock was so exposed that most of the team felt that any determined person could break into the room by simply using a credit card or wire coat hanger to move the latch away from the door frame and open the door. The security team was asked if anything else could be done to secure the room.

To add an extra layer of security, we recommended installing a miniature camera with a radar-based motion detector. The camera recorded to an extended-play VHS recorder and was turned on after hours, on weekends, and whenever any fewer than three team members were in the room. With the camera in place, we could monitor anyone entering, moving within, or leaving the room. We selected the radar-based motion detector because we needed to hide the entire apparatus in the conference room. During the day, many client personnel, including suspects, entered our room as a normal course of business, and we did not want any of them to know that the camera had been installed, so it needed to be out of sight. Further, if someone were to break into our room after hours, it was less likely they would uncover our camera and motion detector than if we had used an infrared-based motion detector that could not be hidden.

With the motion detector in place, the camera would automatically turn on when someone entered the room (and we wouldn't be recording hours and hours of no activity). For an extra level of protection, we added a battery backup to the camera and recorder in case power was cut to the room; our camera would run for an additional 60 hours on this battery (to cover a full weekend). In cases of fraud—especially when the dollar amounts involved start to rise—you don't take chances.

15.3.1 TAKE YOUR HANDS OFF THAT KEYBOARD AND SLOWLY BACK AWAY

With the room secure, we proceeded to gather the computers and computer paraphernalia from the suspects. Several liaisons from the client's physical security team worked with us during this process. Their assistance proved an effective means of obtaining computer systems from company personnel (employees and executives), because those personnel were not expecting our request and were not prepared to resist the company's own physical security department. The fact that someone from the corporate security team was doing the confiscating made the process of turning over a computer system fairly tolerable. After all, yell all they might, the employees really had no choice. We needed this to be an exceptionally quick process because we wanted to mitigate the risk of anyone deleting pertinent files or e-mail from the systems we wanted to obtain. Therefore, we made the collection all at once, creating teams equal to the number of suspects.

Once the computers and all paraphernalia had been obtained by the liaison, with someone from our team present, we utilized a tracking form (see Figure 15.1) to ensure that we properly documented the chain of custody. Both team members (liaison and forensic investigator) signed our tracking form, as did the suspect. If anyone refused to sign the form, the refusal was noted and a witness (another employee who happened to be in the area) was asked to sign. (When faced with the threat of involving a witness, most suspects quietly signed.) This process was repeated when the computer was returned to the client.

15.4 DRIVE IMAGING

Imaging a suspect's hard drive is one of the most critical functions of the computer forensic process—arguably *the* most critical element. It is extremely important that no data be written to the suspect's hard drive during this process. To ensure the integrity of the 40+ hard drives to be imaged and analyzed in this case, we used the Linux DD function as the method for imaging.

Using Linux DD means attaching the suspect's hard drive to the analysis system and copying all of its data to a file on the analysis drive. Linux DD makes a bit-for-bit copy of the suspect's drive and writes all of the data to what is commonly

TECHNOLOGY TRACKING FORM

Employee/location the item is assigned to:	
Computer type (laptop, desktop):	
Computer brand:	
Computer model number:	
Computer serial number or service tag number:	
Hard drive brand:	
Hard drive model:	
Hard drive serial number:	
Printed name(s) of person(s) who gave this item to investigative team:	
Signature(s) of person(s) who gave this item to investigative team:	
Date item was given to investigative team:	
Printed name of investigative team employee who received this item:	
Signature of investigative team employee who received this item:	
Date item was returned:	
Printed name(s) of person(s) to whom investigative team returned this item:	
Signature(s) of person(s) to whom investigative team returned this item:	
Printed name of investigative team employee who returned this item:	
Signature of investigative team employee who returned this item:	

Figure 15.1 Chain of Custody Tracking Form

referred to as a **raw data file.** This file contains everything that was originally stored on the suspect's drive, including the logical file structure and unallocated space. By using a large hard drive (300GB) for our analysis drive, we were able to store up to five or six suspects' raw data files on a single drive.

Here's the command for using DD:

```
# > dd if=/dev/hda of=/mnt/image.dd
```

where /dev/hda is the physical address of the suspect's hard drive, and /mnt/image.dd is the raw data file to which the suspect's hard drive is being written.

It is imperative to validate that every bit and byte of the suspect's computer was properly copied to your analysis drive. To accomplish this validation, before using DD we used the MD5 checksum utility, called md5sum, that is built into Linux. We first performed a checksum on the suspect's hard drive, then we used DD to make the image, and finally we performed a checksum on the suspect's raw data file. The results of the two checksum operations were compared to make sure that the contents of the suspect's hard drive and our raw data file were identical.

Here's the command for using the Linux MD5 checksum utility:

```
# > md5sum /dev/hda
77538d7cdb02e592e1787f6905235b89 /dev/hda

# > md5sum /mnt/image.dd
77538d7cdb02e592e1787f6905235b89 /mnt/image.dd
```

Comparing the results of the two checksum actions will tell you if the DD image copy is exactly the same as the original.

15.5 REVIEW OF THE LOGICAL FILE STRUCTURE

After imaging the suspect hard drives, we reviewed the logical file structure. To facilitate this process, our team used the EnCase Forensic Edition software. This is a licensed software tool. By using our Linux servers, previously used for hard drive imaging, as file servers (utilizing Samba as the mechanism for file sharing), our Windows-based analysis machines could access the raw data files that contained images of our suspects' hard drives.

With EnCase as our tool, we opened each raw data file and began our analysis. EnCase has the built-in technology to read the file and present the data as if it were actually connected to a hard drive. The view that is represented is similar to what an average Windows-based computer user sees when accessing the Windows Explorer utility (see Figure 15.2).

A review of logical file structure involves both automated and manual procedures. The computer forensic software being utilized facilitates the automated procedures. By using EnCase, we were able to search through the directories of

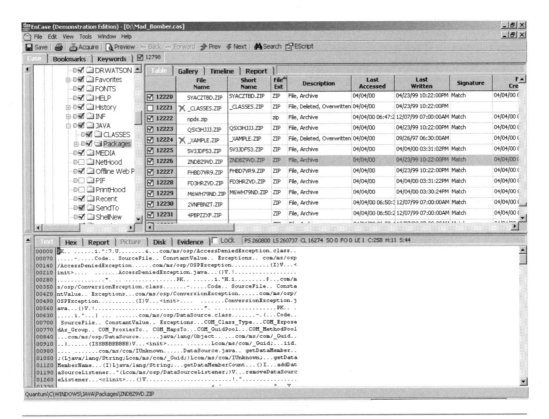

Figure 15.2 EnCase Logical File Structure Review

the suspect's computer system and quickly locate any files that seemed pertinent to our investigation. As a follow-up method, we looked through the directories manually to identify any files that might not have been detected during our automated search with EnCase.

Each file we located that was deemed pertinent to our investigation was copied to the analysis drive, to be included in our computer forensic analysis report. When performing this step it is important to record the logical address of the file. This is the full path name; for example, the full path name of the System32 directory on many Windows NT/2K/XP computers is C:\Winnt\System32.

15.6 REVIEW OF UNALLOCATED SPACE AND FILE SLACK

After completing the logical file structure review, we focused on analyzing the unallocated space and file slack. **Unallocated space**, also called *free space*, is defined as the unused portion of the hard drive; **file slack** is the unused space that is created between the end-of-file marker and the end of the hard drive cluster in which the file is stored. Sometimes data is written to these spaces that may be of value to investigators.

Using a software tool to facilitate the process is the easiest way to accomplish this portion of the analysis. As we had earlier, we used EnCase for this segment of the review. Our approach was twofold: (1) We extracted deleted files out of the unallocated space and subsequently reviewed them for appropriateness, and (2) we performed string searches through the unallocated space and file slack in an attempt to locate data related to the matter being investigated.

Even with the assistance of software tools, this process can be very time-consuming and potentially lengthy. The results of the extraction of deleted files can be voluminous. In this case several thousand files from each hard drive needed to be reviewed.

In addition, all of the identified files must be reviewed. We can't simply review until we find material that we're looking for, or material that helps our case, and stop. That would an unfair and incomplete evaluation of the potential evidence. Therefore, to expedite the process of reviewing files extracted from unallocated space, we use a software utility called dtSearch. With all of our extracted files in one location, we fed our search terms into dtSearch and had it scan through the files to find those that were pertinent to our investigation.

As in logical file structure review, when potential evidence is found, its address on the hard drive must be recorded. However, because unallocated space and file slack are outside of the logical addressing scheme in this review, we must record the physical address of any evidence, essentially including its cluster and sector address (e.g., cluster 11155, sector 357517).

15.7 SMOKING GUN

Although everyone on the investigative team wanted to find a smoking gun, such as an e-mail from a senior executive saying, "I'm going to lie about the numbers to increase my yearly bonus—the SEC be damned," no such e-mail was found. In addition, no single financial report, PowerPoint presentation, or word document clearly indicated that any individual was a party to fraud or that any fraud had indeed taken place.

Instead, the investigation was an iterative process in which we discovered information piece by piece—draft financial reports, reports marked confidential, e-mails between suspects—and shared it with the accountants to review. Each time we gave them some such material, they reviewed it and suggested that we look for more of the same.

Sometimes the accountants came to us with leads. For example, they might ask us to do a search on the name of an off-shore corporation to see what might turn up. In some cases, a great deal of relevant data was discovered; in other cases, nothing came up. In this back-and-forth process, the case for fraud was built.

15.8 REPORTING

When our analysis was complete, we began to draft a report. This is another critical step in the computer forensic process, and we wanted to make sure we got it right.

We met with the lead investigators and attorneys and provided them verbal reports of the results of our analysis, as well as our working papers. We had been working together, so they were aware of the findings for the most part, but a presentation still had to be made to ensure that there were no misunderstandings. In addition, though we had a report format (template) that we were comfortable with, we needed to know how the report should be labeled (e.g., confidential, sensitive, privileged, attorney/client privileged). This is an important consideration, that, in general, is best left to the lawyers.

We agreed to develop our report using Microsoft Word and to include links to pertinent files that would be stored on an accompanying CD-ROM. All the attorney would need to do is insert the CD in a computer, and the report would automatically open for viewing. The attorney could then easily review the report and choose to open any associated files she wished to view.

The report, as well as all data and work papers, would be on the CD-ROM. The written report could certainly be printed in hard copy; the sheer volume of the data, however, made hard copies of the data completely impossible.

15.9 LESSONS LEARNED

Although no smoking gun was found in this investigation, enough evidence was discovered (e.g., key electronic documents, e-mail, spreadsheets, PowerPoint presentations) that, when put together, identified how key executives had committed the fraud and had communicated about their activities. In this particular case, however, all of the information that we uncovered with computer forensics would have to fall into the category of circumstantial evidence. All of it was critical to allowing our team to complete the investigation. However, none of it contained the smoking gun that our computer forensic technicians were hoping for. Fortunately for the investigative team (and the company involved), a whistle-blower and other company employees were willing to talk with the investigating team and provide information that was helpful in uncovering the details of the fraud.

For the sake of fairness, it must be stated that the investigation did exonerate certain of the suspects. And this is a major part of the role of computer forensic professionals. We are charged not only with presenting evidence that an incident did in fact occur, but also with presenting evidence suggesting that the incident did *not* occur, if that is indeed the case.

After the investigation was completed, the lead attorneys from the investigative team provided the complete report to the audit committee. The report outlined specifically which company employees—mainly executives—were involved in the fraud, without attempting to evaluate their culpability. (Lawyers have more leeway in assessing guilt than we do.) The report also contained information about internal control deficiencies that permitted the fraud to occur and ways to mitigate the risk of this type of fraud in the future.

The audit committee took swift and decisive action, firing all of the executives that were involved in the fraud and recommending significant changes to the company's internal financial reporting and control environment.

CYBER EXTORTION

One of the keys to succeeding at extortion is to keep your true identity hidden. The Internet, which allows people to hide behind computers and operate at great distances through electronic networks, is therefore an ideal medium for extortion.

Extortion can be the popular "Give me money or else!" but also comes in more subtle forms. This case study discusses one such situation and describes the process used to track and capture the offending party.

16.1 INTRODUCTION

In this case study we will describe the events and processes related to the computer forensic investigation of a cyber crime incident that involved extortion and the use of a Trojan horse. Along the way, in addition to providing specific details of the case, we will place a great deal of emphasis on our use of forensic tools and procedures so that this discussion will assist the reader in understanding and performing other computer forensic investigations.

One day, we received a call from Ashley Landscapers informing us that one of its employees, Anne Richards, was asking them about how she could rid her personal computer of NetBus. NetBus is a back-door Trojan horse designed for Windows 95/98 (the NetBus GUI is shown in Figure 16.1). Once installed,

Figure 16.1 NetBus Graphical User Interface

NetBus allows anyone who knows the listening port number (the default NetBus port is 12345) and password to control the host remotely. Among other things, NetBus can capture keystrokes in an encrypted file, open and close the CD tray, and control the mouse. NetBus can turn on a microphone, if present, potentially giving the attacker the ability to listen to any audio (including voices) near the computer.

Apparently Richards had found that NetBus was installed on her home computer. She used her home computer to dial in to work remotely, and she was concerned about a possible compromise of work data.

Initial questioning of the victim (Anne Richards) indicated that she believed that her PC was "infected" because it was telling her so. We were glad to be speaking with her over the phone and not in person, for we would have looked at her like she was crazy. She went on to explain that she had been receiving a daily pop-up message for the previous six days indicating that her PC was infected by NetBus/ Back Orifice and that the infection could be removed, for a price, by a company called Moser Computers. An e-mail address for Moser Computers was included in the message.

Richards had rightly considered this an act of extortion and had eventually reported the event to her employer, who in turn contacted us. By using a search engine and searching for "Moser Computers," we were able to track the e-mail address to a Cody Moser, who worked for Moser Computers. This information was turned over to the local police, who were asked to interview Cody Moser. Chief Andy Summers handled the case. The chief was able to obtain a statement of admission from Cody Moser declaring that he had sent the NetBus Trojan horse to the victim's PC.

> **ASIDE:** Intentionally loading or installing a remote-control Trojan horse such as Net-Bus or Back Orifice on another person's computer without that person's knowledge and consent is illegal. However, it is not our intent here to imply that Cody Moser admitted to willingly performing this act with the intent to break the law. We are simply saying that he admitted doing it, without asserting anything about whether or not he knew he was, in fact, breaking the law at the time.

Moser claimed that he searched the Internet for vulnerable computers, and when one presented itself, he loaded the Trojan horse and then marketed his firm's computer security services to the system owner (through the pop-up messages).

Questioning disclosed that Moser had specifically targeted Anne Richards and sent her an e-mail that contained NetBus. Richards had inadvertently loaded the Trojan horse on her computer when she clicked on an attachment in her e-mail titled "Credit Report." The text in the e-mail message indicated that a random check of her credit history had indicated several late and missed payments. The message requested her to verify the validity of the attached credit report and send it back to her local credit agency.

> **ASIDE:** You should *never* open an e-mail attachment when you are not 100 percent sure of its contents. A Trojan horse can easily be sent through an attachment, and generally it requires only that the user open (click on) the attachment. You should also have up-to-date virus protection software that can check all attachments and e-mails before they are received, opened, or sent.

Moser also indicated that he had not taken any personal or Ashley Landscapers company information from Richards' computer and that he had made no attempts to further compromise Ashley Landscapers' network infrastructure. He claimed that his goal was merely to build a computer security consulting practice by demonstrating the lack of security in his prospective client's computers. He further admitted to using the same tactics with other individuals and firms, some of whom had become clients and had retained Moser Computers to secure, or "lock down," their networking environment.

Chief Summers was waiting to see if Anne Richards wanted to press any charges. Though the perpetrator in this case had admitted to the wrongful act, the local police were not in a position to pursue the matter further unless the victim was willing to press charges. Prosecution of any cyber crime demands that evidence be handled and preserved in certain ways (in accordance with specific guidelines of computer evidence admissibility), most of which had not been followed in this case. Even if a victim wants to press charges, taking a case to the district attorney requires that it be a strong case supported by the required evidence. An additional consideration is the very nature of the crime and how difficult it will be to explain to a possibly nontechnical jury how such a thing happened.

16.2 TO PRESS OR NOT TO PRESS CHARGES

We told Richards that she should start documenting everything possible, including conversations, work done to date, and all dates and times that might be relevant. We explained the concept of chain of custody (COC) and how important it was.

Chain of custody is the legal concept whereby you need to be able to show to a court that all evidence was in your possession at all times from the time it was collected until the time it was presented to the court. Any gap in time could be enough reason to throw out the entire case.

> **ASIDE:** Section 14.5 in Chapter 14 contains an explanation of the chain of custody, along with a sample evidence COC form that anyone can use (Figure 14.2). We will discuss the importance of ensuring proper control over the chain of custody throughout this case study.

Richards was instructed not to do anything more on her computer until we could process it for evidence. Although we did not necessarily disbelieve Moser's statement that he had made no effort to further compromise the computer aside from loading the tool, due diligence dictated that a thorough examination of the machine was necessary. In addition, there was the concern that with a remote-control tool on the machine, other unauthorized users might have been given access to the computer.

Therefore, at the request of Ashley Landscapers and Police Chief Summers, who was not prepared to perform a computer forensic evaluation, we made plans to seize the computer to analyze it for all potential and relevant evidence it might contain. We would need to proceed carefully so as not to spoil or taint the evidence in any fashion, because the evidence would likely be required if Richards decided to press charges.

This case is unlike most cases, in which the goal is to obtain a statement of admission from the culprit. Here we already *had* that admission before we started the investigation. Therefore, the goal became to perform the forensic examination in order to collect the evidence to support or contradict the statement of admission. (Statements are never retracted, are they?)

We also learned from the victim of the alleged attack that although she occasionally dialed in to her workplace from home, she had not been keeping up with her virus protection. She had continued to use her computer for six days even after receiving the extortion notifications. This was the first lesson learned from this case. If you have a strong reason to believe your machine has been compromised (and pop-up messages from unknown parties constitute a strong reason), then you need to stop using that computer until the infection is completely wiped out and the security hole is plugged.

The PC in question needed to be processed for evidence. Specific procedures needed to be followed. A road trip was needed. We had to get to that computer as soon as possible.

We prepared a forensic tool bag that included the software listed in Table 16.1 and the hardware listed in Table 16.2.

Table 16.1 Software Used for a Forensic Investigation

Forensic software from New Technologies, Inc.

Norton Utilities

Norton AntiVirus

DOS boot disk with drivers and backup software

Utilities disk

Table 16.2 Hardware and Supplies Used for a Forensic Investigation

Portable parallel port Travan 3 tape backup drive

Handheld mini cassette recorder

Cassette tapes

Camera

Film

Audio recorder

Backup batteries

Extra hard drives (2)

Computer repair toolkit with antistatic wrist strap

TR-3 extra tape backup cartridges by Verbatim (6)

Diskettes (50) with labels

Evidence labels

Chain of custody forms

Masking tape

Markers

The ways in which the software were used will become apparent in the description of the case study. New Technologies, Inc. (NTI) produces a great many tools for computer forensic investigations. The use of several NTI tools will be discussed in this case study.

Of the hardware items listed, the cassette recorder and camera are for recording any notes and thoughts during the investigation and for taking pictures of the computers and devices to be investigated. Film and backup batteries for these devices are important. The masking tape is used to mark wires and connection ends. Sometimes you will need to remove components from within a computer or disconnect computers from a network, and having the masking tape to help mark the connections is useful.

The antistatic wrist strap is necessary because static electricity and computers don't function very well together. The TR-3 extra tape backup cartridges store up to 2.2GB of data uncompressed or 4.4GB in compressed form—excellent for backing up the victim's disk drive. The evidence labels and chain of custody forms are absolutely necessary if the evidence is to be used in a court of law.

We needed to address a couple of things with the client immediately upon arriving on-site. The things Richards needed to do immediately to limit any further compromise of the network and to secure the evidence for examination:

- Change all her passwords at work.
- Check with her employer on all accesses attempted with her user ID and password. If the employer was not logging remote IDs and passwords, they needed to start doing so immediately.

Richards' log-on ID and password were changed at work. She also changed all personal passwords that existed on her home PC. Checking the remote-access logs at her work indicated that Richards' user ID had logged on numerous times during the time frame in which the PC appeared to have been compromised. These log-on sessions each took place during normal working hours and coincided with dates that Richards was scheduled to be working from home. They ranged in time from 30 minutes to two hours. Fortunately, logging had already been enabled in this case. The remote-access logs and other system logs were captured and stored securely.

ASIDE: Turning logging on in the middle of an investigation can invalidate the use of that log as primary evidence. Although the log could be used as corroborating evidence, it would not meet one of the federal guidelines regarding computer evidence admissibility—the guideline that all evidence used in a case must have been gathered in the normal course of business. See Section 14.6 in Chapter 14 for a layperson's explanation of this and other federal guidelines of computer evidence admissibility.

16.3 THE INVESTIGATION

Now we were ready to start the formal investigation. As we discussed in Chapter 14, this process is guided by the four A's of computer forensics:

1. **A**cquire
2. **A**uthenticate
3. **A**nalyze
4. **A**rchive

16.3.1 ACQUIRE EVIDENCE

The first step is to acquire and secure all evidence. All evidence needs to be preserved in its original condition; it must not be altered in any way. This means that in order to analyze the computer and its files and logs, we would first have to make a mirror image copy of the machine, not a file-by-file copy. We'll discuss this process in greater depth shortly.

It is important to make sure that all material, data, computers, and information are gathered and processed in a manner that protects their evidentiary value. The following detailed instructions help ensure that this processing is performed properly:

1. **Document the configuration of the system under investigation**. This is the point at which you should take pictures of the system, including any peripherals, from all angles. If you have to disconnect any cables, attach masking tape to each cable end and mark on the tape the device to which the cable was connected.

2. **Shut down the computer and/or hardware**. This may already have been done by the time the computer forensic investigator arrives on the scene, as was the

case in this particular investigation. General computer forensic safeguards dictate that a suspect computer should be shut down in case there is a destructive process running in the background. If a computer is on and you need to process it as evidence, document what's on the screen before you shut it down (pictures and printouts of the screen are helpful here). It is also recommended that you remove any network connectivity.

3. **Establish and maintain a chain of custody.** A chain of custody form must be completed for every device seized. A separate form must be filled out for each component, such as the hard drive, if it is removed from the system for any reason. The paperwork can be tedious, but it is highly important. See Section 14.5 of Chapter 14 for a detailed explanation of chain of custody, along with a sample COC form that anyone can use (Figure 14.2).

4. **Secure the computer.** If you are not in a good location—that is, a place where you have enough room, resources, or the privacy necessary to complete your review—the computer should be transported to a secure location. Generally, we like to bring everything back to our lab; however, this itself poses significant challenges and requires us to maintain a fully locked-down, secure facility. In addition, clients may not want what might be crucial evidence leaving their location. So, we can commandeer an office or conference room for the period of the investigation. If you are doing this, be sure to warn the client that this may be for quite some time—depending on the amount of evidence to review—and make sure that the room can be secured.

5. **Back up the original hard drive.** An original hard drive must *never* be altered or directly examined. Let's repeat that. An original hard drive must *never* be altered or directly examined. Get the point? The backup that is created should be a mirror image, or bit stream, backup, of the hard drive, not a file-by-file backup.

Remember, we cannot take the chance of anything happening to potentially spoil the evidentiary value of the hard drive, including writing to or deleting anything from the hard drive. We make a mirror image and work with the mirror image in an effort to protect the original hard drive.

The choice of backup tool is up to you. The important point is that the backup software and/or hardware used must have been tested in court and have withstood defense challenges. Check with the manufacturer to see if it has or uses commercial forensic software products like EnCase or SafeBack that have been tested. Later in this discussion we'll cover the general techniques used in forensic backups.

To make the backup image, we need to create a boot disk with the appropriate drivers and backup software. A boot disk ensures that no possible evidence is altered or destroyed through hard-drive boot sequences.

We boot to DOS using MS-DOS version 6.22 when using NTI's forensic utilities. Unlike other available forensic utilities, NTI's utilities require a user to boot to DOS. Most computers can boot by a floppy. You should verify that a computer's boot order is set to boot from the floppy drive before the hard drive.

How can you do this, you ask? Insert a write-protected DOS boot diskette into the floppy disk drive of the system under investigation. Turn on the computer and go into the CMOS BIOS area that contains a lot of high-level computer information. To get into the CMOS BIOS area, you will need to press a key or key combination when booting up the computer. Consult an owner's manual for the proper combination of keys before trying any of the following. We have encountered a few key combinations for accessing the CMOS BIOS, as shown in Table 16.3. As the table suggests, the world is full of IBM-compatibles, and appropriately, there is a great deal of variety in the key combinations that apply.

When you are in the CMOS BIOS area, look for the boot sequence and make sure that the floppy drive comes before the hard drive in that sequence. You could also

Table 16.3 Key Combinations to Enter the CMOS BIOS for Various Computers

Computer	Key Combination
IBM	**F1**
IBM-compatibles	**Delete, Ctrl-Alt-Esc, Ctrl-Alt-Enter, Ctrl-Alt-F2**
Dell	**F12**
Compaq	**F10**
Apple	**Ctrl-o-f**

apply the same process to boot from a CD. Remember to save any changes when you exit the CMOS BIOS, if you did in fact make any changes. You will need to reverse this process later so that you can return the computer to its original state, so be sure to keep track of how things were when you found them.

You should never boot from a suspect hard drive, because doing so might cause you to alter and/or lose evidence. And if you do alter any part of the evidence, all other evidence may also come under suspicion.

Before backing up the hard drive, we use the NTI (www.forensics-intl.com) utility GetTime to document the CMOS date and time on the suspect computer. First we boot to DOS using a DOS boot disk as already specified. Then we insert the disk containing the NTI GETTIME.EXE utility. The utility is run with the following command:

```
A:> GETTIME
```

The results of the file will be saved on the diskette in the following format:

```
STM-MMDD.00X
```

where MM is the month, DD is the day, and X is the file occurrence number.

We compare this system date and time to the current (or actual) date and time on a watch and document any differences on paper, and then we edit GETTIME.DOC later in the investigation, noting the source of the actual date and time—for example, a Lance Hawk Timex wristwatch. GETTIME.DOC should then be edited and printed (but not on the suspect machine and printer). Here is a sample printout of a GETTIME.DOC (not from the current case).

```
Forensic System Status Documentation Tool  GETTIME.EXE Version 2.0
-----------------------------------------------------------------
Licensed to Lance Hawk
-----------------------------------------------------------------

      System Time set at 12:28:10
      System Date set at 02-18-2003
-----------------------------------------------------------------
```

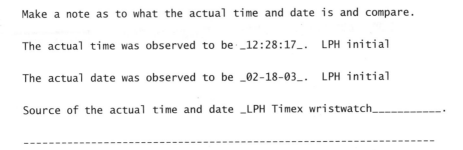

```
Make a note as to what the actual time and date is and compare.

The actual time was observed to be _12:28:17_.  LPH initial

The actual date was observed to be _02-18-03_.  LPH initial

Source of the actual time and date _LPH Timex wristwatch_____.

---------------------------------------------------------------
```

After using GetTime, we use PTable, another utility from NTI, to document and analyze the hard-disk partitions. This analysis identifies the specific type of partitions, thereby suggesting which specific forensic software we should use.

You can use DOS redirection to document PTable and print the results to a file:

```
A:\PTABLE > PTABLE.DOC
```

Sample output of this tool (again not from the current case) looks like this:

```
PTable version 1.5 -- Partition Table Analysis tool by NTI
Build date Thu Nov 09 12:49:00pm 2000

The following Hard Disk partitions were found on this system:
        XBIOS          |  Begining  |   Ending   |  Size in Kbytes
  Vol   HD System      | Cyl Head Sec | Cyl Head Sec |(1 Kb = 1024 bytes)
Boot C: 80 FAT16 > 32Mb |   0   1   1 | 1021  63  63 |   2060320
Boot    81 DiskMgr DDO  |   0   0  10 | 1459 255  63 |  11773435
```

PTable indicated that FAT16 (Windows 95 before release 2) was on the computer being investigated. Note that the second line of the output specifies DiskMgr, which is a program that was used to get around previous drive size limitations in FAT16 file systems. After ascertaining that the backup software worked with the operating system as indicated by the PTable utility, we begin the backup process.

Here are some other systems you might see:

- **FAT32** (for Windows 95 release 2, Windows 98, Windows ME, and Windows 2000)

- **NTFS** (for Windows NT, Windows 2000, and Windows XP)
- **VFAT** (for Windows 95 and Windows NT 3.5)
- **HPFS** (for OS/2 and Windows NT)

Remember, not every backup software can work with every operating system. Sometimes it takes a bit of effort to identify a good match. It is also important to make sure you have a stable and effective version of the backup software—one that you have experience with and confidence will work effectively. In the absence of confidence, get the latest version. Unfortunately, however, there is no substitute for experience.

If any diskettes are involved in the investigation, you should make mirror image or bit stream backups of them as well. You can use the DOS DISKCOPY command with the /V (verification) switch. Note that whatever software you use to create the mirror image backup, it must have been tested in court and have withstood defense challenges. Contact the vendor for confirmation and proof.

The acquisition processes used to create a mirror image backup are different depending on the situation. Different software, hardware, and processes may be required depending on the acquisition method used. Section 14.2.1 in Chapter 14 included a partial list of methods that we have used with some success. In this particular case we used the tape drive acquisition method. Tape drive acquisition involves acquiring the data from the computer under examination by using a tape or Jaz drive. The connection is generally through a SCSI or parallel port. The basic setup is illustrated in Figure 16.2.

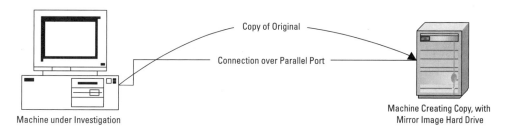

Figure 16.2 Configuration for Making a Mirror Image Copy of the Original Hard Drive

16.3.2 AUTHENTICATE THE EVIDENCE

Next you need to authenticate the evidence—that is, to show that the copy of the evidence you have acquired is indeed a mirror image of the original and has not been altered. The copy is to be used in the investigation. The necessary testing and examination will always be done with the copy. Therefore, it is crucial that the copy be an exact mirror image of the original.

Original evidence is *never* directly examined. Original evidence is only copied, and in turn the copy is examined. Sometimes two mirror images of the original are made in case it becomes necessary to have a second working copy of the evidence.

As you may have guessed, there are indeed some specific steps for properly authenticating evidence.

1. **Authenticate the data on all storage devices**. We use the NTI tool CRCMd5 for mathematical authentication of the data. CRCMd5 will obtain a CRC checksum and an MD5 digest,[1] which can be used to verify that the data has not been compromised or changed and can be admitted as evidence. (Naturally, of course, the final decisions as to whether any piece of evidence can be admitted into a court of law will depend on the judge and the attorneys involved.)

   To generate a CRC checksum and MD5 digest for all files on the C: drive and redirect the output as headerless text to the file A:\CRCMD5.doc, we use the following command:

   ```
   A:\CRCMD5 C: /s >CRCMD5.DOC
   ```

   Following is a typical listing created using CRCMd5. Note that only the root directory, C:, and the first subdirectory, \DOS, are listed. A full listing of a hard drive would be much longer. The /s option will list corresponding directories and subdirectories. The field ATTR is for file attributes such as H (hidden), R (read-only), A (archive), and S (system).

---

1. The CRC checksum and MD5 digest values were defined in Section 14.2.2.

Sample Directory C:\

FILE NAME	LENGTH	DATE	ATTR	CRC-32	----------MD5 DIGEST------------		
===========	========	======	======	========	===================================
SUHDLOG.DAT	6451	05/05/01	HR	893c0a4c	5043dd2cb91f7cf5	d47e05b55c2ee057
SUHDLOG.BAK	19627	05/05/01	HR	c04c766a	6bfbb3b0ad3f65ba	73ea2dc5fca5abbc
COMMAND.DOS	54619	09/30/93	R	acd2e2f6	c98e0df201047722	fec01cfda0db3ce0
MSDOS.SYS	1646	05/05/01	HRS	85f4670a	aa145c54695534ad	a649ebd87428068c
SUHDLOG.---	7738	10/23/96	HR	b0db49d3	ef44981ab1b9a3ab	942243215671e6c4
BOOTLOG.PRV	29183	05/11/01	AH	e7fafd55	dd73b113c8dfc74c	31923e6fb89e277b
CONFIG.OLD	109	10/23/96		ec283c0e	df90cdb4b7bf95d3	4b011fd0eae1c6df
AUTOEXEC.OLD	84	10/24/96		dbf90dcd	b4e3576a12571f3d	97f39a362f47d1bf
CONFIG.DOS	204	10/23/96		702ee315	591afd8239dd94b2	5b504ba21ae5d0a4
AUTOEXEC.DOS	90	10/23/96		93cba1fe	6cb0636e47c71f68	f5b4d479759d0029
SCANDISK.LOG	407	06/14/02	A	7b9c52d9	0ba1c4dd2c15feaa	605c22a1a2a6900d
BOOTLOG.TXT	29900	05/11/01	AH	39ceaf1f	4d28a4e2c7bcd92c	52f7f024c57cf788
DRVSPACE.BIN	65271	08/24/96	HRS	c9192b9a	cbfed93d55e7d249	8822281cfba12793
MSDOS.---	22	10/23/96	H	62e00f4b	724880b1fdde31c4	d298f49bbdb1e479
SETUPLOG.TXT	64000	05/05/01	AH	aacd5430	fd9977580d9833f1	a260d7626230a0df
DETLOG.OLD	37527	05/05/01	H S	8e69df9a	abfed8e5160e28ed	9e54fbe29bb2683b
DETLOG.TXT	70712	05/05/01	AH S	8265e1d3	ce9714ee2450f257	a5d6eaaebd9551b4
NETLOG.TXT	1179	05/05/01	A	ac37036b	8372623a1e4e208e	012778b504bf11d2
DRV.TXT	37	01/11/99		2afe1c95	fbf2b369c182aaff	69b8490c4e7e7cde
DRVBIN.W95	71287	07/11/95	H S	46d9da28	2c38baabdd0bbe36	77eeb0f3841c2ed4
SCAN111	611	01/11/99		8ac88f80	377b23ee691d4781	bb735cf25dd07935
DBLBIN.W95	71287	07/11/95	H S	46d9da28	2c38baabdd0bbe36	77eeb0f3841c2ed4
CONFIG.001	69	05/11/01	A	8045c988	e0b2f45c4fcc24d6	9bbee4401d50859e
__OFIDX.FFL	24576	10/24/96	AH	714cb119	272c8d65cf80e35d	2eeec5f56bf65896
__OFIDX0.FFX	217088	10/24/96	AH	7307a71a	afbe7f147bde88b7	1494d2b8f00595c1
__OFIDX.FFA	4998	10/24/96	AH	7fde0cf1	e9a6c5e38aec0ede	702a053c9c011f50
CONFIG.BAK	69	05/05/01	A	8045c988	e0b2f45c4fcc24d6	9bbee4401d50859e
COMMAND.COM	93812	08/24/96	A	e4f5d88a	087f030e5515db37	78617b6ac41bb0c9
COPY(B~1.BAT	96	10/24/96		c4aa8f9d	f7618ae5697a2c41	fa74ad99659cc8d3
CONFIG.SYS	69	05/11/01	A	8045c988	e0b2f45c4fcc24d6	9bbee4401d50859e
IO.DOS	40566	09/30/93	HRS	9ae24bc8	819d3376886ea555	45515b790332265a
TOMBPATH.BAT	20	05/10/99	A	c7812113	735ffa0b9d627bfd	b7424e64c0f2c5a9
COPYOF~1.BAT	129	06/24/97		6d402d6e	df2a3dad0d64b102	a997ed780bdf60bf
SETSOUND.ZIP	225655	02/10/97		8e48a45a	f5c5da6ba0b2f2c2	d2d1db5c577db9e8
INDEX.EXE	4225	02/23/97		d14dc300	9edab41a38dc9a22	3e739418c4cab585
AUTOEXEC.NAV	135	03/30/99	A	173cd57f	ae5d1889398a9c04	6a791ea769ee34ef
DBLSPACE.BIN	65271	08/24/96	HRS	c9192b9a	cbfed93d55e7d249	8822281cfba12793
AUTOEXEC.002	147	05/06/01	A	84742f2f	d38ada016be17e18	32cd29dff27ee49d

```
PAGECNT.H          357 03/21/01 A        27f97f7 650c5170f87d9854 fe4d85340e001297
CONFIG.SYD         273 05/11/01 A        482677f0 3abe15000251a0dc 743c469ac7f6c129
DBLSPACE.INI        84 08/02/97   HRS    1c61d555 67b0b294b23e3255 3a389943e2a7199f
SETUPLOG.OLD     45647 05/05/01   H      5b8cf0f2 a784aa81542e3f58 dd251694bf62e1d9
SHOCKW~1.EXE         0 07/21/97                 0 0000000000000000 0000000000000000
AUTOEXEC.001       139 04/20/98          6ac0fb38 84563fecd73180b6 112c1a77c1c369ac
MBRBAK.DM          512 05/04/98          cd970690 2967121506f394ea fc9a7a52649ce75e
AUTOEXEC.BAK       147 05/05/01 A         390c66a 7b3cb7dfce1ce4f3 5460f9f9e285d488
AUTOEXEC.BAT       147 05/06/01 A        84742f2f d38ada016be17e18 32cd29dff27ee49d
MSDOS.DOS        38138 09/30/93   HRS    c05f942b 75959bc417c19135 b982f7959ee9c92a
MSDOS.BAK         1634 05/05/01   HRS    e0fd5720 489bd95374137f8f 6f0ac31d3f8a0114
IO.SYS          214836 08/24/96   HRS    ef1122a2 35c813f9f84e68f0 1b675cec3841b435
MSDOS.001         1634 05/05/01   HRS    e0fd5720 489bd95374137f8f 6f0ac31d3f8a0114
VERSIGN.P12       4390 06/01/99 A        a2f5bdaa 58ca2a10c69c3ea1 f1e1dd4b37f1830a
CONFIG.002          69 05/11/01 A        8045c988 e0b2f45c4fcc24d6 9bbee4401d50859e
AUTOEXEC.003       147 05/06/01 A        84742f2f d38ada016be17e18 32cd29dff27ee49d
MSDOS.002         1646 05/05/01   HRS    85f4670a aa145c54695534ad a649ebd87428068c
APCIPUB.CRT        803 06/01/99 A        854ffcea 694ccaf3ace11a1b 4bf0c6a826fe5f43
LOGO.SYS        129078 08/24/96   H      d0b0b399 534407f0fb482094 8e322aa7cf5e4990
SYSTEM.1ST     3090692 05/05/01   HRS    2e54a6bc 5bf804a8354a0c6d 9cc44dad90b9f445
FAX.DOC             69 06/03/00 A        d7d3ed34 492d4e5034d4a4e0 6e76d0928fd2dab7
TUBPATH.BAT         22 07/18/00 A        9862b95c cfce16f3de43e403 0394cc2cbdc86c40
SCHDPLUS.INI        49 05/10/00 A        2774fe6b 6e820d2dc6f611e4 6d3e11ac3c79f5b1
AUTOEXEC.BIT       135 06/11/99 A        173cd57f ae5d1889398a9c04 6a791ea769ee34ef
LOG.TXT              0 05/28/02 A               0 0000000000000000 0000000000000000
STUB.LOG         20592 11/05/01 A        c4151e53 a4d68c70c3b80ea7 330d30f78df7dd26
FILE0000.CHK     65536 08/11/01 A        3fe787b7 b9fbac09adcf7703 7b7dccd048065430
FILE0001.CHK     65536 08/11/01 A        5df9e9b6 f64890fabde53fe4 d72c362c6941bb4c
NULL            139755 08/12/96          fd697908 c0474be805eb2dba 268fe2f0a5f09bf9
FILE0002.CHK     32768 12/19/01          eead474b 04e504b5f5d2e57a d8680310201daacc
FILE0003.CHK     32768 12/19/01          1f7b4bed 654f2d05362cc24e 9159d21b5c63a90e
FILE0004.CHK    163840 02/03/02 A        f37f7aeb 95fa92aa95f9e3d9 0e92551237c7bcca
FILE0005.CHK     32768 06/09/02          a1ca65d8 5dad8ae776faaaeb 6d16523a1fc9575b
FILE0006.CHK    524288 06/09/02          69bd8640 f1c46f802c50d08a 418569d555ac4052
```

Directory C:\DOS

```
FILE NAME       LENGTH    DATE    ATTR  CRC-32   -----------MD5 DIGEST------------
=========       ======    ====    ====  ======   ================================
DRVSPACE.BIN     71287 07/11/95          46d9da28 2c38baabdd0bbe36 77eeb0f3841c2ed4
DBLSPACE.BAT       403 07/11/95          f4351167 9e5203f68b75adda a024f1d2681b3eac
DEFRAG.BAT         339 07/11/95          b835a5e7 816c38b511e60efb 025888a53a54ad08
```

DRVSPACE.BAT	329	07/11/95	7495220d	7570d72a0e5d6cd4	5040fbc8c5ed1c07
DBLSPACE.BIN	71287	07/11/95	46d9da28	2c38baabdd0bbe36	77eeb0f3841c2ed4
DBLSPACE.SYS	15831	07/11/95	275747b6	d6c4c40caf932c45	fc264e09c800b915
DRVSPACE.SYS	15831	07/11/95	275747b6	d6c4c40caf932c45	fc264e09c800b915
SCANDISK.BAT	152	07/11/95	7bc0179c	9d6bd9bd69e039f2	b5afbbf424d934f4
EXPAND.EXE	16129	09/30/93	a09fcf14	917a703374f842a2	ab2cfdbb9454f9e4
OSETUP.EXE	160720	08/21/95	61369f4a	5d9031f28a8aee63	e335505155c51d12
OSETUP.INF	1820	11/26/95	b148e66	ae843a7ac45a8ed3	6ca6e813e091bb2b
MSD.PIF	967	05/25/97	ce53b3f3	ac7a150fd2420e36	09defb877dd89c0a
OSETUP.SYS	39	08/24/95	36ab9958	e8dd24773c2e804e	61d3f10734fc1e13
UNDELETE.PIF	967	12/02/96	2c94e232	20be2e556ef88e79	c0d52b6910b2348b
QBASIC.EXE	194309	09/30/93	4ead2021	f84f0bf74b830603	a29f77b11b9e4833
APPEND.EXE	10774	09/30/93	746f5417	487d985dc691564f	75ebacb4b757496d
DBLWIN.HLP	8597	09/30/93	549ad7fb	8e21a3f32ea7d5ed	35a68331269b3827
DISKCOMP.COM	10748	09/30/93	755975cf	7d44b8da2489675d	a0fd42a2f96986ea
DOSHELP.HLP	5667	09/30/93	ff56ae42	69c4969a52f121bf	fa227fa192db577c
DRIVER.SYS	5406	09/30/93	ede07ee0	7daa31644808b693	d9f3c6441193db77
FASTHELP.EXE	11481	09/30/93	97adaf5c	89ee3f94f207bd74	b2c16bd27e531b9f
FASTOPEN.EXE	12082	09/30/93	bc0da3ec	dce3ebff45016ff1	6416a1ceb631971c
GRAPHICS.COM	19742	09/30/93	ec264b82	33f61083be04f8e3	50a65c2b50d7e08d
HELP.COM	413	09/30/93	1b5ac11c	1caba11891a5d217	571a133be8bb8d02
HIMEM.SYS	29136	09/30/93	ded7aa9b	d96aaa22ca28b8d5	5570429e4e8617e7
INTERLNK.EXE	17197	09/30/93	a28591a7	871dad393adba453	7e763ad59302ab18
INTERSVR.EXE	37426	09/30/93	fd2d05a1	aa04841234ddb0aa	11529df3380f60cc
POWER.EXE	8052	09/30/93	d529a7ca	fc5cad5db544c4d4	bc55aeda598a0feb
VFINTD.386	5295	09/30/93	c2b4053d	4e3983e1c564548f	936c5c53a1cca58c
CHKSTATE.SYS	41600	09/30/93	3068202e	6548811e80d36d49	76052e05e31742ed
DBLSPACE.HLP	80724	09/30/93	aaea18f0	6ec26081adf4de8b	af290653b3ced234
DBLSPACE.INF	2620	09/30/93	93390092	aa25125463591c43	e7c5629f5d0b8766
LOADFIX.COM	1131	09/30/93	f18750e4	536460507b20ae0f	03d7bee8111028cf
MEMMAKER.EXE	119557	09/30/93	18a76de6	d11ca5b9e7de7c43	4b0812958e1081da
MEMMAKER.HLP	17237	09/30/93	55fbe1e9	2327811fca14b947	79328982d65cae65
MEMMAKER.INF	2911	09/30/93	f0ebded	f746b7e9546e1926	9a4cfa738d73634d
MSD.COM	867	09/30/93	906fbec	3faf9b29a9da858a	277d2efc755de974
MSD.EXE	158470	09/30/93	cea66e61	c0dfb48743671254	fe9cae9e2a121c47
QBASIC.HLP	130881	09/30/93	7f4661e3	4d0b9e7d5a07d717	23e725c2bb07fb82
REPLACE.EXE	20274	09/30/93	2504d5d0	698cebe154201ba8	ff0cf2c27055420d
HELP.HLP	296844	09/30/93	e71c82d2	d8819c8f1878f97f	a2c3aa1b18d4730b
MONOUMB.386	8783	09/30/93	dda52144	0d33605d20095399	c95a571b603f8214
PRINT.EXE	15656	09/30/93	6296d9ca	fc274a56dec9b54a	be0ed7a0a66ee5d3
MSBACKDB.OVL	63098	09/30/93	80e78ab4	482749de78c50211	8849b37cdfa9c7c2
MSBACKDR.OVL	66906	09/30/93	1db43d73	77d58bbb60a334e1	6a7405fe10b6bf4e

MSBACKFB.OVL	69066	09/30/93		7bdb32d9	64042a5393614854	13d068255a526081
MSBACKUP.HLP	314236	09/30/93		41aeeca8	caf7fabf1f00a8fd	adc8e357f2717815
MSBACKFR.OVL	72474	09/30/93		a79bfd3b	140e33ae31b5a010	b221462cc5cb220e
MSBACKUP.EXE	5506	09/30/93		414cd7ba	de179cd16a93ad99	5137ce19b13264b1
MSBACKUP.OVL	133952	09/30/93		3d651b78	7421fe10fb604c56	9e1841eb95b1e6ea
MSBCONFG.HLP	45780	09/30/93		628c578e	7931cb2ee3b2e066	a7f12c5f2db4de39
MSBCONFG.OVL	47210	09/30/93		bd7dbd58	9ac5dae8b233c69f	240e3f13d9cafd3c
UNDELETE.EXE	26416	09/30/93		2f93da27	08e89ceded01795b	fcbcbcb23614c0fd
DELOLDOS.EXE	17726	09/30/93		3104d974	8be0bcbe10f228dc	0e975981816fdd33
EGA2.CPI	58870	09/30/93		b8687ca7	8db749e70a40d0ac	ea9ffa79feea167a
GRAPHICS.PRO	21232	09/30/93		46773d28	bc33aa625d6b807f	718627386df78426
KEYBRD2.SYS	39366	09/30/93		56e926cc	37947b5d0ead0e94	3d106d18deca7f2d
MSAV.EXE	172198	09/30/93		efeb9fe	86bd0f47510685a4	4ae0a107e73f735f
MSAV.HLP	23891	09/30/93		7f86b41e	81794ce01e09f897	79dd862bc3085315
MSAVHELP.OVL	29828	09/30/93		ecb96b99	a8e8e7250d0913e5	782ce5672d6f47af
MSAVIRUS.LST	35520	09/30/93		681de2dd	a013ef863fac849a	4c701d5c0fa2eab0
MSTOOLS.DLL	13424	09/30/93		a1e80c84	2a0f3394baf18b04	05da2572534c0806
RESTORE.EXE	38342	09/30/93		90ca6338	84b19d2e9b417196	ae850329837a82d1
SIZER.EXE	7169	09/30/93		3ac84f33	03fe65eeada86c0c	dbb26e74359e4d70
SMARTMON.EXE	28672	09/30/93		8b98a1fc	50b4fbf5d54c14a6	3ab54a48cce4bb93
SMARTMON.HLP	10727	09/30/93		9deb9138	a330c99a7564de2f	1f0254746660f0b8
TREE.COM	6945	09/30/93		55a44b3b	dace1ce32e1439d7	b887b3961bb06603
UNFORMAT.COM	12738	09/30/93		f3e18fed	acc51c467657abb8	41b372fc1e4b2c0b
VSAFE.COM	62576	09/30/93		73c43615	fbb097049d67acea	c4b33fef32908619
COMMAND.COM	54619	09/30/93		acd2e2f6	c98e0df201047722	fec01cfda0db3ce0
$WPM1D1F.DOC	32256	02/05/02	A	84e9c585	38a3db70a945119f	bb62d685cf164c48
~HP3A37.TMP	0	04/03/02	A	0	0000000000000000	0000000000000000
~GL_0967.EXE	2560	01/27/99		268204cf	815372073da85b20	98a37ded84083c8a
$WPM17FC.DOT	98816	03/25/02	A	6e6f4710	f714ac19fb8ff6a2	2e4d3ad0ef704dad
~HP2D38.TMP	0	04/04/02	A	0	0000000000000000	0000000000000000
~WRA0001.WBK	14848	01/11/98		944bcf1	e615eba6e10ead4b	9edbca15fe609d3f
REG_MIN.BMP	75178	07/27/95		a2087d6f	5edacfe6a300b0ad	9c54a0575ace976b
SAVER.DLL	8384	05/23/96		1d371d40	4616d40302fde3b6	30bd53954a0b098f
REGISTER.BMP	75178	06/02/95		30410f56	093df32e537f7efd	384b540c1838e6fe
TPRLOGO6.BMP	45382	10/10/95		e1e16950	69c1eecf6ec23d0b	1b332a76abfa6a0b
CANCEL2.BMP	73150	10/03/95		d69e80eb	aebd56e9662e502e	58fdbf5034de3479
CANCEL2B.BMP	73150	10/05/95		6be52870	ca79920b75fdcfdf	30a0387b3aa57a04
~WRA0000.WBK	14336	01/11/98		b36bc934	49c6699926fc47fc	2780693c1f71f46b
GOODBYE.BMP	61078	10/06/95		e54e8614	58f5c6a11e5c5443	8bc16336aeb00f4d
GROUP2A.BMP	46658	10/06/95		53dd7025	8e6ed8cc13b46d0a	e54dd85fb83a4377
LOCATIO2.BMP	57010	10/03/95		961251fc	9e49aa2eb59e5f41	48a08aa6e9322879
OPTION2A.BMP	52558	10/06/95		bcc6892a	c3e6ab479bdeff4d	be5036e3cf6cb7f6
PATH2.BMP	57010	10/03/95		c235603f	b79db8a46062d37a	c04181ab8604fb2d

~EMF3E12.TMP	518524	01/20/02	A	a71d6a4e	78b76e5227a8ac49	0486d8c777559d2b
~WRS0000.TMP	1562112	10/23/02	A	8cab7312	dee5f50571e5927a	30008aa8082e050d
OFFICE~2.TXT	1469	01/13/02	A	329687e1	f1edf6bb9d2e9a40	4988d75d7a2ebb3a
HPISTR.HPI	1515	07/13/99	A	656eb419	10261e4b64ab367b	279e08f55d5ee665
HPILOG01.TXT	6422	07/13/99	A	f594d6fe	e6fa2d506d068720	3dca73b8d985c785
HPFINST.DLL	172032	04/09/99	A	d0cd67cf	f436781b108e326e	3065da1b2a15a194
KAMAL.DOC	25088	01/31/99		4aee35d3	9ba3a9cee97bdba5	da41d6dcee748557
HPFIUI.EXE	291840	04/09/99	A	ae0860e3	f12741d7a3e936a3	ac11f2cc2bce1fca
TCUPDV.TXT	330	02/18/01	A	526668a8	b00a391b927a60f3	157d274dd370c79d
INC.HPI	24199	04/09/99	A	295593fe	8407a19b8ec0000a	547d13a5f4201eee
MASTER.HPI	17228	04/09/99	A	59d792fc	3c8e11852b3bdeef	bdd6b31d8433a351
INLINE.BMP	26196	04/09/99	A	54a29725	ccdf6814a0b3a407	8beb74e8a5b090da
APPS.HPI	64707	04/09/99	A	99f846d7	7a2897317d88c2c1	d883f73150f2317f
$WPM2B5A.DOC	26624	01/20/99		c5909fb5	7003499d71779fa0	80dc96a8a2960bc2
$WPM4F67.DOC	26624	01/21/99		c5909fb5	7003499d71779fa0	80dc96a8a2960bc2
~WRS0603.TMP	1605120	10/23/02	A	d517096c	bbccda544ee6a96f	4928eed84eba2a8d
STATUS.BMP	26196	04/09/99	A	e639847	e2ad3eca6464ae42	9456e55a4a81335f
PFLIC.TXT	5029	04/09/99	A	7e168f6d	7b8c852a4f1e05e9	37a414d2f51f82b8
LICENSE.BMP	26838	04/09/99	A	ae91e5d3	3d77986da050355f	18089784a19c0e28
HPILOG02.TXT	2764	07/13/99	A	27eb5a2e	9d82497146761d65	fe1c1994ae42c974
HPILOG03.TXT	71662	07/13/99	A	ef54cbbb	74986567717448f7	8e06175570c734c0
CONGRAT.BMP	26838	04/09/99	A	bac3166	6328f3188d425659	3c56c8b81cbda604
USB.DOC	40448	04/09/99	A	717b2c29	1b56b9ec05af65b7	76a17855678023a6
HPILOG00.TXT	56947	07/13/99	A	2d9925f2	aa02f1800fc00ddf	68062eb86acc6a79
~WRL1839.TMP	12288	10/23/02	H	3b9dff63	e8ff21e4eb16aafe	e60fcda9fd7363ad
$WPM1F28.EML	118	01/05/00	A	eb607e47	c8b1dc0fa7de2b8e	985c72ab88876dd9
$WPM3682.EML	118	01/05/00	A	eb607e47	c8b1dc0fa7de2b8e	985c72ab88876dd9
$WPM699F.EML	118	01/05/00	A	eb607e47	c8b1dc0fa7de2b8e	985c72ab88876dd9
OFFICE~1.TXT	59193	01/13/02	A	5c97d6ee	51b45cf6d586be3e	b1f59835ebc98a9c
TCUPD.EXE	3927588	02/18/01	A	89441031	1365a8693594d6fc	4f367a6639891dd8
~WRD0001.DOC	0	04/25/00	A	0	0000000000000000	0000000000000000
OFFICE~4.TXT	1469	01/13/02	A	7a71dd5d	7be56cabfb56d9a8	7172d82b2bcea18e
OFFICE~3.TXT	23215	01/13/02	A	cbd0349d	7fe6dc53bd83dcca	60a69f48621c23c7
_INS0576._MP	642560	05/10/00	A	567dbef7	c29ba4f6c99ef491	d869f28ca18701d5
ZDATAI50.DLL	45056	05/10/00	A	57e374ef	e5871671de890057	88d0459d43ccba45
_WUTL950.DLL	40448	05/10/00	A	2d93ba52	dfb40e2a94cab5b7	abe275c908bd0f44
RNLOG.TXT	12591	12/14/99	A	d0aa3451	70d41aef84925a8c	455768b6fb43557a
$WPM5C61.ZIP	387303	10/15/00	A	5b02cc0c	09aeb0f46f6b58cd	3b0e942041e7fac7
~WRD3168.DOC	81	12/06/00	A	391304e2	3fef7605e01208ea	2f2837e1bcec17d1
~WRD0497.DOC	0	04/01/01	A	0	0000000000000000	0000000000000000
MF0215AU.EXE	4129397	05/16/01	A	f9f74eb1	f84ae68c45c189fc	9d92864849578a38
$WPM2E54.EXE	897536	06/21/01	A	a774dfe3	45cb63f277973c35	fd0b49263f63d9c1
$WPM6534.DOC	0	12/04/01	A	0	0000000000000000	0000000000000000

Once we have the checksum and digest information for the C: drive, we can compare these values to those of the copy (which we calculate immediately after making the copy), and if the values match, we can assume that on the bit stream level they are identical.

The CRC checksum and MD5 digest, or hash table, are one-way functions that map input (in this case all the data on the hard drive) to unique output. It is mathematically inconceivable for multiple inputs to map to the same output. If the input is changed in any way, even in one single bit position (or in an even number of bit positions), then the output will be changed. Therefore, when the results of running the CRCMd5 tool on the original hard drive are compared to those from the copy, if the copy is in fact an accurate mirror image, the results should be the same.

> **ASIDE:** Remember to run CRCMd5 against all media seized and copies made!

2. **Swap the drives**. Remove the original hard drive and label it with information as entered on the chain of custody form. Secure the original hard drive. Depending on the acquisition method used (see Section 16.3.1 for a description of methods), you will most likely be examining the hard-drive copy in a forensic computer or in one similar to the computer being investigated. You will need to be careful here so that you do not run into BIOS and hard-drive geometry issues.

   Insert the mirrored hard drive into the forensic computer for further analysis. Insert a DOS boot disk into the floppy drive. Run PTable and compare with the original. Note that the space occupied may differ because the hard-drive copy may not map to the exact size of the original. This difference should not affect the CRC checksum or MD5 digest values, nor will it affect the examination of the evidence. Run CRCMd5 against the copy and compare as discussed earlier.

16.3.3 ANALYZE THE EVIDENCE

This is where the real investigation begins. We will begin to analyze the copy of the data. Original evidence is *never* directly analyzed. Original evidence is only acquired, copied, and archived. (We mention this several times for its importance.) Of all the forensic processing steps, analyzing the evidence will likely take the longest amount of time, depending on the amount of analysis required and the size of the victim's hard drive.

Before you learn how to search and analyze files, you will need to understand the terms *file slack* and *unallocated space*. As described in Section 14.2.3 in Chapter 14, there are three basic areas to search for data on a disk: normal files, file slack, and unallocated space.

Normal files are the files we are all familiar with—the files that users create, read, edit, open, and close on a daily basis. **File slack** is space that consists of memory dumps as files are closed. Data dumped from memory is stored at the end of each normal file that had additional space allocated to it that remains unused. To view what is in this space, you need forensics software or a hex editor. NTI has a software tool, GetSlack, that allows you to capture all file slack to one physical file that can then be searched repeatedly.

Unallocated space is the space occupied by erased or deleted files. Whenever a file is deleted in Windows or DOS, what is deleted is not the actual content of the physical file, but the pointer or index to the file. The physical memory on which the file was written is marked as available (for new data to be saved to). One can easily recover unallocated space with an undelete program or forensics software. NTI's GetFree tool allows you to capture all unallocated space to one physical file that can then be searched repeatedly with tools similar to those used in searching file slack.

Now as we proceed to the examination of the files, file slack, and unallocated space, it is important to first determine our search criteria. This is where the "game" is won or lost.

To search a Windows 95 machine, we have always had the most success with NTI's TextSearch Plus tool. Here's how to use it.

First insert your DOS boot disk. After booting to the floppy drive, which is often the A: drive, insert the TextSearch Plus disk and enter the following command to execute the program:

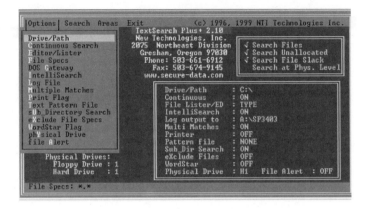

Figure 16.3 TextSearch Plus Menu

```
A:\> txtsrchp
```

You will get the menu shown in Figure 16.3, with the following pull-down menu options: **Options**, **Search**, **Areas**, and **Exit**.

First select the areas to be searched by clicking on **Areas**. Placing a check mark by the **Search Files**, **Search Unallocated**, and **Search File Slack** options (using **Enter** to toggle) indicates that you want those three areas to be searched, as shown in the upper right corner of Figure 16.3 and in Figure 16.4.

Use the arrow keys to select the Drive/Path option, as shown in the upper left corner of Figure 16.3. A window in which the drive path to be searched can be entered will pop up. Type in the logical drive to be searched, in this case C:\ (as shown in the lower right corner of Figure 16.3 and reproduced in Figure 16.5)

Figure 16.4 TextSearch Plus Menu with Areas Selected

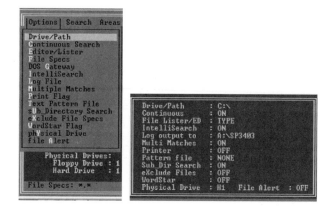

Figure 16.5 TextSearch Plus Menu Options Areas and Selections

and press **Enter** to return to the main menu, having selected the areas to be searched.

Next go to the **Search** pull-down menu option, then proceed by entering the words to search for. The type of investigation performed will dictate the keywords to search for. In this case we searched for the words *Moser*, *NetBus*, *Orifice*, and *password*. You can type up to 120 search words of up to 30 characters each. Each search word must be separated by a carriage return (pressing **Enter**). Pressing **F6** will terminate the keyword input. Note that the list of keywords is not saved. It is recommended that you save the keywords in a file for the purposes of documentation. The search will then be conducted, and results (hits on the keywords) will be printed out in their order of appearance within the normal files, unallocated space, and slack space (in that order). Be careful what you search for! Tailor the search to the investigation at hand and be as specific as you can.

Next go to the **Options** pull-down menu option, illustrated in Figure 16.5. Use the arrow keys to get to the continuous-search option (**Continuous**). The field should say "ON." If the continuous-search option is not enabled, the software will pause every time it finds a match. But if continuous searching is on, it will log every match it finds without pausing. Also on this screen, verify that the **IntelliSearch** option is "ON." Select **Log File** to ensure that the log is being written. Verify that the **Multiple Matches** option is "ON," as indicated in Figure 16.5 to allow the software to look for all matches or hits for the keywords selected.

In the lower left of the main screen (see Figure 16.3), verify that **File Specs** is set to "*.*" (star-dot-star). This is the default for any file of any file type.

Type in the following:

```
A:\ filename.doc      SP3403.DOC
```

Generally it is a good idea to use a descriptive file name that clearly identifies the investigation being conducted. All search results will then be logged to this file on the diskette in the floppy drive. You do not want to write to the mirror image of the evidence drive.

We will discuss the output from the search, and our findings, in the next section.

16.3.4 ARCHIVE THE EVIDENCE AND RESULTS

Just because the investigation has been completed doesn't mean our work is over. The last step, but an important one, is to securely archive all evidence and software that was used to acquire, authenticate, and analyze the data.

> **ASIDE:** General computer forensic theory teaches three A's: acquire, authenticate, and analyze. We have added this fourth step, archive, because proper record keeping and data handling is so important to the potential use of evidence in a court of law.

You will need to make copies of all software used in the forensic review (including backup software and drivers, boot disks, all NTI software, and virus software) and store them securely with the other evidence. You need to do this in case you ever have to re-create the steps taken, in which case you will need the original software used, not an updated version of the software.

16.4 LESSONS LEARNED

In this particular case, the review of the logs and the results of the forensic investigation suggested that Cody Moser had not attempted to steal Ashley Landscapers' or Anne Richards' corporate or personal information or to penetrate the network any further. Therefore, although the exploit of loading a Trojan horse file onto Richards' computer is a crime, our client was satisfied in having Cody Moser identify the process he had used and promise never to do it again, and in having the hole "plugged."

As mentioned earlier, it is important to be very proactive in responding to potential cyber incidents. Although Anne Richards should be commended for taking the actions she did in informing her firm and the police, she really should have taken those actions days earlier.

It is also important to note that although the business strategy of finding and exploiting security holes in the computing infrastructure of potential clients prior to their knowledge and consent may appear to be an effective marketing tool, you shouldn't actually do it. This approach is analogous to the fire department setting fire to a house and, once it is burning, asking, "Do you want us to come and put it out?"

In one incident at an established, professional security consulting firm, a (single) security professional (not the authors) compromised a potential client network to capture some files, just to show those files during the client presentation. This was done in an effort to win the client by proving both the individual's technical capabilities and the client's vulnerability. Although that goal might have been achieved, in actuality the individual was immediately let go and the firm did not win the engagement.

16.5 WHAT WOULD BE DONE DIFFERENTLY TODAY?

The forensics "tool bag" has changed dramatically. There are new varieties of both hardware and software to consider.

16.5.1 HARDWARE

We use a portable computer evidence seizure, preview, and analysis system called Road MASSter. The system can capture hard drives at a rate of 1GB per minute. It also contains many other great features necessary in computer forensic evidence processing: the ability to acquire, authenticate, and analyze various types of hardware in a timely and secure fashion.

Digital cameras are a must. Digital pictures can attach directly to an electronic chain of custody form. This is better life through technology. Note, however, that a chain of custody must be established for any digital memory cards that you use.

16.5.2 SOFTWARE

We still use NTI software, but we also use the NTFS suite of software, including the tool DiskSearch Pro, to do Windows 2000 forensic reviews. Another alternative to the NTI suite is EnCase by Guidance Software. Although EnCase and the NTI suite do similar things, EnCase combines all the tools into one.

What Are Ports?

Every computer has many ports, or access channels, for data to travel both to and from another computer or user. Ports are given standardized numbers so that one port is used to send data and another port receives data. Port numbers are assigned by the Internet Assigned Numbers Authority (IANA, at http://www.iana.org). The port number is included as part of the address given to a packet. Ports can have numbers from 0 to 65535.

Ports 0 through 1023 are generally well-known ports and should be used only by users or processes with powerful privileges. For example, Web servers receive traffic typically over port 80, and SNMP traps are communicated over port 161. Ports 1024 through 49151 are registered and generally used by ordinary users and processes. Ports 49152 through 65535 are considered dynamic and/or private ports.

If we were to use the analogy of a house, ports on a computer are like the doors and windows into the house. The object in security is to lock as many doors and windows, or ports, as possible and allow only specific ingress and egress through the front door.

CONCLUSION

FURTHER INVESTIGATIONS

In the Introduction we said that this book, this collection of case studies, would be like a tour of many of the issues that a cyber security professional must be prepared to face. Any such tour, while valuable and entertaining, is restricted to showing only part of the overall picture.

In this Conclusion we will briefly talk about some of the other topics that come up in security and must be at least understood by the well-rounded security professional. Again, we had to make choices about what to include and what not to include,[1] and after a few knock-down, drag-out fights, the following topics were selected:

- Public key infrastructure
- Identity management
- Single sign-on
- Biometrics

---

1. If the readership level on this book is high enough, we hope to cover these topics in depth in a second edition.

- Secure architecture
- Firewalls and VPNs
- The home user
- Identity theft

PUBLIC KEY INFRASTRUCTURE

Almost no security book would be complete without at least a mention of public key infrastructure (PKI). This technology is so well documented that we will skip any technical descriptions here. In fact, let's cut right to the chase: Although PKI has not enjoyed the widespread deployment that was often predicted, it is making inroads in the federal sector—especially for its capability to provide secure e-mail and offer nonrepudiation through encryption based on a public/private key pair and digital signatures.

Also it is making its way into the underlying operating systems (especially network operating systems) as a part of the infrastructure itself, most notably through efforts at Microsoft to incorporate PKI technology into Windows XP and its .NET environment.

Still, any large-scale deployment of PKI is a long-term effort and generally financially costly, partly because many challenges must be tackled during a PKI deployment.

USER ROLES

Chief among the PKI deployment challenges is the need to develop user roles prior to deployment. The user certificate that contains the public key can also store access rights and privileges and can be used not only to prove an end user's identity but also to provide potentially very fine-grained access control.

COMPONENTS

A long list of servers and devices can be included in a PKI deployment. Figure C.1 shows the major components of an operational PKI solution. Only the highlighted items are needed for pilot implementations.

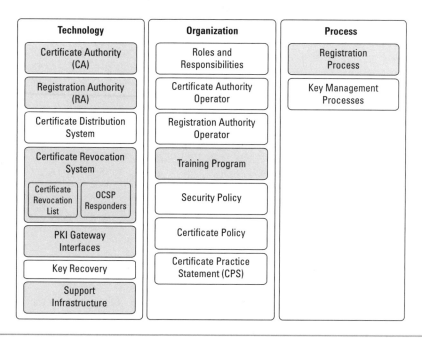

Figure C.1 Components of a PKI Solution

Some would argue that a security policy, as well as a key recovery process, is essential even before a pilot is attempted. That is certainly an acceptable view. Many also say that given that the certificate distribution system and key management process are two of the more challenging aspects of PKI, they should be developed at least in the early stages of a pilot, if not ironed out beforehand. Again, one can see the logic of such statements. Certainly, the key management process should be well understood prior to any full-scale deployment.

SCALABILITY

Another issue is the scalability of the PKI solution. PKI is often piloted for a small number of users and a limited number of applications. However, a full-scale deployment is sometimes considered for a large number of users interfacing with numerous applications. The more users that the system has, and the more applications that those users interface with (increasing the rights and privileges that must be disclosed), the exponentially more complex a system becomes, as Figure C.2 shows.

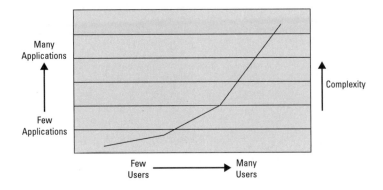

Figure C.2 Increase in Complexity of a PKI Based on the Number of Users and Applications Involved

IN-HOUSE VERSUS OUTSOURCING

A decision that must be made by those implementing a PKI is whether or not to manage the certificate authority (CA) in-house or to outsource the entire certificate creation, maintenance, and revocation systems. Companies such as VeriSign act as managed service providers (following essentially the application service provider [ASP] model) and handle all aspects of the CA. This approach speeds the process of getting a PKI system up and ready to go, but it offers less control. Often it is not clear which solution will be the least expensive. In many cases, outsourcing the CA will obviate any support infrastructure other than a Web browser through which to access the certificates.

CROSS-CERTIFICATION

Unless the PKI is being established strictly for communication with individuals within an organization (nodes on the same tree), the ability to exchange and validate credentials between two or more CAs is very important. Enabling users with certificates signed by separate CAs remains an issue in part because of the lack of standards. The Federal PKI Steering Committee and other organizations are working to develop standards that will facilitate the cross-certification of CAs. **Cross-certification** is the process by which Alice's root CA vouches for Bob's root CA, allowing Alice and other members on her tree to be confident that Bob is who he says he is.

IDENTITY MANAGEMENT

Identity management (IM) is—we apologize in advance for the way this sounds—a process for conveniently managing all the identities on a network. That's it, nothing more. One may ask, What exactly is an identity? An **identity** is essentially a user account. An employee has an account to be able to access the office network. That account (typically the Windows or Unix account that the employee accesses upon turning on his computer) is an identity. The first two columns in Table C.1 show an example.

In a larger sense, the identity can be considered all of the descriptive user information that is associated with a particular account, such as information stored in the Unix gcos fields. Each user likely also has an account on the corporate e-mail server. The user name for the e-mail account generally determines the e-mail address (e.g., *user_name*@company.com). However, this user name need not be the same one that is associated with the network account (as Table C.1 shows). The employee may also report his hours worked and expenses through an application—with a separate user name (again, see Table C.1).

Corporations run numerous other applications—such as databases, billing applications, payroll applications, applications to track supplies, and countless others—that employees can access. Generally, when these applications are installed, there is no absolute necessity to tie the database of users to an existing user account database. In fact, in large corporations, especially those that have been in business for some time, likely more applications exist than people know about. Further, there are likely countless individual user accounts—or identities.

Therefore, an identity can be any specific user account and password pair. It makes sense to tie all of a person's user accounts together into a common identity, if for no other reason than to be able to manage them more easily. An IM solution does this.

Table C.1 The "Identity" of the User Known as The Edge

Actual Name	Network Account	E-mail Account	Time and Expense Account
The Edge	Guitarist	Mail_Me	Pay_Me

There are numerous security benefits to creating a common identity for a single user's multiple accounts. First, without being able to track identities, it can be hard to know who has access to what data. Second, and more importantly, it is very hard to know who has accessed what data. Identity management makes it easier to know what's going on with access to data. If critical data falls into the wrong hands, it may be impossible to find out how it happened and who is responsible. Those concerned with corporate espionage will realize that this is an entirely unacceptable scenario.

Identity management doesn't have to aggregate all user accounts and/or passwords into the same user name and/or password (this process is called *synchronizing user credentials*), but it can be used to do this. IM is an important first step in providing single sign-on, discussed next.

When IM solutions were first introduced to the market, the better ones were fairly expensive. The prices have come down, but IM solutions can still be pricy because the process is fairly involved. And given the fact that applications themselves are hard to track, and user names across multiple user accounts sometimes share little or no common information (e.g., "Guitarist" and "Pay_Me"), figuring out which accounts should be attached to the same person is sometimes a manual process. The size of this task affects both the costs and the time involved in a full-fledged implementation of an IM solution.

SINGLE SIGN-ON

Single sign-on (SSO) can take one of two forms:

1. Upon supplying user credentials (typically the user name and password) to sign onto the network, the user immediately has access to all applications to which she has been granted access rights. To make immediate access like this possible, the system transparently passes the appropriate set of credentials to an application when access to that application is requested.

2. All of a user's multiple accounts (with separate credentials) are reconciled into a single user name and password (i.e., the user credentials are synchronized).

Although these two options are similar—in fact, some might say that the first option is true SSO, whereas the second is actually just an effective stepping-stone—there is a difference: The first option does not imply that the user credentials for all accounts have to be the same. One of the perceived security holes of an SSO infrastructure is that if a single password is lost, whoever has it can potentially access all of the user's accounts; whereas if the passwords are different, this may not be true.

SSO may be provided to the user from a specific physical location, such as the office desktop. A hacker with a stolen password who is attempting remote access may not be able to access applications with this stolen password. Indeed, that password need not even be the correct remote-access password. This is at least something of a protective barrier. In addition, if it is known that a password is lost, simply changing that one password should return the system to its previous level of security without a large-scale password-changing exercise.

The benefit of the second SSO option is that it makes it significantly easier to manage accounts and to concisely define a full set of user credentials. For this reason, many defense agencies are considering an SSO solution (incorporating both definitions) to assist in their current large-scale rollout of the Common Access Card (CAC) solution.

RETURN ON INVESTMENT

An SSO project is certainly an area where a return on investment (ROI) can make the difference in convincing a hesitant client to go forward. The savings from having an SSO capability can be more significant than one may originally think.

LOG-IN TIME REDUCTION

The most commonly discussed savings is the reduction in log-in time. Instead of typing the user name and password for each of numerous applications, it is necessary to do this only when logging into the network, therefore conceivably only once a day. To calculate the potential savings, we can estimate the number of log-ins that will be saved per day (converted to year), multiplied by the length of time

Table C.2 Savings from Log-in Time Reduction

Number of Daily Log-ins without SSO	Number of Daily Log-ins with SSO	Seconds per Log-in per Day	Users	Average User Salary	Yearly Cost Reduction
6	2	15	1000	$50,000	$108,333

(converted to hours) it takes to enter user name/password credentials, the number of users, and the average salary (again, on an hourly basis) and we arrive at a savings of over $108,000 per year, as shown in Table C.2. (Note that we settled on a $50,000 average salary through no scientific calculation at all.)

This savings will manifest itself in terms of time saved from entering credentials that can go toward greater productivity.

Help Desk Call Reduction

Perhaps the most common help desk call is to request a password change. An SSO solution can reduce the number of such calls because the number of applications for which passwords will need to be remembered is reduced. The average number of password reset calls per user per year is between 3 and 4,[2] and each call costs an average of $20.[3] Assuming that this number drops to between 1 and 2 (it can't go any lower), we get a savings of $40,000 per 1000 users, as Table C.3 shows.

This savings would allow, conceivably, a reduction in the number of help desk staff or the reallocation of that staff to other endeavors.

Table C.3 Savings from Help Desk Call Reduction

Number of Password Resets per User per Year without SSO	Number of Password Resets per User per Year with SSO	Users	Costs per Call	Savings
3.5	1.5	1000	$20	$40,000

2. The Gartner Group (http://www3.gartner.com).
3. The META Group (http://www.metagroup.com).

Additional Savings

SSO doesn't have to be restricted to humans. If an individual software application needs to access another application, potentially residing within a separate stovepipe, to either access or transfer data, an SSO architecture can be designed to provide transparent access between the two. An estimated 35 percent of IT personnel's time is devoted to creating linkages between existing systems or applications.[4] If an SSO can help save a majority of this 35 percent, the yearly savings can be astronomical in terms of increased productivity or reduced staffing requirements.

BIOMETRICS

Biometrics is a New Age or *Star Trek* technology whose time has very likely nearly come. One of the initial concerns with biometrics was that users would find the technology too intrusive and not accept it. Attitudes have been changing, though, and biometrics is now being positioned as a technology that can increase security while actually making things more convenient! That's unique.

Imagine a scenario in which a company wants to protect access to data and feels that data is often compromised by unauthorized users gaining access through unprotected screens that belong to authorized users who have logged in and simply walked away from their desks—taking, for example, long coffee or smoking breaks. A potential solution is to configure the Windows screen saver to lock the screen after a short period of inactivity (say, 5 minutes or 30 seconds). But if this interval is too long (5 minutes), it may not be effective in thwarting this threat. And if it is too short (30 seconds), it may simply annoy end users and lead to problems. Enter biometrics.

A fingerprint-scanning device attached to each desktop or laptop can be used to deactivate the screen lock. Instead of hitting **Ctrl-Alt-Delete** and entering a user name and password, the user would only need to touch the finger pad for the split second required for the system to compare her fingerprint to the fingerprint on file and the screen would unlock.

---

4. Forrester Research (http://www.forrester.com).

In addition, given that it is harder to possess someone's face or fingerprint than to have that person's user name and password, biometrics provides a more secure access control system. (Note, however, that the thresholds for the biometric system must be set carefully.) Biometrics is also being considered for inclusion in smart-card implementation such as the Defense Department's CAC program.

SECURE ARCHITECTURE

More and more, security professionals are being called in at the architecture design phase—which is a good thing. As of even three years ago, most security measures were being retrofitted into network systems that were designed for efficiency, speed, communications, redundancy—anything but security. Finally, those in power are beginning to realize that security can be both cheaper and more effective if it is designed into networks from the get-go.

Designing secure architecture does involve making trade-offs between convenience and security, or between cost and security, and sometimes both. Security professionals need to remain vigilant in explaining to system owners and customers the need to include security issues in the initial design phases of their projects by having a team member (at least in a consulting capacity) devoted to that subject rather than trying just to plug up holes after the fact.

FIREWALLS AND VPNS

The concept of a firewall is similar to that of the Great Wall of China—a structure designed to keep the unwanted out and allow only the wanted to pass. By its very nature, it is a defensive construct. Virtual private networks (VPNs), on the other hand, are similar to the tunnels dug by the Viet Cong, and more recently by Al Qaeda. Those who know the locations of the tunnels and how to access them are allowed secure access to and communication between multiple places through an otherwise insecure medium. VPNs are commonly used to allow remote access to the company's network and applications, such as e-mail, to employees who work off-site (see Figure C.3).

When properly managed and deployed, these can be very powerful tools for protecting networks and data.

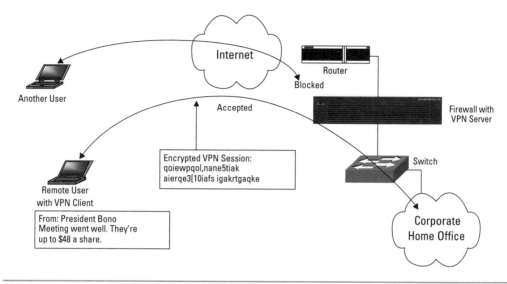

Figure C.3 Firewall and VPN Server Appliance

Firewalls have been around long enough to have become almost standard office equipment. VPNs are not quite so popular, especially because there are so many competing remote-access solutions; however, they are the solution of choice when what's needed is secure, remote access to networks and data over the public Internet.

THE HOME USER

As more and more people take their work home with them, and as IT permeates the home environment, we must start thinking of protecting the home PC with at least the same security measures that are available (or assumed to be available) in the workplace.

Taking work home is nothing new; in fact, it's a part of the culture. Working at home is just another way to increase productivity. From the basic office worker to senior personnel at the Central Intelligence Agency, everyone takes work home. So why wouldn't those who like to engage in corporate espionage, identity theft, and blackmail catch on and start to target the home machines of their victims in an effort to capture what they seek?

It's also interesting that a great deal of spam actually comes from compromised home PC systems without the knowledge of the owners. Many home users simply do not monitor what their own machines are doing. Home users who have always-on Internet connections tend to take advantage of this feature and leave their machines on whether they're using them or not, and whether they're at home or not. Unmonitored machines connected to the Internet—that sounds like a great target for spammers!

We recommend installing antivirus software and a desktop firewall (even one of the free versions) on all home PCs. If you have a wireless network, you should seriously consider limiting the network to a specified set of MAC addresses and using a pass phrase–based encryption scheme. No, it's not foolproof, but it's a start. And you should periodically check to see how much data your machine is sending out. You can do this easily (and cheaply) by looking at the network icon that is usually on the task bar. Generally, the amount of data received should far exceed the amount of data transmitted.

IDENTITY THEFT

Do you like to pretend you're someone else? When I was younger, I liked to be Joe Theismann, starting quarterback for the Super Bowl champion Washington Redskins. (I was also Larry Bird, the forward for the most successful basketball franchise ever, the Boston Celtics.) And who wouldn't want to be the fictional Michael Corleone of *The Godfather*, or Neo of *Matrix* fame? Well, make-believe as a child is acceptable (as long as it ends, I guess, but I'm not a child psychologist), but when grown-ups pretend to be someone they're not and try to spend money in that persona, it is a crime.

With the increased accessibility of information these days, adopting someone else's identity has become all too easy. **Identity theft** is simply spending (or stealing) money on another person's credit. Often all it requires is a few details of the individual, such as home address, full name, mother's maiden name, Social Security number, bank information, credit card numbers. (Not even all of these may be necessary.)

The problem is that the crimes and debts are attributed to the real person—who is innocent—and the merchants that sold goods on this credit are out both the goods and the payments. The credit card companies are squeezed between the honest members that they have to protect and the honest merchants who are their business partners. And someone somewhere has a brand-new 63-inch plasma television for free.

Developing processes and technologies to limit and eliminate as far as possible the threat of identity theft is a major area of practical research within the security field. Protecting data held in storage at companies, banks, schools, and other holders of databases is also a critical component.

KEEPING UP WITH THE LATEST TRENDS

One thing we have not discussed in this book is the simple act of keeping up with the latest trends. Because the IT industry itself is changing and growing over time, certainly the security considerations (potential holes and solutions) are changing right along with it. Security professionals must make the necessary effort to stay abreast of these changes, just as doctors, accountants, and lawyers have to be aware of new research, procedures, standards, and laws.

Staying current can involve everything from reading books and periodicals, to attending industry conferences, to being active on mailing lists and playing with new products.

The worst situation is being in an interview and being asked a technical question (such as, What are the safe-harbor provisions of the Digital Millennium Copyright Act? or Can you export 128-bit encryption keys?)[5] and responding with an answer that has been refuted or changed by recent disclosures. Avoid these situations. They call into question your technical qualifications, damage your reputation (not to mention your ego), and certainly don't help land the job.

---

5. In answer to the first question, we refer the reader to the act itself, available at http://www.copyright.gov/legislation/dmca.pdf. The answer to the second question is yes.

RECOMMENDED READING

We refer the interested reader to the following books and Web sites for further reading and information on the topics discussed in this book. Although a complete listing of references is impossible, we are confident that this list is a good starting point. These sources will be updated periodically on the book's Web site, http://www.Gsecurity.com/DefendIT.

GENERAL TOPICS

There are many, many general security books on the market. Feel free to select a favorite. A good primer for anyone is *Computer Security: Art and Science*, by Matt Bishop (Addison-Wesley, 2003). Two others are

Network Security: The Complete Reference, by Mark Rhodes-Ousley, Roberta Bragg, and Keith Strassberg (McGraw-Hill Osborne Media, 2002)

Microsoft Encyclopedia of Security, by Mitch Tulloch (Microsoft Press, 2003)

In addition to books, there are many Web sites dedicated to information security, including the following:

SANS Institute: http://www.sans.org

Internet Storm Center (operated by SANS): http://isc.incidents.org

InfoSysSec: http://www.infosyssec.com

NMAP

There can be no better reference than the official Nmap site: http://www.insecure.org/nmap.

SECURE ARCHITECTURE

Practical Guide for Implementing Secure Intranets and Extranets, by Kaustubh Phaltankar and Vinton G. Cerf (Artech House, 2000)

DENIAL OF SERVICE

Good sources of tools and analysis are

RFC 2267: "Network Ingress Filtering" (http://rfc-2267.rfc-index.com/rfc-2267-8.htm)

RFC 2827: "Network Ingress Filtering: Defeating Denial of Service Attacks Which Employ IP Source Address Spoofing" (http://www.ietf.org/rfc/rfc2827.txt)

Packet Storm distributed attack tools (http://packetstormsecurity.nl/distributed)

Distributed denial of service (DDoS) attacks/tools (http://staff.washington.edu/dittrich/misc/ddos)

WIRELESS

A good selection of wireless security books includes

How Secure Is Your Wireless Network? Safeguarding Your Wi-Fi LAN, by Lee Barken (Prentice Hall PTR, 2003)

Real 802.11 Security: Wi-Fi Protected Access and 802.11i, by Jon Edney and William A. Arbaugh (Addison-Wesley, 2004)

Wireless Security Essentials: Defending Mobile Systems from Data Piracy, by Russell Dean Vines (Wiley, 2002)

VIRUSES

Many antivirus vendors maintain a great deal of virus-related information on their Web sites, including McAfee (http://www.mcafee.com) and F-Secure (http://www.f-secure.com/virus-info).

WEB SECURITY

Web Hacking: Attacks and Defense, by Stuart McClure, Saumil Shah, and Shreeraj Shah (Addison-Wesley, 2003)

INTRUSION DETECTION SYSTEMS

Network Intrusion Detection, Third Edition, by Stephen Northcutt and Judy Novak (New Riders, 2003)

DISASTER RECOVERY

We recommend *Disaster Recovery Planning: Strategies for Protecting Critical Information Assets*, by Jon William Toigo (Prentice Hall PTR, 2000). Another good resource is the article "Developing a Continuity-of-Operations Plan," by Ajay Gupta, which appeared on InformIT (www.informit.com) on July 26, 2002, and is available in the archives.

SECURITY POLICY

Although the case study presented in Chapter 10 is fairly detailed, *Writing Information Security Policies*, by Scott Barman (New Riders, 2001), adds additional information about and insight into the process. The SANS Institute provides several template policies and additional resources on its Web site: http://www.sans.org/resources/policies.

HIPAA

To become familiar with the HIPAA regulations, it is a good idea to read the act itself. The act and additional information are available on an informational Web site, http://www.hhs.gov/ocr/hipaa, established by the Office for Civil Rights. In addition, the HIPAAdvisory Web site, http://www.hipaadvisory.com, is a good informational site.

WAR DIALING

Reluctant as we are to cite ourselves, few books deal with the subject of war dialing. Chapter 6, Dial-In Penetration, in *Hack I.T.—Security through Penetration Testing*, by T. J. Klevinsky, Scott Laliberte, and Ajay Gupta (Addison-Wesley, 2002), is a good source of information on the topic.

SOCIAL ENGINEERING

We recommend *The Art of Deception: Controlling the Human Element of Security*, by Kevin D. Mitnick, William L. Simon, and Steve Wozniak (Wiley, 2002). We also suggest Chapter 8, Social Engineering, in *Hack I.T.—Security through Penetration Testing*, by T. J. Klevinsky, Scott Laliberte, and Ajay Gupta (Addison-Wesley, 2002); and the article "The Art of Social Engineering," by Ajay Gupta, which was published August 23, 2002, on InformIT (www.informit.com) and can be found in the archives.

COMPUTER FORENSICS

There are several good introductions to computer forensics, including

Computer Forensics: Computer Crime Scene Investigations, by John Vacca (Charles River Media, 2002)

Computer Forensics: Incident Response Essentials, by Warren G. Kruse II and Jay G. Heiser (Addison-Wesley, 2002)

Incident Response: Investigating Computer Crime, by Chris Prosise and Kevin Mandia (McGraw-Hill Osborne Media, 2001)

Cyber Crime Investigator's Field Guide, by Bruce Middleton (Auerbach Publications, 2001)

PUBLIC KEY INFRASTRUCTURE

The Federal PKI Steering Committee Web site is a good first reference on the topic: http://www.cio.gov/fpkisc. In addition, two suggested titles are

Planning for PKI: Best Practices Guide for Deploying Public Key Infrastructure, by Russ Housley (Wiley, 2001)

Understanding PKI: Concepts, Standards, and Deployment Considerations, Second Edition, by Carlisle Adams and Steve Lloyd (Addison-Wesley, 2003)

IDENTITY MANAGEMENT

Identity management is still a relatively new area, and the identity management vendors are the best place for information on the topic—though you will have to read through the marketing push and product descriptions. Some vendors include

Waveset (http://www.waveset.com), recently purchased by Sun

Jamcracker (http://www.jamcracker.com)

Courion (http://www.courion.com)

BIOMETRICS

Biometrics and Network Security, by Paul Reid (Prentice Hall PTR, 2003)

FIREWALLS AND VPNS

We suggest two classic books on the subject:

Firewalls and Internet Security: Repelling the Wily Hacker, Second Edition, by William R. Cheswick, Steven M. Bellovin, and Aviel D. Rubin (Addison-Wesley, 2003)

Building Internet Firewalls, Second Edition, by Elizabeth D. Zwicky, Simon Cooper, and D. Brent Chapman (O'Reilly, 2000)

HOME SECURITY

Home Networking for Dummies, Second Edition, by Kathy Ivens (Wiley, 2003)

IDENTIFY THEFT

The Federal Trade Commission has set up a good informational Web site on this topic: http://www.consumer.gov/idtheft.

INDEX